OFFBEAT

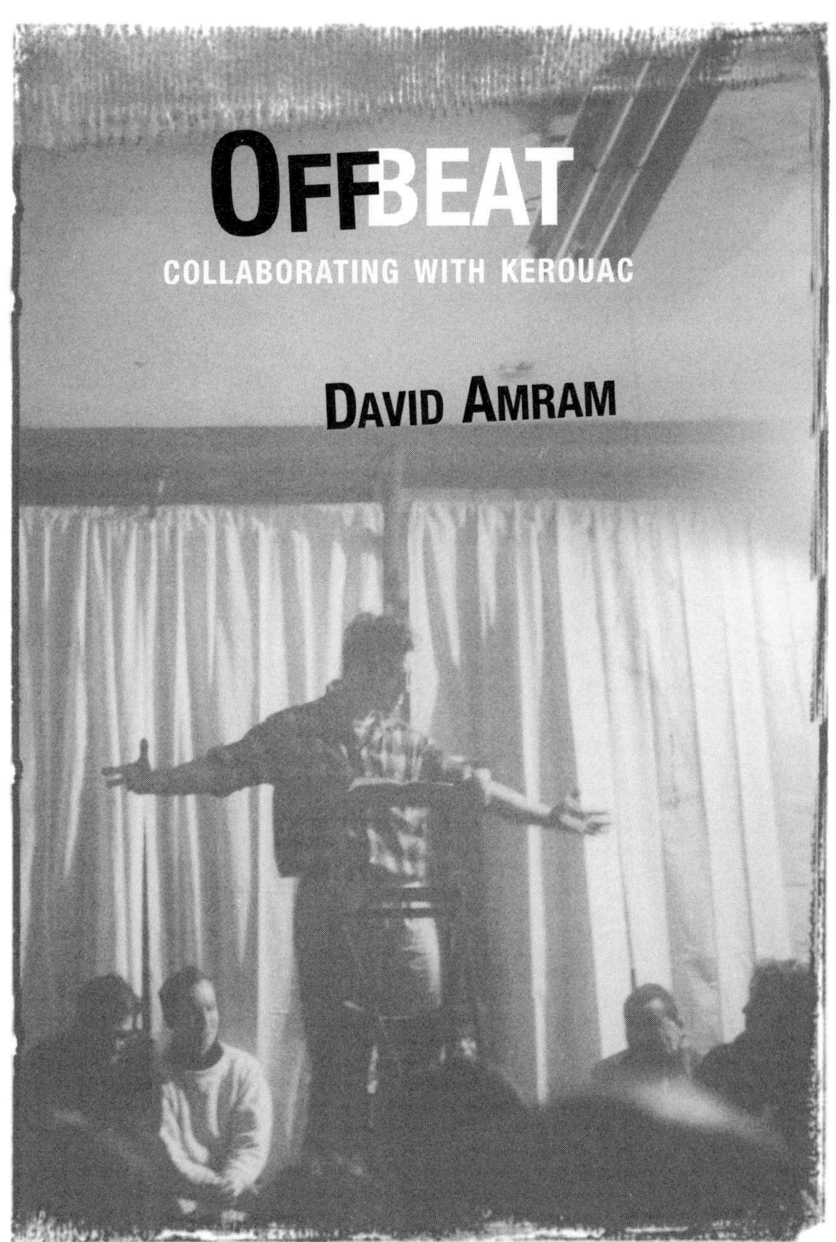

OFFBEAT

COLLABORATING WITH KEROUAC

DAVID AMRAM

THUNDER'S MOUTH PRESS • NEW YORK

OFFBEAT: COLLABORATING WITH KEROUAC

Published by
Thunder's Mouth Press
An Imprint of Avalon Publishing Group Incorporated
161 William St., 16th Floor
New York, NY 10038

Book design by Michael Walters

Library of Congress Control Number: 2001097351

ISBN 1-56025-362-2

9 8 7 6 5 4 3 2 1

Printed in the United States of America
Distributed by Publishers Group West

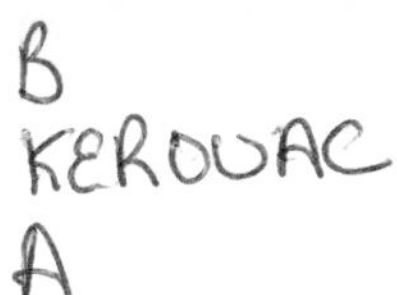

Foreword

The collaboration that Jack Kerouac and I began in 1956 happened naturally. Our chance meeting and friendship was a direct result of how we lived our lives. Each day was a new adventure. Each day was a struggle for survival. Each day was a celebration of life, and a new day in school as prize students in our own homemade University of Hang-out-ology. We both had our own paths we were pursuing. It turned out our mutual love of and participation in the French language, sports, music, romance and the search for a family, traveling, languages, and the yin and yang of spontaneity and formality—all this gave us a basis for an enduring friendship.

Jack reminded me of my uncle David Amram, a merchant seaman in the 1920s for the Grace Lines, who was full of wonder and adventure every day of his life, and whose zest for new experiences and ability to be part of every situation and share these experiences taught me how to remain open and honest.

I was able to share family stories with Jack as he shared his with me. When I met him, he was bursting with energy. He knew *On the Road* was finally going to be published, and he was hopeful that his other books already written would finally get into print. Like most of us, he was a vessel with eighty-five percent of his cargo in storage beneath the waters, ready for a landing in the Port of New York, the great arbiter of all the arts in the 1950s.

We were called Outsiders, but we considered ourselves Insiders. We were later called ahead of our time, but we knew we were right on time. We were told we were offbeat, but we felt we were on the case. There was a small group of us who figured out that the unrecorded geniuses of eclectic speech, the undocumented poetry of the streets, and the brilliant improvisations of the jazz masters shared one thing in common with the treasures of European classical literature and music: That common bond was an exquisite choice of words and an exquisite choice of notes.

All we wanted was to have our work made available. Gregory Corso and Dan Wakefield both told me at different times in 1999 that they would be judged and remembered by their books on the shelf. In 1956, most of our shelves were nearly empty, but Jack and I and hundreds of others we knew had already created enough unpublished work to build a stack of shelves. By 1956, when we met, we both knew we were ready, even if there was not yet a place card with our names inscribed at the table.

By the time I began collaborating with Kerouac, I was able to utilize skills I had already acquired from writing music for the theater and film. I was working as a jazz French hornist blessed to have already played with many of the masters of this most sophisticated music, and I also had my own band. I was a composer of symphonies, chamber music, and choral works, an improviser of words and music, and a budding conductor.

Jack also had acquired skills as an improviser of words and music, scat singing, writing, and the ability to create countless characters with his voice. We were often told at the loft parties where we performed that he looked like a lumberjack and I looked like a hayseed.

The idea that either of us would end up in some people's minds as original members of a Beat Generation autocracy would have been greeted with roars of laughter. The two things that our network of friends shared was an outrageous sense of individualism and a desire to free ourselves from the stifling conformity of the 1950s. None of us had a desire to become members of the Elks Club, the Rotary Club, the Masons, the Chamber of Commerce, the Shriners, or the Beat Generation. Jack and John Clellon Holmes were referring to a Beat Generation in a literary way, not as two journalists documenting a new global movement like the *Ten Days that Shook the World.* The whole idea of a Beat Generation as an exclusive group was the exact opposite of the one principle all of us shared—loving kindness and compassion toward all and a seat at the table for anyone with an open heart.

Jack was our reporter.

In the new millennium, there is a whole generation of young people who read his books. This new generation considers him, like Melville, Twain, Dickens, and many of the great writers of the twentieth century, an author whose works have enriched the body of English letters.

I was with Jack in the glory days and the dark days and nights as well. Like many other of Jack's friends who appear in this memoir, I remained loyal to Jack through the years and still do today. As we all grow older, Father Time (and Mother Time as well) thins the ranks of those of us who were close to him. With that sort of loss weighing on me, I called Lawrence Ferlinghetti in 1995 and shared my concern with him.

"Why don't you write a book yourself about the experiences you shared?" he said. "Don't be flowery. Just tell what happened. You were there."

I began to go over old notes, letters, hundreds of interviews I had given to others, diaries, and all the conversations with Jack that remained so vivid in my mind. If I had to write an objective biography of someone I didn't know, it would take the rest of my life just to research what was already documented, and try to interview hundreds of people to gather information, if the subject still had people alive who knew him. But in my case, I had such a wealth of experiences with Jack, past and present, that it was almost like interviewing myself. I was also fortunate to have John Sampas, Jack's brother-in-law and executor of his estate, to check dates, names, places, and facts in Jack's journals.

In the process of writing about the years of my friendship with Jack, I have tried to honor some wonderful people, places, and experiences I have been lucky enough to have been involved in as part of my life. I have spent time with many of Jack's friends who were with him through the good years and the tough years—Joyce

Johnson, Carolyn Cassady, Billy Koumantzelis, Stanley Twardowicz, Ramblin' Jack Elliot, Gregory Corso, Lawrence Ferlinghetti, Dody Muller, Philip Lamantia, Howard Hart, Bob Creeley, Dizzy Gillespie, Dan Wakefield, George Plimpton, Steve Allen, John Clellon Holmes, Allen Ginsberg, Neal Cassady, Jerry Newman, Zoot Sims, Al Cohen, Barney Rossett, Pepper Adams, and Herb Gold (one of the first to separate Jack from the Beatnik myth). There have been hundreds of others as well whom I have talked to; most of their stories have yet to be documented.

In addition to primary sources, I have met people of all ages whose lives are touched by Jack's work. They range in age from people older than myself who tell me they are so happy to see Jack and other artists of our era finally get their due, to kids in the first grade for whom I play the many styles of music from around the world that Jack and I cared about. I often include some of his work in my concerts for young people, where I create a spontaneous accompaniment to his words, as we often did together beginning in 1956.

Over the decades, there are special moments with Jack that I have recounted hundreds of times. There are other experiences we shared that stay in my mind every day. When Gregory Corso was terminally ill, I spent hours by his bedside talking of our shared adventures with Jack and Allen, and some of them are recounted in this book. I read these passages to Gregory, at his apartment and on the phone, to be sure I got them right.

I hope this book will encourage present and future scholars of Jack's work, as well as his devoted readers, to reexamine our era and search for a broader picture than the one painted so far. We need to become more familiar with the artistic output of so many others of our era, some of whom I have mentioned. They and their work finally deserve to be judged solely on creative merit, not by the label attached to them. Many of them influenced Jack as much as he influenced them.

Jack Kerouac and those of us who were his friends were repelled and hurt by labels that denigrated anyone's race, religion, or nationality. We never dreamed we would become labeled ourselves as emblematic of a nonexistent "movement" whose presumed values were used to discredit us from having anything of substance to offer the world.

The French Impressionists, the great composers known as the Russian Five, the Dadaists, and many others made a conscious decision to create a movement. We, in contrast, were a floating group of friends who shared many ideas and ideals. Above all, we were militantly free spirits who scrupulously avoided joining anything, or telling anybody what to do or how to think. The long overdue awareness of this is finally helping to put the Beatnik myth, the collective albatross around our necks, into the landfill of trash culture, along with the hula hoop, the padded bra, and all the stereotypes used to dismiss many significant artists of our era as being subhuman Cro-Magnon barbarians, because of the Beat stereotype to which they have been assigned.

I also hope this book will encourage readers to pursue their own creativity in their daily lives and to dare to joyously collaborate with others in different fields than their own.

Whether we combine words and music, play tennis or stickball, create your own dance or theater, have jam sessions or back porch Southern style picking parties, Latin American *descargas* or your own homemade 12-step program discussion and hangout group sessions with your neighbors, all of us can enrich our lives and the lives of others by reaching out to open the doors of perception.

We also realize that in the new millennium the creation of new works of art built to last does not require the artist to become a slave to drugs or alcohol. We are finally beginning to understand that creativity is a natural gift from the Great Creator, which we are all blessed with at birth. We can see now that the nineteenth-century idea of romanticizing the artist as the ultimate advertisement for self-destruction and addiction succeeded in keeping the artists' productions in a state of obscurity and their salaries down.

If there had been the awareness that alcoholism was a disease in the 1950s, Jack would probably still be with us today, along with an army of others who killed themselves looking for salvation at the bottom of a bottle. Drinking during our era was not only considered admirable, it was assumed that all real men could reach a higher plateau of personal heroism and super-macho masculinity by demonstrating how much they could drink. It was also assumed that being a chronic drinker was a necessary part of being a successful artist in the 1950s. Hollywood movies of our era portrayed men and women smoking up a storm and getting blasted on alcohol. This was always presented in a sympathetic way.

The horror of becoming an alcoholic was always hidden by colorful expressions that made out-of-control drinking seem like a fun time for the whole family. Being stoned out of your skull, torn up, wasted, wrecked, ripped, juiced, fried, blasted, way out there, high as a kite, gone . . . all these were affectionate ways of depicting the pleasures of imbibing in liquid refreshments until you passed out, often in a sea of your own vomit, got into a car crash, or died before your time. My own early years, as I described them in my autobiography, *Vibrations,* were no model for a health regime. If I had continued along that path, I would not be alive today to write this memoir.

Jack deserves to be remembered not only for his unique gifts as an author but for his shining character and strength to persevere in spite of illness during the last years of his life. He never stopped writing and he never stopped dreaming of the day that America would learn to love itself and all its people learn to love one another.

John Sampas expressed it best when he gave me a statement to read during a ceremony honoring Jack, sponsored by the New York City Landmarks Commission, where I played and spoke. A plaque was placed on the side of the house in Queens, New York, where Jack, his mother, and father had once lived. The event celebrated Jack's literary output.

The final lines of John's note said it all.

"Jack's road was a long and tortuous one, but he triumphed in the end."

All the experiences I describe in this book about our times together, and the spirit of those early times that endures today, are meant to celebrate Jack's final triumph. His work endures and flourishes. He is understood and beloved by virtue of the words he wrote, translated now in many languages. He left us all with a better world. He continues to inspire millions. I hope this book can do the same.

Book One

Children of the American Bop Night

Collaborating with Kerouac was as natural as breathing. That is because the breath and breadth of Jack's rhythms were so natural that even the most stodgy musician or listener or reader could feel those rhythms and cadences, those breathless flowing phrases, the subtle use of dynamics that are fundamental to the oral (i.e., spoken) and aural (i.e., to be listened to) tradition of all musical and poetic forms of expression.

Whoa, you might say. Why such a long sentence? Because Jack himself spoke, wrote, improvised, and sang in long flowing phrases, like the music of Franz Schubert, George Gershwin, Hector Berlioz, Haydn, Charlie Parker, Lester Young, Billie Holiday, like the poetry of Walt Whitman, Dylan Thomas, Baudelaire, Céline, Langston Hughes, and other lyric artists whose work we both loved and admired.

The 1950s were the pinnacle years for great conversationalists and great rappers, the last generation to grow up reading voraciously, traveling by extension of the thumb, and trusting the Great Creator to get you to your destination. Part of the requirement of being a successful hitchhiker was to engage your patron saint of the moment, the person who picked you up, in conversations about anything and everything.

Storytelling was still practiced as a people-to-people activity. Television and the Internet were not yet born. Entertainment and communication came from the interaction of people with each other. Many of the greatest poets, authors, and jazz artists, whether reading or playing in public, could carry on for hours for an audience of one other person. Our expectations and goals were to achieve excellence, with the hope that once we did, someone out there would dig it.

"Just find one person and play for that person all night long, Dave," Charlie Mingus told me in the fall of 1955, when I had just arrived in New York and was fortunate enough to be chosen by him to be in his quintet. "All you need is one person in your whole life to really be listening."

Jack was one of those people who listened and observed as well as he wrote and performed. When Jack and I first began performing together in 1956, we would run across one another at BYOB parties, often held at painters' lofts. The guests would bring wine, beer, Dr. Brown's Black Cherry Soda, sometimes just paper cups, or potato chips, graham crackers, or a musical instrument, a new poem, a song, a monologue from Shakespeare, or Lord Buckley's latest comedic-philosophical rap, or simply their unadorned selves, looking for romance, fun, excitement, and a chance to celebrate Friday and Saturday night, where you could stay up till dawn, because you didn't have to go to your day job the next day.

This was the New York where Jack and I each felt most at home—an environment that was inclusive, informal, almost rural, temporarily created for a few hours in the midst of the vast sky-scrapered metropolis, where we miraculously found temporary cocoons of warmth and camaraderie. These party environments were like back porch Lukenbach, Texas, picking parties in the summer, or Lowell, Massachusetts, get-togethers over beer with Acadian accordions and singing of old songs, or the pubs of Dublin, Ireland, where unheralded natural poets celebrated the rising of the moon, or great jam sessions in the South, like the ones with Charlie Parker and Dizzy Gillespie in my basement apartment in 1951–52 in Washington, D.C., before I met Jack.

These informal, spontaneous gatherings were like magic. Years later, Jack talked about these New York all-night weekend bashes that we shared, but when he and I first performed together we hardly said a word to each other. Just as I was blessed to play with

Thelonious Monk, Miles Davis, Bud Powell, and scores of other great musicians who never said much and let their music do the talking, Jack and I had that same musician's ESP. It was an unspoken communication that came to us naturally. I would play while he read or improvised words, and I knew exactly what to do. We both knew how to *listen,* to lay back, to breathe together, to curb aggression and search for harmony, to tune into one another and surrender ourselves to the particular rhythm and pulse of the evening.

That rhythm and pulse was always connected to the Native American drum we both felt so strongly, the African drum that permeated all the great music of our time, the drum of the Middle East, and the soulful song-stories, prayers, and chants of the Catholic Church that Jack had in his bones and the Jewish liturgical wailing of ancient songs that reverberated in my unconscious. As soon as we were done performing, we would give each other a wink, a nod, or a smile, and become part of the party, flirting with young women and searching for food, drink, and adventure.

Several months after we had crossed paths many times, my weekend excursions to these parties temporarily came to a halt, and I began an eleven-week-long stint with my quartet at the Five Spot, a funky bar in the Bowery that became the hangout for painters like Franz Kline, Willem de Kooning, Joan Mitchell, Alfred Leslie (who later directed the film *Pull My Daisy* that Jack and I collaborated on), and Larry Rivers (who appeared in *Pull My Daisy* as a saxophone-playing railroad train conductor, modeled after Neal Cassady).

The Five Spot welcomed everyone—artists, moving men, postal workers, winos, office workers, and off-duty firemen—and you could get a huge pitcher of beer for 75 cents. My quartet was sometimes joined by as many as eighteen musicians (on the night when the whole Woody Herman Band sat in with us). Late at night, poets and actors would sometimes join us, reciting poetry or improvising verse with music. This was never planned. Our era was always *in*-clusive, not *ex*-clusive. Jazz was about sharing and spontaneity.

Jack was often there, and all of us in the quartet could always feel his presence the minute he arrived. We could telepathically feel his power as a listener, just as we could feel his ability to observe, reflected in his dark, brooding eyes. I remembered our great encounters at the weekend loft parties where we played together. *On the Road* was not yet published, and the terrible pressures of celebrity were still to come. Even though he often sat alone, like a wayward meditative Canadian lumberjack in his plaid red-checkered work shirt, he always exuded a special energy. He was that one special person Mingus alluded to, the one we always knew we could play for. We began to know one another as two fellow transplanted hicks, trying to relate to Golgothian New York City. Jack was from Lowell, Massachusetts, and I was brought up on a farm in Feasterville, Pennsylvania. Even though we had both seen a lot of the world, we still had the bond of being outsiders in New York City. Like so many of our friends, we were looked upon as offbeat characters, searching for hidden treasures that we knew we would find in our everyday lives, if we left ourselves open to appreciate everything that surrounded us.

Jack told me how being a football player had opened the doors for him to leave Lowell, go to an Eastern prep school, and be accepted at Columbia University, and I told Jack about my childhood growing up on a farm in Feasterville, Pennsylvania, always dreaming of becoming a musician. I described the trauma of moving to Washington, D.C., at the age of twelve, and deciding to become a musician and composer, the joy of my job as a part-time gym teacher at a French school, then being drafted into the army and beginning my travels around the world.

We found we shared a mutual interest in sports and speaking fractured French, which often annoyed the 4 A.M. stoned-out customers at Bickford's greasy spoon, where we would congregate after the Five Spot closed, to eat hamburgers with fried onions and mayonnaise on English muffins, while we drank coffee and planned our conquest of New York.

A few months later, after my eleven-week engagement at the Five Spot was over, poet and drummer Howard Hart and San

Francisco poet Philip Lamantia climbed up the six flights of stairs to my tiny apartment on Christopher Street, which was always open to guests, and told me of their idea to give a jazz-poetry reading in New York City.

"It will be the first one," said Howard Hart, in his hyper-breathless style. "Jack said he'll do it with us. He'll be the MC, and you and he can do all that spontaneous stuff where you both make up rhymed scat-verses and accompany each other, and Philip and I will read from poems we've written out. We'll give you carbon copies of our poems to look at. We can even rehearse, but I know you and Jack don't need to. You guys already can do it naturally better than anyone else."

When I read some typed copies of Howard's and Philip's poems, which Howard had brought with him, I understood why Jack wanted to do a planned reading with them. Their poems were lyrical, original, honest, touching, with brilliant flights of fancy, combined with contemporary sounds of everyday urban life.

"Where are we going to do it, and when?" I asked. "I don't know if I'll have much time to rehearse. I'm writing music for Joe Papp's Free Shakespeare in Central Park, and working part-time in the post office, playing with my band and composing music too. I've always played with Jack spontaneously without ever planning anything."

"Don't worry," said Howard. "It will happen when and where it's supposed to happen, and we'll all be there together."

The next day we met with Jack at my sixth-floor walk-up. I could hear Jack bellowing as he climbed the stairs.

"Merde alors!" said Jack. "I've ascended the cherubic heights to join the lonely bell ringer up in the tower of St. Amram's Synagogue. Get an elevator, Davey. These six flights will be responsible for your premature demise. *A la santé* and *lechayim."* Jack pulled a bottle of Thunderbird wine from his red-checked lumber jacket, removed it from its soiled brown paper bag, and took an enormous gulp.

"We'll make history, Davey. The mad poets and sainted musicians will make New York City become the new international shrine for Buddhalike meditation. All the jaded big-city Philistines will smile at one another as we lay our scatological tomes on their weary souls. Let's play something for Philip and Howard to show these boys how Baudelaire and Erik Satie are reborn in Greenwich Village."

I began playing the 12-bar blues, and Jack and I made up verses, played and scat-sang four-bar breaks, while Howard took a pair of wire brushes from his jacket and played drum parts on a phone book. Philip Lamantia watched us in amazement.

"My God, Jack. I wish everyone in San Francisco could see this. I didn't know you could sing."

"I can't," said Jack. "That's the voice of the Holy Spirit coming through me. Like Stravinsky said about composing *Sacré du Printemps*: 'I'm merely the vessel through which this new creation was given to the world.' "

"I see New York's helping you to overcome your shyness and modesty," said Philip, laughing.

"Naw, I'm *serious,* man," said Jack. "When Davey and I start *cooking,* I feel like I'm flying. Like Charlie Parker. A bird in flight. He didn't *talk* about it. He *did* it."

"*We'll* do it," said Howard.

"I'll drink to that," said Jack. "Let's get some more wine and go out to the Cafe Figaro and meet some beautiful gals. And we'll discuss our plans to invade New York's literary jungle, and overwhelm the masses with our spontaneous madness."

We ambled down the six flights of stairs and headed towards the Cafe Figaro. We walked in silence for a few blocks. Jack turned to me as we crossed Sheridan Square.

"Did you ever feel you knew someone all your life when you met them?"

"Yes, Jack. I felt that with you, the first time we played together at one of those loft parties, but never would have said it."

"You didn't need to say it," said Jack.

We walked to the Figaro and sat in the back room. I took out my horn, and we gave an impromptu improvised performance. Brooklyn Bernie, an old Village moving man, applauded and came over to our table.

"I'll tell ya what, Dave. I'll buy all you guys free coffee, sandwiches, and pastry if you'll let me recite 'The Rime of the Ancient Mariner' with you, all right? Listen, Dave, you play the horn, like the sea sounds making the boat rock, and you other guys hum when I signal you. I always wanted to do this at the Figaro. This is my *chance*!"

Then he whispered confidentially, "There's a bunch of bee-*yoo*-tiful young ladies from Barnard College and Mt. Holyoke College for Women sitting up in the front two tables by the window. They're here to meet some real bohemian artists. What you guys are doin' . . . no offense, but it's too *weird*, it's too far out, but when they hear *me* do 'The Rime of the Ancient Mariner' . . . they'll *flip out*! And I'll buy you all whatever you want."

"I accept your kind offer," said Philip. "I'll have the apple turnover, a double espresso, and salmon platter."

"I'll have the same," said Howard.

"I'm not hungry. I'm thirsty," said Jack. "I'll take a sip of whatever holy spirits are in that bottle I see in the side pocket of your coat."

"I'm starving, Bernie," I said. "I'll have the vegetarian special plate, a tuna roll, a cappuccino, and toasted bagel with lox, onions, and cream cheese, with a side order of coleslaw and French fries."

Brooklyn Bernie, the moving man, ordered us our feast. After we chowed down, Jack and I did a few impromptu numbers, punctuated by Jack taking loud slurps of Wild Turkey whiskey from Brooklyn Bernie's brown-bagged bottle, before launching into his next improvised story-song-poem. Jack sat down and attacked my remaining coleslaw and French fries. Brooklyn Bernie took a huge belt from his near-empty bottle of Wild Turkey, cleared his throat, and climbed on top of his chair, waving his arms to let the patrons of the Cafe Figaro know it was show time.

The denizens of the Cafe Figaro were used to unannounced performances by anyone who felt like giving impromptu readings of their latest poems, monologues from Shakespeare or Chekhov, ranting and raving about world politics, or delivering homemade public service announcements requesting a place to stay for the night.

Brooklyn Bernie clapped his hands, gestured like a crazed symphony conductor from his chair-podium for quiet, and launched into a raspy-voiced version of *The Rime of the Ancient Mariner*. No one paid any attention. He gave Howard, Jack, Philip, and myself signals to accompany him with sound effects suggesting the sea, but his ship was sinking rapidly. He was receiving the fabled New York freeze. The customers began talking to each other, gradually drowning him out. Many of them turned their chairs so that gradually Bernie could see a room filled with people whose backs were turned towards him.

"He's like Ralph Ellison's Invisible Man," whispered Howard. "No one knows he's here."

Brooklyn Bernie concluded and was rewarded by withering silence and cold stares of contempt. We could feel his despair. Jack leaped up and started singing "Pennies from Heaven," interspersing "Bernie from Brooklyn" into the lyrics, while I accompanied him. Jack made up a whole song about Brooklyn Bernie coming through the rain to make Manhattan his new home, and what a *moving man* this moving man was. At the end, the whole Figaro crowd burst into applause and laughter, and one of the women from the table full of intellectual lovelies invited us to join them. We were asked to go with them to a friend's loft, where we partied till dawn. Brooklyn Bernie was in heaven and was having an elated conversation with a gorgeous philosophy major which was prematurely terminated when he passed out in the armchair he was emoting from.

There was an old upright piano in their loft, and Jack played his particular style of crashing Beethoven-esque chords while I was scat-singing. I backed him up when he sang, spoke, or scatted, and we traded rhymed verses together, with Jack playing the bongos. His natural musicality and style of poetic speaking was extraordinary, and the young women were transfixed to see someone who looked more like Paul Bunyan than a tortured introspective poet emoting streams of dialogue, stories, songs, and poetry that all made sense.

That night we knew we could do anything, anywhere, for anybody, and that people who were there with us would no longer be the traditional passive audience. All of us would feel part of one another, sharing in the moment, knowing it would never happen in the same way again.

Howard Hart and Philip Lamantia got up and read their poems. Accompanied by Brooklyn Bernie's snores, my French horn, and, at times, the old upright piano I played, their performance, like their poetry, was powerful, lyrical, intense, severe, sincere, and disciplined. Their formality fit perfectly with the totally spontaneous moments that Jack and I had created earlier in the evening. That night in the spring of 1957, Philip, Howard, Jack, and I gave what later became the basis for the first jazz-poetry reading in New York City.

Finally the sun came up, and the gorgeous philosophy major, Helen, put an afghan blanket over Brooklyn Bernie's slumbering hulk, and listening to his loud snores we ate an omelet of hot dogs, mushrooms, Swiss cheese, canned peas, olives, and strawberry yogurt that I whipped up as a culinary thank-you bouquet to our hostesses for allowing us to have what became our only rehearsal for our future public performances, although, of course, we didn't know it at the time.

I staggered home, slowly climbed the six flights of stairs, and collapsed into an early-morning 8 A.M. slumber. At noon, there was a loud pounding on my door. Howard Hart, knowing it was never locked, burst into the room. "My God, man. What a night! I've got a terrible hangover, but we've got to be at the Museum of Modern Art in an hour. I called Frank O'Hara, and he made an appointment to see the events coordinator at 1:30. He's going to try to get us a jazz-poetry reading at the Museum this fall. We're ready to storm the Bastille of uptown uptightness in the Big Apple. Jack's still sleeping, so we'll meet Frank O'Hara and Philip in eighty-five minutes. Get dressed. Hurry up! Wear anything."

I threw on my old gray sweater, no socks, mismatching sneakers, and paint-stained jeans.

"I hope I look okay," I said.

"You're fine," said Howard. "Frank O'Hara will take care of

everything. We're going to make history. Roll over, Picasso, Frank O'Hara's going to let us play the Museum of Modern Art Jazz-Poetry Blues!"

Frank O'Hara was highly respected in the uptown world and was established as an important figure in New York's cultural life. Aside from his gifts as a poet, he was much beloved by all of us and acknowledged as a link to the burgeoning community of artists, poets, painters, musicians, and friends who later became known (or some of us did, through no effort on our part) as the founding members of the Beat Generation, a term most of us had never heard of at the time.

We got to the Museum two minutes early, gave Frank O'Hara and Philip Lamantia a hug, and were escorted into the event coordinator's plush office. The man in charge of performance events at the Museum listened patiently as Frank extolled the virtues of Howard Hart, Philip Lamantia, Jack Kerouac, and myself. I noticed the events coordinator was wearing an elegant crushed velvet jacket and smoked French Gitanes cigarettes from a long ivory cigarette holder. He was wearing patent leather shoes. He eyed my sockless mismatched sneakers and grimaced. After a glowing report of nearly half an hour, I thought Frank O'Hara's recommendation of our list of achievements would make us candidates for the Nobel Peace Prize.

"Frank, let's be brutally honest," said the events coordinator. "These two poets and Amram are just about totally unknown, outside of the downtown bohemian circles. The Museum of Modern Art is not a talent show for hopeful emerging artists. We have an international reputation to uphold. And that Jack Kerouac. I've met him at the Cedar Tavern. He acts like a *truck driver*! He's a *total* unknown and so *gauche*! We would *never* have someone so crude appear at one of our events. I didn't even know he was a writer. I can't believe Viking is going to publish a novel of his this fall. Do you think he wrote it himself?"

Philip looked dismayed. Howard looked at me despairingly. "Let's split," he murmured. We walked towards the exit of the Museum.

"What will we tell Jack?" said Philip, in a glum tone.

"He'll roar with laughter," said Frank O'Hara. "Especially the part about him looking like a truck driver and not being able to write a book. Jack's already written *eleven* books. *The Town and the City* was marvelous, even though my colleagues here at the Museum *refused* to read it because it never made the best-seller list. Don't despair. When my colleague loses his job as the events coordinator at the Museum and is selling lingerie somewhere, all of *you* will be scaling the heights and opening doors to new vistas.

"Do it *down*town, where you're already loved. It was a mistake for me to try to break down the walls of pretension here at the Museum. When you get better known, they'll *fawn* and *grovel* all over you . . . at least until you fall out of fashion. Do it *down*town. Let's try the Brata Art Gallery on East 10th Street. You've already played for their art openings, David. The artists all remember you from your stint this past winter at the Five Spot with your quartet. They know your scores for the Free Shakespeare in the Park you just started composing, and they've heard you with Mingus. They trust my judgment of the value of your poetry, Howard and Philip. And they love Jack, and sense he is a genius, as we all do. Let's do it *down*town."

We went downtown, and I called up Jack and told him the whole story. As Frank predicted, he roared with laughter.

"*Je m'en fou,* Davey. Let's go hang out in the Village and *épater la bourgeoisie*. This may be the holy night that you find the dream-wife life-companion you've searched for on your musicological field trips through the lonely streets of Auld Manhattoes [that was Jack's affectionate nickname for downtown New York]. You need to find a soul mate. You can write symphonies and cook omelets for her. I don't need to look anymore. I'm cool, Dave. I have sweet Joyce, the finest woman on Earth. We should both get married tonight at City Hall and celebrate with a champagne dinner in your Mt. Everest walk-up Himalayan-high cabin in the sky on Christopher Street. We can serenade our new young wives with our Rimbaud-Baudelaire-Lester Young-Thelonious Monk-Bartok-Kerouacian inspired soulful ditties."

I grabbed my French horn, Jack packed up his notebooks, and we strolled through Greenwich Village. I sat in with Art Blakely's band at a nearby jazz club for a set, and then we wandered over to the Cafe Figaro. Brooklyn Bernie, the moving man, wearing the same clothes he'd had on when we left him snoring earlier the same day, greeted us in his loud raspy voice.

"Jack, Dave, let's do 'The Rime of the Ancient Mariner.'"

The manager of the Figaro came over immediately.

"Listen, Bernie, no offense, but you almost emptied the house last night. I'll buy you all supper if you'll promise to keep quiet Face it, Bernie. 'The Rime of the Ancient Mariner' doesn't go over with the weekend crowd. Let Jack and Dave do their spontaneous stuff. New York's a tough town. Stick to moving furniture."

Bernie looked crestfallen.

"Let Bernie play the bongo drums, and accompany us with his highly evolved moving man rhythms," said Jack graciously.

The manager handed Bernie the house set of bongos, and Jack made up a new version of "Brooklyn Bernie, the Moving Man, a Moving Man."

Everyone in the Figaro was snapping their fingers and singing along in a rhymed choral refrain I made up from Jack's words.

"Thank you, Jack," said Bernie, after the twenty-five-minute improvised tribute celebrating Bernie, his native Brooklyn, the Brooklyn Dodgers, and Hart Crane on the Brooklyn Bridge. As everyone applauded, Jack lifted Bernie's hand up as if he were the new heavyweight champion of the world.

Bernie was beaming. "Jack," he said. "You're a generous soul, you're what we call in Yiddish a real *mensch*. You gotta lotta *neshuma*. That means soul, man."

"Merci," said Jack. "I come from Soul People. The Kerouacs have been on a long journey since the twelfth century, in France, Canada, and the U.S. and I feel reverberations of some lost memories of Iroquois ancestors in my blood everywhere I go. I have dreams about them. I'm never lost. Jesus and St. Francis and Buddha guide me on my journey, and you, Bernie, are the reincarnation of the Ancient Mariner, a landlubber, trapped in a port of call. You're in dry dock on a pier crowded with Philistines. But despair not, Bernie, I have the sacred wine to anoint your tortured soul."

Jack pulled out a fresh bottle of Thunderbird wine and we surreptitiously poured it into coffee cups and drank it all. Bernie staggered off to take the subway back to Brooklyn, and Jack and I went up to my apartment and played music and talked till dawn.

He told me stories about his travels, and how we could someday create a band of musicians from all over the world and combine them with a symphony orchestra. How we would write a huge piece like the Berlioz Requiem for chorus, band, and orchestra, and tour the world, inviting local poets and jazz and folk players to join in at each concert. We would give our guest artists—the poets and jazz musicians—a special ten minutes when we would all improvise, while the symphony orchestra players watched us on stage from behind their music stands.

"We can open up the doors, the minds, and hearts of everybody," said Jack. "Music and words are all part of the same cloth. Like yin and yang, they give the perfect balance to existence. The perfect duality."

A few months later, in early October of 1957, Howard, Philip, Jack, and I gave the first-ever jazz-poetry reading in New York City at the Brata Art Gallery on East 10th Street. It was an event that Frank O'Hara had helped to organize. There were no posters and no advertising. Just a mimeographed typewritten handbill that we handed out at the Cedar Tavern, the Five Spot, the Cafe Figaro, Kettle of Fish, White Horse Tavern, and San Remo.

The Brata was packed. We did what we had done before, at parties, park benches, and friends' houses. We had no idea if anyone would even come, or if they would like it. Philip reminded me in 2001, when we had a reunion in San Francisco, that forty-four years earlier we said a communal prayer before walking over to the Brata for our great adventure. Philip, Howard, and Jack used to take me to Mass in the Village, so we were used to praying together. The reading proved to be memorable. We didn't know it at the time, but the seeds were sown.

Shortly after our Brata performance, Jack was offered a chance to play at the Village Vanguard on December 19, and get paid. He called me from Florida, full of excitement.

"I'm joining the pantheon of the great souls of jazz who burn like Charlie Parker with a hard and gemlike flame," he said, paraphrasing Walter Pater's motto that we always used to energize each other.

After a disastrous week at the Vanguard he was terminated. I wasn't able to be there to cheer him up and make him know that every word he spoke or read would be treasured. The musicians who were at the Vanguard, meeting Jack for the first time in that tiny dressing room, didn't know what he was capable of doing. They weren't aware of his musical gifts or the extent of his love and knowledge of music. One of the bartenders told me that when Jack felt a freeze from the musicians backstage, he drank so much he wasn't able to show the audience or the musicians what he was capable of.

"He was such a beautiful cat," said the bartender. "The musicians who squeezed in and out of that telephone booth they called a dressing room saw this guy who looked like a dock worker or a moving man, wearing a necktie and carrying a bunch of papers and a little notebook. Only musicians were allowed go in the back to that tiny room. That was the inner sanctum for musicians only and their old ladies and close friends. When Jack walked in unannounced to the back room, J. J. Johnson and his band thought someone had wandered in off the street, and gave Jack the freeze. J.J. would have flipped out if he'd known that Jack was able to sing him his recorded trombone solos on those records he'd made with Charlie Parker. Jack was too shy to say anything to either J.J. or the cats in J.J.'s band. You should have been there. He needed to have someone with him he knew was on his side, to introduce him to everybody. I heard him carry on with you for hours at different loft parties where you jammed out together and when he'd sit in with you and your band at the Five Spot. He was fantastic when he was feeling right. This was the first time he ever performed in a club as a featured performer. The pressure got to him. He couldn't handle it. I've seen seasoned cats who have been playing for years crack under the pressure of playing for the first time in New York as a headliner. You need someone in your corner. He didn't have anybody back there with him to cool out the scene. He was lost."

Since Jack was in town and now suddenly available, someone from the Circle in the Square Theater thought it would be a good idea to throw together a Friday midnight show to close out the year.

"The Village is so packed with school kids on vacation and people recovering from Christmas that there should be a good turnout just from people walking by," said the woman who worked in the box office. "We'll let everybody in free and see if we can start a series. Your type of crowd stays up all night hanging out anyway. I'd love to see it myself. I hear you're both fantastic when you work together."

"We never know what's going to happen, but something always does happen and it's different every time," I said.

"I'll notify our lighting designer," she said. "He is very creative and he's a fan of you both."

Friday, December 27, 1957, we performed our first midnight show at the Circle in the Square Theater. Since Jack's engagement at the Vanguard had been terminated, he was free.

"Now that you've had two days off, it's time to come out of retirement and make your big comeback," I told him.

Someone at the Circle in the Square printed up a stack of black-and-white flyers at the last minute. Even with no announcements, the theater was packed, just through word of mouth, and the distribution by hand of the flyers to all our favorite Village haunts. Philip was back in town from San Francisco for a few days and Howard Hart was raring to go. I took off from my night time job at the post office, and the Jazz-Poetry Trio was ready for anything.

At about 11:30 P.M. we all ambled into the lobby of the Circle in the Square and then hung out in front of the theater, talking to old friends, and inviting anyone who passed by to come in out of the cold and join us for this free event. The woman at the box office told us she planned to have more midnight readings with us after the first of the year.

"Look at all these people," she said, as Howard, Philip, Jack, and I, joined now by other friends and strangers, continued handing out flyers to bemused curiosity seekers who stumbled into the theater through the snow. I still have a copy of the original flyer from that reading. Over the last forty years, copies of that flyer have circulated around the world. We had no idea that what we did that night would have the effect it did. We were just having fun, and trying to undo the unhappy experience Jack had suffered at the Vanguard.

Because the Vanguard engagement had been such a disaster, no press came to our midnight show, and they missed an unforgettable evening. At about 12:30, one of the ushers came out in front of the theater where we were all standing around, talking, joking, and continuing to greet passersby. The theater was now packed.

"Gentlemen, may we begin?" she said politely.

"It's show time!" shouted Howard Hart. "Let's hit it."

We all walked to the center of the stage and started our totally unrehearsed and improvised program.

The Circle in the Square lighting designer improvised with us throughout the night. I told him as we were walking into the theater that he must forget about his previous experiences as a lighting designer and make himself part of the band.

"Wail on those lights," said Jack. "Be like Picasso playing a bass solo."

"Do what the words and music tell you to do," I said. "You'll feel it. We'll follow you and you follow us and we'll all follow each other and we can't go wrong."

"That concludes our rehearsal," said Jack.

"I'm ready," said the lighting designer. "Fire away. I'm ready to play my ax."

A minute later, the theater went pitch black, and all kinds of strange colors came from different angles, fading and blinking, like a Technicolor horror movie. As I started playing the piano to set the tone for whatever the evening might turn out to be, the lighting designer suddenly got a demonic grin. He seemed in a trance as he pushed and pulled every dimmer switch and lever on his mixing board, like a new-millennium DJ showing off his scratching technique at a hip-hop party. This incredible display was ten years before so-called psychedelic lighting came into existence.

He must have utilized everything in his lifetime of experience in the theater, flashing all the different-colored lights, dimming and brightening every lamp at different angles and tempos, blinking and pulsating, contrasting different hues, creating instant blackouts and even beaming lights in the audience's faces from time to time, all synchronized to the rhythms of the poetry and music. At one point, he cut out all the lights and focused what looked like a searchlight right at Jack's head, making Jack bend over and shield his whole face like a deer caught in the headlights of an eighteen-wheeler. Then Jack, seemingly nonplussed, made up a whole rap about driving down a dark two-lane highway in the Black Hills of South Dakota and being blinded by a speeding trucker who was bearing down relentlessly in the wrong lane, trying to get home early to make love to his new bride on their farm in North Carolina. Meanwhile, the lights changed to make the theater resemble the inside of a planetarium. The designer added one small light projected against the aurora borealis tableaux, with his left hand making shadows of different kinds of animals and birds in flight, all in tempo with the music.

When Jack, Howard, and Philip disappeared after intermission, squinting to regain their eyesight as well as their composure, they decided to celebrate their *succès d'estime.* They continued reading their poems to anyone who happened to be in Sheridan Square Park, fortified with Thunderbird wine. When the perplexed usher told me we had to resume, even though the whole theater and street outside had turned into a good-natured block party, I obliged by going on stage to play the piano and make up rhymed scat-songs, based on suggestions from the audience to fill up time till Jack and the poets returned from their wine-tasting expedition.

Suddenly, it seemed overnight jazz-poetry was the new hot thing, and that was the last thing we ever had in mind. We weren't trying to franchise ourselves or our work, or be trendsetters. We both had our life's work. Jack had his books to write and I had my music to compose. When we worked together, aside from the fun we had, we shared an interest in finding new ways of combining the spoken word with music, without any preconceived formulas. We worked together with a mutual respect and understanding of the jazz tradition. Always listen. Always follow one another and always go with what the moment tells you to do. We didn't stay exclusively in the idioms of the many worlds of jazz. My music and Jack's reading and even his occasional singing of the words were done differently each time. The style of music depended on the feelings of the moment. It always came out right. It was something we did together for the joy of doing it. Our message was for everyone present to celebrate that passing moment in time.

In the beginning of March 1958, Howard, Philip, and Jack, along with Joyce Johnson and a group of merrymaking friends, went to Brooklyn College where Jack was supposed to talk about *On the Road* and the literary influences in his work. He decided to bring us along to give him moral support. The bottles of Thunderbird started appearing and by the time we got out to Brooklyn College an hour behind schedule, all of us were quite torn up. The place was packed. Jack was one of the shyest people I'd ever met in my life when he was sober. Because he had struggled so long before he'd been discovered as a writer, his overwhelming success and the sudden pressures were more than he could handle. When he was around a lot of people he didn't know, the only way he could face them was by drinking. Still he always maintained his sweetness and kindness.

As we lurched into Boylan Hall at Brooklyn College, the students looked astonished at the sight of us. The English professor, though, was very cool. He introduced Jack, who told a few stories and anecdotes and then said that in the tradition of the Zen master, he would let the students ask questions. When someone asked a long involved question about whether or not Stendhal or Proust was more of an influence on his work and whether or not Céline influenced him stylistically in any way, Jack said, "You've got the answer in your question, and it's a beautiful answer." He was putting everybody on in a way, but in another way he was trying to show them that the writer says it all in his writing and for him to answer the question academically would be dishonest. The students grew increasingly hostile; they wanted to be told something definite.

One student got up and said, "How come I love your books and the characters in your books and I hate you?"

"You don't hate me," said Jack. "You love me and I love you." It went on like this and the rumbling and the confusion grew more intense till finally a cute little fellow with Harpo Marx curly hair, bright blue eyes, and an insane leprechaun smile raised his hand and stood up. "Jack," he said, "when you take those trips out across the country hitchhiking, walking, bicycling, sleeping out in the fields at night, traveling on freighters to foreign countries, and when you go to Mexico and out into the desert—doesn't your mother ever get worried?" Everybody in the place cracked up. He had brought the house down with his question and good vibrations were restored.

After that Philip began to read some poetry, Howard read some poetry, Jack read some poetry, I played the horn, and what started out as chaos became very beautiful. The students loved it. The English professor was happy because although this was not what he had expected, he wanted to show his class that writers or artists were real human beings. Some of the students, including the young guy who'd asked Jack about his mother, stayed afterward. He introduced himself as Lenny Gross, an aspiring writer. He and some other students invited us out. We stayed up most of the night partying and ended up in Manhattan. It was the greatest group of students I'd ever met and it made me feel that I was back in school again, except the kids were so much hipper than the kids I had known.

On March 22, Jack and I did our final midnight Circle in the Square performance. We could have easily exploited what had now become a fad, but that was the last thing we were interested in doing. We were now searching for new ways of collaborating. We continued to play together anywhere and everywhere the spirit moved us, but we both felt we wanted to do something that would also utilize our classical backgrounds. We somehow sensed that this would happen naturally, as long as we didn't allow ourselves to be devoured by the Beatnik Ogre that had arrived like Godzilla to stomp us all into a mashed mound of mediocrity. We vowed never to forget who we were or to allow ourselves to become the imbeciles this new consumer fad told us we should become.

"I want to be Lamont Cranston again," said Jack. "The invisible man. Thank God I found a place to live in Northport. New York is killing me, even though I love it. I need peace and quiet, to write. I'm a writer, Davey, not a performing seal."

Jack was moving with his mother to Northport, Long Island, and we knew that we could continue to stay in touch, whenever he would make his forays into the city.

A Night of Poetry on the Bowery

"Davey, check out the stars in the few feet of sky visible to the oh-so-naked eye here in Auld Manhattoes," said Jack. It was a clear night and you could see a few stars poking through the murky carbon monoxide–filled air of downtown New York.

We were walking down 8th Street with Allen Ginsberg and Gregory Corso, checking out old friends, rapping with strangers and hanging out in the style that was still the major source of Saturday night entertainment for most downtown New Yorkers during the twilight of the 1950s.

"I just checked out those few feet of sky," I said to Jack. I pointed down to the glistening asphalt, strewn with candy bar wrappers, pizza crusts, cigarette butts, shreds of discarded newspapers, half-eaten souvlakis being eyed by an occasional rat, and various fast food meals recently upchucked by passing revelers.

"Now I'm checking out the diamonds in the sidewalk that you always talk about," I said, stepping over the remains of a falafel and pita sandwich.

"Check out that chick," said Gregory in a raspy voice, ogling a tall young brunette with a drop-dead figure, wearing a plaid skirt, bobby sox, and penny loafers. She was furiously chewing bubble gum while adjusting her pigtails.

"She's an old lover of mine," said Allen, giving Gregory a stern look.

"What?" said Gregory incredulously. "You don't dig chicks.

Whaadda ya trying to lay on us, Allen? You don't go near broads unless it's a business matter."

"I never said I did, Gregory," said Allen patiently. "That chick as you call her is a guy. A transvestite. We spent some time together."

"Well," said Gregory, "there goes my night of passion."

"The night's still young," said Jack.

"Yeah," said Gregory, "but it'll stay young and I'll grow old before I score when I'm with you guys. All we do is talk and listen to Amram play his horn and b.s. with every stranger that walks up to talk to us and then Jack starts his rap and it's five A.M. and poor Gregory goes home all alone, to a poet's solitary room while all the fine chicks are with someone else."

"Well, Gregory," said Allen. "Let's go to my place for another night of music, tea drinking, meditating, wine sipping, and poetry-rap exchanges."

"Awright," said Gregory. "Maybe we'll meet some fantastic young Lower East Side beauty on the way."

We walked towards Allen's house. Allen and Gregory started arguing about the great English poet William Blake, with Gregory screaming at Allen and then laughing slyly when startled passersby stared at him.

"Hey Jack, Dave. Did you see that guy? He thought I was going to kill Allen. All I was doing was talking about syntax and imagery, haah hah HAH!"

Gregory loved to put people on, and continued his routine as we ambled slowly along, stopping to talk to anybody and everybody and enjoying a Saturday night of aimlessly wandering down the street. Jack was now famous but with Gregory carrying on with his street theater antics he was able to slouch down with the collar of his lumber jacket turned up, his baseball hat pulled down, and do what he enjoyed doing the most: observing and blending in with everyone else.

Gregory at this point had drawn a crowd of people who thought they were going to witness a fight as he continued shouting at Allen.

"Hit him," said a husky young high school–age kid with a crew cut wearing a Tenafly, New Jersey, high school football jacket.

"I'm gonna hit him with the *truth,*" shouted Gregory.

"How many of you kids know who Blake is?"

"What team does he play for?" asked the kid with the Tenafly High jacket.

"He plays for the Great Poets," said Gregory.

"I never heard of the Great Poets," said the kid. "Are they in the Big Ten?"

"Yes, they are," said Gregory. "They're football immortals. Ask my friend Jack here. He played for Columbia."

"I've heard of Columbia," said the kid, his eyes brightening. "What position did you play, Jack?"

"I was in the backfield but I broke my leg and that ended it for me," said Jack, looking morose. "I loved the game more than it loved me."

"What do you do now?" asked the kid.

"I try to stop my friends from killing each other," said Jack. "Gregory, Allen, stop it. Let's go. We're almost at the Bowery."

The kid walked off and Gregory continued shouting at Allen. Jack and I were a few paces behind, walking in silence. Jack gave me a motion with his hand as he did when we performed together and I knew he wanted to convey a message. It was an upward flipping of the thumb and fingers as if you were shooing a fly from the top of your hand and it usually meant to check something out in silence.

Jack motioned with his eyes towards the little bag he had with him and took out a small notebook, and when we passed a bright street lamp, he showed me some sketches he had made and some watercolors. One of them was a picture of red brick buildings rising above a waterfall.

"That's beautiful, man," I said.

"That's my homage to Lowell," said Jack. "I still see those falls in my dreams and my mind's eye. Dody Muller is my mentor, along with Matisse, Renoir, Picasso, and Tintoretto, but she is mad at me again. I'm not sure I'll keep these, but maybe I will. I might Scotch tape them on some gloomy Bowery wall, like Walt Whitman and Johnny Appleseed sowing seeds for future generations and sitting back in their rocking chairs as old men and watching someone discover them and become inspired."

"They call that littering," said Gregory. "Save 'em, Jack. Save everything. You picked Burroughs' smacked-out scribbles off the floor and made a book out of them." Then he got a devilish gleam in his eye. "Do the same with your art work. You could have a show, man, and get all the rich people who put you down to dress up and come to your art opening. There'd be food, drink, and all kinds of women falling all over you, the way it was when *On the Road* came out. You'd be a star again. The instant celebrity shot. Jack Kerouac returns . . . on canvas!"

"Nahh," said Jack, looking hurt. Gregory, Allen, and I started laughing. His face clouded and we saw in his eyes the pain of reliving in a flash the incredible overnight success that so quickly turned to critical savaging.

"I don't need success. I just need people to read my books. I'm an *author*. I paint and draw for Jesus and my own satisfaction."

"Well, Jesus wouldn't have been adverse to your making some money," said Allen. "I can get you an art dealer. I know art patrons—big money, yearning to be connected and rise above the nouveau riche dilettantes they compete with for attention. You'd be a natural. Poor French-Canadian boy from Lowell mill town comes to New York, is celebrated and then rejected by New York's tastemakers, turns to painting and becomes a star again. Like the painters Grandma Moses or Horace Pippin. You could be an icon for primitivism, where there's a lot of *money*."

"Allen," said Jack. "I never wrote or painted, sketched or drew, read in public or did anything other than heartbreak day jobs for money. I write and do art work for the love of bearing witness and telling stories in any medium to *share* my story."

"It's the St. Francis Shot," said Gregory.

"Yes," said Allen. "But never overlook the commercial potential of what you do."

"You can't sell Buddha, Jesus, Moses, Mohammed, or the American-Indian's Great Creator," said Jack.

"Put up a sign on this red brick building right now, Jack," said Gregory. "Spirituality is not for sale in this neighborhood."

"It's all for sale," said Allen sternly. "The capitalistic system guarantees a price on everyone's head."

"If you lived in Russia, you would have been eating whatever scraps of garbage you could dig up and clearing out latrines in Siberia for the last twenty years," said Jack. "Capitalism and materialism are two different things."

"Well, the more capital you have, the more material you can buy," said Gregory. "Who's got two dollars to get a hit of wine, pot, speed, smack, or mescaline from somebody?"

"Give me the two dollars," said a voice from the sidewalk.

Huddled up with his knees drawn to his chest, a middle-aged black man was sipping on the remains of a bottle of Thunderbird wine.

"Ahhh, Thunderbird wine, the drink of all sainted poets," said Jack, his face brightening. *"Quel bouquet! Quel goût!"*

"You want a hit?" said the huddled up man, handing the near-empty flask to Jack.

"Merci, mon frère," said Jack, slowly leaning forward and gently taking the bottle as if to show the man he appreciated his generosity in sharing the last few ounces of relief from the pain and loneliness of the world. Jack drained the remains, wiped his mouth with the sleeve of his ever-present red and black lumberjack shirt, and gently returned the empty bottle by the man's side, as if he were at a dinner table in someone's home.

"That was perfection," said Jack. "Let's get some more."

"All right," said the man, slowly rising to his feet.

"I'm Buddy. They call me Buddy the Wino down here. But I'm no wino. I just like to get high, you dig? A wino just gets juiced twenty-five hours a day till he drops dead. I like to get *high,* so I can get next to those deep feelings. You know where I'm coming from? You boys dig what I'm sayin'? I like to get my head straight. I'm a dreamer and a player, not no juice-head."

"Me too," said Gregory. "I'm a poet, looking for nirvana. Where can we buy something to get our heads all messed up?"

"Who got five bucks?" said Buddy.

There was a pause. We all thought about how to get some remaining money from your pocket, feeling with the tips of your fingers to make sure you left some there in order to get home safely in case the panhandler turned out to be a mugger.

Allen, Jack and I got five dollars in single bills and change and gave it to Buddy.

"I got to speak to my distributor," said Buddy. "Hey, Rocco," he shouted through cupped hands.

"On the way, Buddy," answered a gravely voice. Around the corner of the building appeared a familiar face. It was Rocco, the pot salesman and army dropout who had lived on the New York streets for over twenty years and survived by panhandling, selling weed, and working odd jobs. He was a good buddy of my first composition teacher, Charles Mills, who was also a friend and drinking buddy of Jack and all of us.

"Ah hah!" said Rocco. "Gregory, Jack, and Allen, the three musketeers. And Amram, the music man. Would you boys like to indulge in any nefarious substances?"

"How 'bout some Thunderbird, Rocco," said Jack.

"Excellent choice," said Rocco, in a stentorian maître d' voice. "We're having a sale right now. This particular bottle of fine wine is an excellent year, just manufactured a month ago, and better for the heart and liver than drinking sterno or rubbing alcohol and orange juice. If you're sleeping on the street, the combination of a bottle of this and wrapping yourself in the Sunday edition of *The New York Times* guarantees a good night's sleep. Of course you boys would most likely want to take the Book Review Section out to save for your erudition, rather than your insulation."

"Hah-hah, very funny, Rocco," said Gregory. "Cut the crap and get us some wine."

"I have it right here in my wine cellar," said Rocco. He lifted a steel trap door from the sidewalk, used for entering the basement of buildings, rummaged around, and emerged with two bottles. One was full, one was half empty.

"I use this one for quality control, but I'll throw it in as part of the special sale, and we'll all drink it on the way to Allen's house."

"Who said we're going to my house?" said Allen.

"Where else?" said Rocco. "Mind if I come along?"

"Do I have a choice?" asked Allen.

"I knew I was welcome," said Rocco.

"C'mon, Buddy. Hang some with these young cats. Boys, I'm glad to see all of your bad reviews and recent put-downs in the press haven't driven you all to despair or departure. We need you all here in New York. I want to hip Buddy to the vegetarian underground intelligentsia in action. I was too young to ever meet Edna St. Vincent Millay, Edgar Allen Poe, O. Henry, Eugene O'Neill, and all the other heavy cats and kitties that were around the Village. After I quit my day job and started living in the streets, the only way I could get close to the happenings was to hang out in Washington Square Park in the summer, and outside the jazz clubs and BYOB parties at painters' lofts. I got to meet some great heads. But Jack, after *On the Road* came out, it messed things up for everybody. Things will never be the same. Suddenly there was money to be made from being a Beatnik, and everything changed. Everybody turned cold. The only ones left to hang out with are you guys and the jazz musicians, the painters and moving men, waitresses and bartenders that still care about being real."

"Ah, the pain of crushed idealism and lost youth," said Gregory. "You're breaking my heart, Rocco. Let's drink that wine and score some dope and you'll get over it right away."

"I have a leftover sample packed from my weekend special," said Rocco, drawing a rolled-up grease stained brown paper bag full of Mexican weed from his raggedy coat. "We'll roll up a few bombers and have a reunion when we get to Allen's place."

"Now you're talkin'," said Gregory. "Now all we need is a few broads."

We trudged up the stairs to Allen's apartment and all sat down wherever we could clear space, passed around the wine, all drinking it from the bottle, except for Gregory, who insisted on pouring his share into a small saucepan and drinking it while holding his pinky finger up as if he were at a tea party.

"Elegance is wherever you decide it should be," said Gregory, slurping his wine from the saucepan, his voice echoing as he spoke. "Any command performance of my work demands high decorum. Gimme some more wine and pass that joint."

Allen stood up, and we all quieted down. He looked like an

overweight, stoned-out Abe Lincoln, without the top hat, and when he spoke his face became intense and his eyes focused on all of us, in two different directions. It was hard to tell if he was angry or off in another world, exorcising demons. Half of his face was angry, the other somewhat smiling. But when he recited poetry, whether it was his own or someone else's, his voice had a soothing hypnotic effect on everyone. Allen began to emote like a crazed Hassidic rabbi delivering a sermon.

"We are gathered here, old comrades in the arts, with our new friend Buddy."

"That's Buddy, the *Wino*!" said Buddy, puffing on a huge cigar-sized marijuana joint, wrapped in part of the sports section of the *New York Post*.

"There's thousands of Buddys in New York, but only *one* Buddy the Wino. And you lookin' at him right now."

"Yes, yes. I stand corrected," said Allen. "Buddy the Wino."

"And don't forget the holy man of Washington Square: Rocco, born and bred New York veteran of the 101st Airborne, who chose to reject earthly possessions to live a life on the streets, like a Jacobean worker priest, to help his brothers and sisters to find salvation in the living hell of New York's cruel Bowery nights," said Jack, finishing off the first bottle of Rocco's special Thunderbird wine bargain sale.

"There's no place to hang out anymore in the cold weather," said Rocco. "All the coffee shops and jazz clubs and old restaurants are booming now. You guys started a trend that is pricing us all out, including yourselves. Where's all your royalties and advances, Jack?"

"Gone," said Jack wearily, fluttering his fingers in the air like a dancer. "I got my mother a home," he said proudly. "She'll never work in a goddam factory again for the rest of her life. I'm surviving. I'm still writing all the time. And painting . . . And I have some poetry I was going to read."

"Let's hear it now," said Rocco, passing the second bottle of wine around. *Salut, à la santé, lecheyim, schlonshon, Prost* . . . whatever language, this wine tastes so good on a cold winter night, it's like the nectar of the gods."

"An interesting turn of phrase," said Allen, professorially, as he took a tentative sip of the somewhat rancid half-empty bottle of Thunderbird that we were passing around.

"I left it open for two days on top of a radiator in the storeroom of this basement," said Rocco, sheepishly. "It tastes a little fruity. Read your poem, Jack. I remember when you and Amram did those jazz-poetry readings in '57. Stirred things up. Now nobody remembers."

"It's good we are doing this at my place," said Allen. "It's too cold outside and if Amram doesn't start playing his horn too loudly, we won't have the neighbors call the cops for disturbing the peace. I'd like to begin by reading a love poem."

We all quieted down, Gregory took a last swig from his saucepan full of wine, and Allen began reading. He was developing his style, modeled after Jack's, and while at this time in his life he had no natural sense of music or rhythm, which he later developed to a higher level, he had the intensity and amazing voice that made everything he read capture your attention.

While he was reading, Buddy the Wino would occasionally nod his head in appreciation, while Rocco fought to keep his head from falling to his chest as he began to nod out.

"Yes, yes," said Gregory when Allen was done.

"I could definitely dig that," said Rocco, awakening from his semi-slumber.

"Nice, that was choice," said Buddy.

"Very tasty, Allen," I said.

"The voice of Allen is heard in the land," said Jack.

"Thank you," said Allen. "It's nice to read like this, without a mob of people, cameras, tape recorders, and detractors. Read one, Gregory."

"Nah," said Gregory. "You guys are the performers. I've got them down on paper. History will judge me by what I leave on the shelf. I don't need the limelight. I'm a *poet*. I'm not a songwriter or a movie star. All I need is a refresher for my saucepan, another joint, and a fine woman, which I'll never find hanging out with you guys. I have a date at the San Remo with a beautiful waitress from the Kettle of Fish at 10:30, so I'm splitting after Jack reads a few new poems. I'll see you at the Cedar Tavern tomorrow night, Dave, and you can meet my new true love, if she remembers to show up. She likes classical music, Dave, and she wants to hear some of your symphony pieces. But if you play her anything, remember she's with *me*."

"I know, Gregory," I said.

"True love knows no bounds, Gregory," said Allen. "Caring means sharing."

"Save the neo-Buddhist crap, Allen," snapped Gregory. "If she's with me, she's *mine*."

"We don't own each other's souls or bodies," said Allen gently.

"That's true," said Gregory. "But I don't want anybody messing with my romantic attachments."

"No romance without finance," said Rocco. "That's Dizzy Gillespie's famous saying. How 'bout five dollars so I can give Gregory a hit of speed to guarantee his sparkling personality to emerge from the debilitating effects of this evening's soiree?"

"Nah," said Gregory. "One more poem and I'm outta here."

Jack stood up and opened his knapsack. Inside was a roll of paper that looked like a scroll of shelving paper. I noticed there was typing on it. He began to unroll it, like an old Hebrew scroll that you would see in temple, like the miniature scroll my great-great-grandfather Moses Ben Judah, aka Moses Amram, brought on the boat with him when he landed in the port of Savannah in the mid-1800s and which was passed on to members of our family through the generations.

Jack and I used to talk for hours about the sanctity of ancient artifacts. Old Jewish documents, the hieroglyphics of Egypt, the Book of the Dead, the 10,000-year-old Lascaux cave paintings, the Easter Island statues, Stonehenge . . . all the surviving relics of antiquity and how their presence today telescoped time and made the past present, and the present past. I suddenly wondered when I saw Jack's scroll if he felt this was something he was leaving, like a time traveler, to the future, or if he had gone back into the past and somehow retrieved it.

"You're looking kind of stoned-out there, Dave," said Rocco, interrupting my thoughts.

"Oh, excuse me," I said. "I was just wondering . . . Jack, tell me what that scroll is."

"Those are some poems, Davey, about Mexico. They deal with the past, way before me, and my recent sojourn there, and with the ancient spirits of the Mexican Indians. I could hear their voices in my dreams at night, speaking in Toltec when I was there. I thought I could feel the spirit of my Iroquois Indian forbears in Canada who married Frenchmen. I had dreams I heard them speaking to me through their Mexican-Indian cousins in a language I never heard before, in dreams that were so real I had to capture them, so I typed them out on this little scroll. I've done this before but never mentioned it to you. Allen and Gregory know. It doesn't matter if anyone knows anymore how I approach my work. It's the writing that counts. Methodology is for pedants. Poetry is for all time."

Jack put down the scroll and began to read "Orizaba 210 Blues" from a small notebook in his musical Lowell accented speech, and we were suddenly transported from Allen's New York City Lower East Side apartment to the dingy streets of Mexico City.

Jack continued to read other poems, unwinding the scroll he carried with him. During certain moments of each poem, Buddy became animated, slapping his leg and shouting, "Yes, yes," like you hear in a sanctified church call and response.

"Blow, Jack, blow, baby!" shouted Rocco, as Jack continued reading. Allen and Gregory closed their eyes and rocked back and forth. Jack pointed with one finger to my French horn case and bag of whistles, which was my signal to accompany him.

Jack was the most generous of all of us, and always promoted others to be in the spotlight, but because there were only six of us in the room, he read for half an hour, poem after poem of a series we now know as *Mexico City Blues*, until the scroll was nearly completely rolled up. He also read others from the small notebooks. I played whatever came to me that the poem suggested, as I always have done. All the images and the stories that fill the pages of Jack's poetry and prose made you think of more musical ideas than you could ever have time to use in a lifetime. It was more intense with the six of us in the room than it would have been playing for a large group of people. We were creating something just for the six of us. We all sat in silence after Jack was done reading.

"Brother Jack, you're sumpthin' else," said Buddy. "You took me right there with you."

"You nailed it, Jack," said Rocco. "You took us all down to Mexico."

"This must be published," said Allen. "I'm going to make some calls."

"I'm late for my date, but it's worth missing my new true love to hear that, Jack," said Gregory. "You're a true poet."

I was speechless after hearing as well as playing for Jack's "Orizaba 210 Blues" and *Mexico City Blues*. This was the first time I even knew the names of what Jack was reading. I never knew whether it was something he wrote, something someone else had written, or whether it was pure imagination. I knew that whatever he did would happen only one time, so I relished each precious second. This time I knew these poems were his own and that he had written them down. I knew that others could experience the messages of these beautiful evocative poems, which sounded so spontaneous but were so beautifully crafted, capturing the essence of his experiences in Mexico. Whether you were there the night he read them in his magnificent natural style, or whether you read them in the silence of your room, which I did many times since that night, they always rang true. I understood why so many poets held Jack in such high esteem.

Gregory left, Rocco pulled out another joint, and Allen read some more.

"You cats are crazy," said Buddy. "I could have been a singer. I dig show business, but I don't want nobody in my life to answer to except my own self."

"This is my King Kong weed," said Rocco, pulling out a joint that was wrapped inside a shredded Phillies cigar. "After you smoke this you'll be able to climb the Empire State Building like King Kong did and pull down planes from the air with your bare hands."

"Let's check it out," said Buddy. "I'm all for that."

We passed around the joint and all began coughing violently. Allen lurched over to his icebox and took out a large bottle of prune juice, which we drank, since there was no more wine left.

Jack and I began making up rhymed verses on the spot about everybody in the room, and our shared experiences together. Buddy joined in, throwing out lines as if we had all played and rapped together for years. Rocco and Allen took the saucepan Gregory had been drinking out of and the prune juice bottle and used them to play percussion parts, tapping them with some old greasy unwashed chopsticks that Allen grabbed from the fetid waters of his half filled kitchen sink.

At 4 A.M. we trudged out of Allen's to go back to my 6th Avenue apartment, where Jack was crashing. We said goodbye to Buddy and Rocco.

"Let's do this soon again, fellahs," said Rocco. "Come by and see me. If I'm not in my office in Washington Square Park, I'll be around here. I'm getting some killer weed and uppers from an old Army buddy who just got out of the slammer and is coming to New York. I'll save you some samples and we'll have a party."

"It was a ball," said Buddy. "Stay beautiful. Gimmee two more dollars for some waffles for breakfast. I'll pray for both of you."

We gave Buddy everything we had left in our pockets and walked toward my apartment in the amazingly peaceful 4:15 A.M. New York late night–early morning calm.

"If we hadn't met Buddy I don't know if I ever would have read 'Mexico City Blues' aloud," said Jack.

"Guys like that have so much knowledge of life, and a spirituality they must have acquired because of all they've been through. Dostoyevsky wrote about salvation through suffering. The *penitantes* who participate in Mexican street ceremonies are like Buddy and Rocco. They rise to another level, through their suffering, as if they are bearing their own personal cross for all of us.

"I can't help seeing things this way. You seem to have some instinctive empathy for the Catholic sensibility, Davey, even if you don't understand it. Maybe it's because you still love being

Jewish. Allen doesn't get it. He tries to equate spirituality with politics. Our feelings of divinity, and man's pain in searching for either Jesus or nirvana, have nothing to do with some miserable European sociological intellectual approach towards finding God. All anyone cares about in New York is knowing who deserves the most money and who should wear the crown. Jesus wore the crown, but it was the crown of thorns. Your Moses spent forty years in the desert, looking for a drink of water. Ah-h-h, Davey, life is cruel. But also a joy. I'm hungry, man. That prune juice and King Kong weed gave me an appetite. Make me one of your amazing omelets, where you empty the icebox and fry up everything into an Amramian church and temple melange of spontaneously chosen ingredients. Like a Mahler symphony, concocted on the spot with extra grease. Quebec's cuisine has given me a cast iron stomach. I can't play football anymore, but I can still eat one of your omelets."

I opened up the old icebox and took out everything . . . Swiss cheese, yogurt, onions, peanut butter, pickles, radishes, moldy baked beans, garlic powder, a half-opened can of clam chowder, gefilte fish, creamed herring, nine eggs, threw everything in a big bowl, whipped it up to a frightening-looking morass of slimy goo and dumped it in a hot frying pan full of boiling safflower oil.

"I thought you were on one of your health kicks," said Jack.

"I am," I said. "The safflower oil is organic and low fat."

"Oh, I see," said Jack, in a basso profundo voice, suddenly taking on the role of a federal judge or brain surgeon. "Do you have scientific evidence to support your recipe's nutritional value? Have you documented the number of fatalities in the past decade from your patients who have ingested this concoction?"

"Not yet, Jack, but this will be my latest, greatest, tastiest, nastiest, moving and grooving, survival omelet."

We sat down with two chairs facing the icebox, began eating our omelets on plastic plates on our laps, while reaching into the icebox to sprinkle anything piled up there on top of the omelets for extra flavoring, and finished off two stale half-empty cans of beer and Dr. Brown's Black Cherry Soda.

Jack's face suddenly lit up as he hunched over and reached way in the back of the icebox.

"Voilà!" he shouted. "Look what the chef has hidden in his cupboard." He leaned back and held up a small pair of sneakers, with the left sneaker covered with a mossy green mold sprouting plant-like from a rotted piece of Camembert cheese lodged next to the sneaker's heel.

"It's like a Corso poem," said Jack, laughing. "Fried sneakers."

"Nah," I said. "Those are Janine's. She's mad at me because I couldn't remember where she left them. When Laura came back unexpectedly to stay with me, I hid all Janine's stuff. Then Laura left to go back to her job as a cook in the Merchant Marine, Janine came over and was suspicious that everything looked so orderly."

"You can't fool women about anything," said Jack. "All you can do is be totally honest. No deceitfulness, no *petite bourgeoisie politesse*. Just be real. Your peccadilloes only mean you are fulfilling your destiny as a born sinner. Jesus forgave Mary Magdalene. Janine will forgive you."

We ate our omelets, and Jack talked about *Visions of Cody* till 5 A.M. He was devastated that no one would publish it.

"They're ignoring me. They are saying my time is past. My time is *now*! My time will always be now. Just like Charlie Parker's 1945 masterpiece 'Now's the Time.' My time is now!"

Jack's face clouded over, and he gently placed the scroll of *Mexico City Blues* back in his little bag.

"So much to write about, Davey. The world is hurting, life is being squeezed out of us all by greed and narcissism. Even the artists and poets are betraying our calling. God calls us all to do our work. Laborer, trucker, poet, lawyer, gangster, big-fingered short order cook, all are answering God's call. I am an author! [He always pronounced it "aw-thuh" after a few drinks, in the musical style of Lowell, Massachusetts].

"I am . . . an . . . aw-thuh. History will judge me by my work. By your works ye shall be known. That work you put into that omelet is doing its work on me. I am slipping into the arms of Morpheus."

"I'll give you the bed," I said, moving piles of music, books, and clothes off the couch, which also served as my bed and research center.

"Nah-h," said Jack. "I'll take my usual literary place at the foot of the bed of the master composer, musicologist, romantic, and my own bebop and Berlioz collaborator Monsieur le Maestro Mezz McGillicuddy" (the name later given to me in the film *Pull My Daisy*).

Jack unrolled my sleeping bag and lay down on the linoleum floor.

"I've got to get up in three hours to make a rehearsal," I said.

"*Dors bien* [sleep well]," said Jack. "I'll dream of our mountain farm, where someday we'll all live together, with Neal and Carolyn and their kids, and your wife and kids when you finally get some. I know you've heard this before, Davey, but someday we'll do it. Look, man, look at that bird staring at us through the window."

A bird had landed on the windowsill and had perched on the ledge with its head cocked back. It sat quietly and suddenly let out a high-pitched tweet.

"Dig that!" said Jack, lifting his head up from the cushion on the sleeping bag. "That bird is singing to us. It's the purest music, like Messiaen's *Les Oiseaux Exotiques* with all the different bird calls, like Beethoven's *Pastoral Symphony* in the movement after the ending of the storm, when the flute becomes the bird. Maybe it's Bird himself, Charlie Parker, coming back from his 1955 demise to tell us he is still here, visiting us at chez Amram, singing his sweet song to us, on your sacred sill on an early New York morning, in a new body, still waiting for more music to come after an all-night jam session."

"I'll feed it some of my omelet," I said.

"No, Davey, no!" said Jack. "Please refrain. A few bites of that omelet might kill it."

"Okay," I said. "I'll have a bite for me."

"Save me some," said Jack. "It's powerful enough to cure any hangover."

The bird still sat, cocking its head as Jack began to snore peacefully over the sounds of early morning New York City rush hour traffic.

Another night had turned to day. I set my alarm to wake myself up. I had a rehearsal in a few hours and I knew I had to be there on time. I knew the time I spent with Jack was always precious. Regardless of who we were with or what we did, not a moment was ever wasted.

A Brief University of Hang-out-ology Field Trip

In January of 1959, we collaborated with a once-in-a-lifetime group of artists on the film *Pull My Daisy.* In addition to appearing in the film as Mezz McGillicuddy, the deranged French horn player in the moth-eaten sweater, I composed the entire score for the film and wrote the music for the title song, "Pull My Daisy," with lyrics by Jack, Neal Cassady, and Allen Ginsberg.

The idea of making a film based on Jack's work was easier to talk about than to actually accomplish. Many people felt that the experience of reading *On the Road* was like watching a film, projected on the screen of your mind, as you devoured the pages of his classic adventure story-poem-novel. All of his writing, like his spontaneous raps, conjured up kaleidoscopic imagery that made you feel that you were a member of the cast in a great documentary film about the quintessential America we all longed to be part of. Like most of the high-energy musicians, poets, painters, and assorted dreamers we hung out with, Jack relished every precious moment of each day and night. He often told me his books were sight and sound journeys, told in the style of a great jazz solo, to be shared by the readers, joining him on his endless odyssey.

One afternoon in the middle of November, 1958, Jack came over to my sixth floor walk-up apartment at 114 Christopher Street from his house on Gilbert Street in Northport. "I've got an idea for a short film, Davey, a *petit flic* about a simple afternoon at Neal's house. It's a scene from a play I'd like to write, about what we all mean to one another. Allen Ginsberg, Gregory Corso, and Peter

Orlovsky will play themselves. They are the psychotic poets who drive Neal's wife and everyone else crazy. Larry Rivers is going to be Neal, and you can be Mezz McGillicuddy, the mad French horn–playing optimistic Irish-American nut-case. It will be a silent film, and I can narrate it after it's been shot, while you play the music for me, like a great Charlie Chaplin silent movie. We can do our part together spontaneously, like we've always done, while we're watching the final edited version. We can paint a picture. No one today knows what Beat is about. They certainly have no idea what I'm about, especially if they read articles about me, where I'm misquoted. They're forced to judge me by embittered journalists who gave up their dreams of writing to become slaves to heartless publications run by people who have *never read a word I've written!* They neglect the fact that I'm referring to the beatitudes, and to the beat of everyone's ancestral drum that we carry through our lives, from the time we hear our mother's heartbeat before we are even born. The Beatnik crap is distorting everything all of us are trying to say. It's even distorting history by cheapening the memories of Charlie Parker, Dizzy Gillespie, and Thelonious Monk. In the forties when I heard them at Minton's in Harlem, they were wearing berets and horn-rimmed glasses to show their allegiance with Picasso, Jean-Paul Sartre, and the revolutionary artists, because they wanted the same respect shown to them as American musical visionaries. The Beatnik craze has usurped their dress style, making a joke out of their struggles. The kids today are brainwashed about this. They don't know that bongos are our link to Africa and have religious connotations. They don't know about Afro-Cuban influences on American music, or Chano Pozo or Machito's contributions to the history of jazz right here in New York City. They're just kids, being guided by money-grubbing merchants, who no longer read books or sit in Bhodovista silence, digging the sounds of the last genius pioneers of bop. Allen accuses me of being stuck in the past. I tell him I only want to see this great chapter of history I witnessed recorded. What's new comes from what's old. And if it's of lasting value, it stays new *forever*.

"Our little movie, *notre petit flic,* can hip-a-fy these kids to the ancient happenings of a few years ago. They can see all of us, now dismissed as passé pioneers of the Beat Generation as regular human beings and fellow artists, spending a silly afternoon together in a *tête-à-tête,* till Neal's wife can't stand our mooching and freeloading anymore and throws us all out of her apartment so that she, Neal, and the children can have a few family moments of tranquillity. Ahh. *Ça ne fait rien.* Let's go to Washington Square Park and see if we can meet a gum-chewing chess-master genius and invite some young gals up to your pad. You can cook them a Hector Berlioz–style omelet of leftovers with eggs, and I'll recite them notes from my latest tome."

Jack and I strolled over to the Park. Through the brisk November streets I told him about my new piece for string orchestra, *Autobiography for Strings,* which was going to be premiered in June of 1959 by Maurice Peress at a concert at New York University a few blocks away from where we were walking in the Village.

"It was inspired by what we have done together, combining the spontaneous and the formal," I said. "It's a one-movement piece, using the *sonata allegro* form, with every note written out. I use a lot of jazz harmonies, walking bass lines, and ideas that I've made up on the spot as a player, ideas that are never used by composers in a string orchestra composition. It's not elevator music or commercial shlock-shmaltz Broadway trash. I'm trying to create a piece of music based on the real thing, so orchestral string players can feel that spirit of what it was like for me to play with Mingus and Clifford Brown and Sonny Rollins, Bill Evans, Dizzy, and Monk."

"Stick to your guns, Davey," said Jack. "Do it right and follow your heart. Otherwise the ghosts of Bartok, Gershwin, Schubert, and Charlie Parker will creep beneath your sheets like crawling cockroaches in the silence of the night and make you give penance and recite Hail Marys as they confront you in your *petit chateau,* sliding on the linoleum between symmetrical mounds of pizza crusts and tortured socks."

We walked around the circle surrounding the fountain in Washington Square Park, talking to old acquaintances of ours who knew Jack before he had become so well known. He was always most comfortable with old acquaintances or young people who knew nothing about him but who had a hunger for life. He loved to start a conversation so that he could lay back and listen, once he had initiated a dialogue.

As we gradually strolled through the Park and passed some of the chess players who braved the cold weather, I told Jack about the next orchestral piece I was going to write, inspired in part by some great raps by Lord Buckley, the philosopher-comedian-poet we both admired. Jack could recite some of Lord Buckley's routines, based on stories from the Bible and Shakespeare and told in a street-scat style all his own, with a Winston Churchill–like evangelical furor.

I told Jack it was to be scored for oboe, two horns and strings, combining Elizabethan harmonies similar to the scores I was writing for Joseph Papp's Shakespeare in the Park Production, and classical dramas at the Phoenix Theater, where I had become composer-in-residence. "I'm calling it Shakespearean Concerto," I said. I hummed Jack some of the melodies, one of which was the song "The Wind and the Rain," that I had composed a few months ago in the summer of 1958 for a production in Central Park of *Twelfth Night*. Twenty years later, it became the principal melody for my full-length opera, *Twelfth Night*. When I sang it for the first time to Jack, he nodded his head. "Oh, man, that's nice, and it fits Shakespeare's words. *C'est beau*, Davey."

I explained to Jack that while some of the musical materials for the new piece I was writing sounded like jazz, they would be combined with classically composed counterpoint, using jazz harmonies and occasional Latin American rhythms and other sounds of 1950s New York City street music. I tried to demonstrate to Jack a section in the last movement where the string players gently tapped conga and bongo rhythms on the backs of their instruments, while the oboe played two written-out, twelve-bar blues choruses. As I began to play some of the bongo and conga drum rhythms on my knee and leg with one hand, and the back of an empty park bench with the other hand while singing the oboe part, Jack began to recite a spontaneous monologue in the style of Shakespeare, taking the story from

Twelfth Night of the sea captain from Elyria running his ship aground in the storm and crash-landing in Elmira, Pennsylvania, where Viola, the long lost sibling of Shakespeare's play, joins the viola section of my orchestra to sit in for the eventual premiere of my new Shakespearean Concerto.

"I wish I'd recorded that, Jack," I said.

"*Ça ne fait rien,*" said Jack. "It was too corny. Anyway, it's already been recorded in the sands of time, and is planted in the souls of the nearby chess players and wine-drinking heroes of Washington Square Park. It is now inscribed in their book of life. I'll remember what was worth remembering, and the choice tidbits will appear someday in a future *oeuvre.*" Jack's Shakespearean recitation reminded me of Lord Buckley, as if he were an English literature professor at a faculty tea, holding an imaginary tea cup in the air with his little finger extended. Jack was an exceptionally gifted mimic, able to portray several characters at the same time, all having an imaginary conversation with one another.

We walked back to the circle by the fountain in Washington Square Park, and participated in an informal jam session with some folk guitar players, Latin percussionists, and a West Indian steel drummer street musician who also played a suitcase full of percussion instruments and passed an empty cigar box for donations at the end of each performance. I played my French horn and wooden flutes, and Jack played a set of bongos the steel drummer handed him.

"Hey, man. You're that writer I see sometimes on television."

"That's right," said Jack.

"You're a bad cat, man. I read *The Subterraneans*. Write a book about *me*. I got some *bad* stories."

He spent a half and hour telling Jack and a group of us who gathered around him tales of his childhood in the West Indies. He described how steel drums were built, what they meant to the West Indians, how the British had failed in brainwashing the West Indians when they tried to make them forget their African heritage, and the beauty of the Islands, and the unique qualities of each island. Jack was spellbound, listening intently, nodding his head as if he were a part of every story being told. Again, Jack was that one person Mingus told me about that everyone needed in life to communicate with. Finally, the steel drummer came into the home stretch of a tall tale about a giant fish that would come up to the side of his small sailing dinghy and lie in the water next to his boat when he brought a small steel drum aboard to serenade the huge fish at sunset.

"That fish *loved* to hear me play. He would have followed me on shore, and flapped his way to my home if he'd been able to. Well, I've got to make me some money now."

He began playing, after opening up his cigar box for donations. Jack and I put what we had in the box. The Cafe Figaro always gave us free food and coffee.

"Don't forget to write a book about *me*," he said to Jack, before launching into a Calypso standard.

"These are the great poets and novelists," said Jack, as the drummer finished his song. "No one can ever capture the beauty of their poetry or the perfect structure of their stories. Guys like him remind me of why I wanted to be a writer."

We never met the gal of my dreams that night, or got to talk to the gum-chewing genius chess player that Jack hoped to encounter. Instead of going to the Figaro, we walked over to the Five Spot, so I could sit in for a set with the band that was playing there.

Joe Termini, the original owner of the Five Spot since Cecil Taylor and I first played there in 1956, greeted us warmly.

"Jack, Dave, come on in. Come to the kitchen. I'll make you hamburgers with fried onions and mayonnaise on an English muffin. I remember that's what you like. You guys never come around anymore."

"I'm away a lot," said Jack.

"I'm home writing music," I said sheepishly.

"Remember this?" said Joe, proudly pointing to the wall. There was an issue of *Esquire* with a feature article entitled "Upper and Lower Bohemia." There was a two-page color picture of me playing with my quartet, taken in January of 1957 and published in the July 1957 issue. Beneath the photo was printed the caption

"Dave Amram leads his jazz group at the Five Spot. Peak crowd is about midnight. In quieter moments, a poet will sometimes read his verse to the music."

"That was you they were writing about, Jack," said Joe. "Reading with Dave, in early 1957, before you got famous. Before you guys did the first jazz-poetry reading in New York. I was just hanging on that winter. That was you, Jack. You and Dave and Cecil Taylor helped to make the Five Spot."

"Me and many others," said Jack softly.

"I miss you guys," said Joe Termini. "Oh, boy, what times we had. All the artists, and those crazy people. The old crowd doesn't come here anymore. We're doing great. We've got headliners playing here now. I had to raise my prices. Tourists come from all over the world to see the Five Spot. We're opening up a new club on St. Mark's Place. After thirty years in the bar business, I'm finally making some money. How's Larry Rivers, Alfred Leslie, Robert Frank, and all the old gang?"

"We're about to make a movie together, a few blocks from here," said Jack.

"I'll come see it," said Joe. "I'll tell all my friends. You guys put us on the map. Take some apple pie if you want. Wine, beer, whatever you want, on the house. I've got to take care of the customers."

Joe went out to a packed house, and Jack and I sat in the kitchen and talked to Dennis Charles, the drummer who had played with Cecil Taylor at the end of 1956 and with my quartet for eleven weeks in the beginning of 1957.

"Man, I see you're out there now, Jack. I remember seeing you in early '57 when we played here. You were usually the only cat listening. You sounded good when you read with us too. You're out there now. I see people carrying your books around."

"I hope they read them," said Jack.

Dennis laughed. "I do. You write about it like it really is."

We began to talk about astrology, life in outer space, and John Coltrane's fascination with Albert Einstein. We also demolished a whole apple pie, a rack of hamburgers, and two pitchers of beer. None of us were what we now call health conscious in those days.

We took it for granted that we were indestructible and would live forever.

When we finally got home, Jack collapsed on my couch and I worked on *Autobiography for Strings* till dawn. Jack left New York the next day for one of his journeys.

Spontaneous Commotion: The Making of *Pull My Daisy*

A few weeks later, Alfred Leslie called me. He, composer Edgard Varese, and poet Arnold Weinstein had encouraged me since I first came to New York in 1955 to pursue my dreams of being a composer, combining all the musical styles I felt belonged together. Alfred and Arnold always made me feel anything was possible. They were native-born New Yorkers with soul. They became friends for life.

"David, I have some exciting news," said Alfred. "Jack has written an extraordinary outline for a silent film he would like to have made. It's based on a larger work, but would be perfect as a short documentary. It's a charming vignette, a simple story idea that could be a real addition to the repertoire of the New Cinema. Robert Frank will film it, I'll direct it in my art studio, you'll write the music as well as appear in it, and Jack will narrate it."

"Jack's already told me about it," I said.

"Are you interested?"

"Sure."

"We have a fabulous cast. Only one professional actor, Jack Youngerman's wife, Delphine Seyrig. She only speaks French, but since it's a silent film, it doesn't matter. She has an amazing presence and dignity. Gregory Corso, Allen Ginsberg, and Peter Orlovsky will play themselves. Mary Frank, Dody Muller, Larry Rivers, Alice Neal, and Richard Bellamy have also agreed to do it. We'll all meet next week to go over the outline, and start filming shortly after our get-together. Jack wants you to be yourself, of course, but your character's name is Mezz McGillicuddy, the cheerful composer-French horn player with a zonked-out personality."

"Type casting. I'd be perfect for the part," I said. "Just don't tell any of the great actors whose plays I write music for that I'm appearing in a movie. I don't know how to act. I have enormous respect for those actors and how dedicated they are to their art."

"You're not supposed to act," said Alfred. "None of you should try to act. Since none of you except Delphine Seyrig are actors, you'll all be your delightful crazy anarchistic selves."

"It should be quite a film," I said tentatively.

"Definitely," said Alfred, brimming with confidence and enthusiasm. "We'll fit our filming to everyone's work schedules. Whenever you're free, come over. I know you're composing a score for a Phoenix Theater production, but it's only a few blocks away from my studio. Whenever you drop by, we can film you doing something. Everybody will be floating in and out. It should be fantastic. It can be our way of honoring Jack's work, and the enduring bonds of friendship we all share. This will be our statement: Painters, poets, musicians, photographers, all capturing a moment of our joy together."

"Aren't you going to be in it?" I asked.

Alfred was great looking, with wild black curls and the physique of a champion athlete. (He had been Mr. Bronx a few years earlier in a bodybuilding competition.) He emanated an unlimited *joie de vivre* and charisma that charmed everyone who knew him. He was already acclaimed as an important young American artist, and so articulate and spellbinding in his conversation that the musicians from our quartet at the Five Spot in 1957 still called him "The Professor."

"No, David," said Alfred. "I'll have my hands full just directing. I'll stay behind the camera. I'll try to guide our cast in the telling of Jack's story in a truthful way. No one needs to act. We don't want anything phony. Like a Truffaut film, everyone will be themselves, and yet we'll somehow keep Jack's ideas intact. It will *seem* improvised, but we'll end up having a film that exudes freshness and vitality."

I talked to Robert Frank the next night at the Cedar Tavern. He was acknowledged by all of us as a photographer who transcended the definition of what photography was supposed to be all about. His photographs of ordinary subjects had such a strange beauty that all the abstract painters who rebelled against representational art loved Robert's work. He captured on film what most of us saw every day and never paid attention to. Like Jack, he could see the diamonds in the sidewalk.

Robert was brought up in Switzerland and inspired by the work of the American photographer Walker Evans. He came to America with a vision of his own. There was no one else like him. Robert and his brilliantly talented and beautiful wife, Mary Frank, were always a joy to be with. Both were pure artists, admired and loved by all who knew them.

Robert was quieter and more thoughtful than most of us, but his eyes spoke for him. When he looked your way, you could feel you were in the presence of an old soul, somehow surviving in the wilds of New York. You could feel him seeking, searching, observing and remaining calm even when surrounded by insanity. This was a redeeming quality, considering the impossible task he was about to undertake—filming a group of incorrigible, individualistic, hell-raising, fun-loving lunatics Alfred had assembled for the cast of *Pull My Daisy*.

"I think we'll achieve something of value from this experience," said Robert. "This is a special time, David. A special moment in history that we can capture. All of these people together. This most unlikely cast of characters should be perfect to tell Jack's story. We shall see."

"Robert," I said, "you could photograph an old rusty tin can lying in the gutter and make something beautiful. You're the tops, Pops!"

"You're much too kind," said Robert softly, with the sardonic smile he always had when he was complimented. "I don't need your approval, but I appreciate your enthusiasm. I know you'll do a good job writing the music. As far as your portrayal of your character, Mezz McGillicuddy, in the film, just be yourself. Don't try to act. Jack told us it's really you, but according to his description of your character in the three-page outline he gave us, you're supposed to be a 'hip tape man.' I have no idea what that's supposed to mean. It doesn't matter. We'll capture the special moments. Everyone's diverse personalities will make it somehow work."

The day we finally began filming *Pull My Daisy* (it didn't have that title until later) was a prelude to weeks of chaotic, fun-filled madhouse clowning. Somehow, this endless party was guided by Alfred Leslie's direction and Robert Frank's ability to film the unfilmable. Both of them managed to stay calm, supportive, and organized, day and night, patiently telling the cast exactly what our motivation should be, where we should stand, and what we should say, so Jack could later lip-sync key moments of dialogue when he narrated the film.

"We must be faithful to Jack's story," said Alfred over and over as we all tried to outdo each other by surprising Alfred and Robert with unexpected pranks. Alfred was as meticulous and devoted in trying to coordinate and guide every detail of the film as he was when he was creating one of his masterful oil paintings. We were his palette.

"We're putty in your hands," said Peter Orlovsky.

In one of the first scenes we filmed, Gregory Corso and Allen Ginsberg were supposed to be engaged in a deep conversation about poetry. Before they came into view, the camera made a slow pan, showing every grimy detail of the studio, that had already been trashed by all of us during a cast party three hours before we even started filming.

As the camera was being set to begin the slow pan, Gregory Corso lit up an enormous joint of Mexican pot.

"This is my Oscar-winning shot, Leslie," he shouted, taking a huge drag from the joint and a slug from a gallon bottle of Gallo wine. He looked like a crazed Jerry Lewis. "I'm ready for my close-up as soon as I finish drinking my breakfast." Gregory took another slug from the gallon bottle and sat on the floor with his head between his knees.

"I think they're about to film us, Gregory," said Allen, softly.

"I'm hip, Allen. I'm getting in character," said Gregory, trying futilely to light up the joint of pot that was now extinguished and soaked with the red Gallo wine Gregory had spilled on it.

"Now, Gregory," said Alfred softly, "we're about to embark on a great adventure together. You must remember your character's relationship in this scene with the character of your fellow poet, Allen. You have to concentrate on the melancholy nature and loneliness of the hopeless situation that you and Allen share as poets, trying to survive in a society that ignores its prophets and cultural pioneers. You have to show the feelings of brotherhood that you and Allen share, and the compassion you have for one another in your mutual struggle for acceptance. At the same time, radiate a feeling of strength and optimism to show the audience your underlying heroic nature."

"Got it, Alfie. No problem. Roll it!" said Gregory, who had rolled a fresh joint of pot.

Robert began to slowly pan the camera in a circle, revealing the filthy dishes in the sink, the cockroach-infested stove, and the soiled aromatic underwear and crusty mismatched socks strewn over the back of a broken-down chair.

"All right," whispered Alfred. "In about twenty seconds, you'll be in the shot. Remember, you are both discussing your commitment of bringing new forms to American verse by stretching all the accepted boundaries of twentieth-century poetry. You are cultural pioneers."

"You got it," whispered Gregory. A few seconds later, as the camera completed its slow pan and focused on them, Allen, with one lightning-fast gesture, as swift and unexpected as a champion boxer's sneak right hand lead delivering a knockout punch, dropped his pants and underwear. Before they had hit the floor, wrapping around the bottom of his sneakers, he was drenched with a mixture of red wine, hamburger grease, ketchup, and French fried potatoes, poured over his head by Gregory from a large paper container from the diner down the block.

"How ya like that Stanislovsky method-actor motivation bit, Leslie, hah?" rasped Gregory, the joint of marijuana dangling from his lips. "Is that a Marlon Brando Actors Studio shot, Alfie? Does that show how America treats her poets?"

Allen broke into a buck and wing dance step, flapping his arms as he tripped over his pants and underwear that encircled his feet and Gregory began to somersault on the floor, scooping up stale French fries, some of which he began eating while throwing the others at Robert Frank's camera, while the rest of us watched this unusual interpretation of two poets having a scholarly discussion.

Robert kept the camera rolling. "That's not what we had planned at all, but it's quite interesting," said Alfred, as Gregory knocked over a lamp during one of his somersaults.

Delphine Seyrig, the classically trained French actress, who would later star in *Last Year at Marienbad*, stood by stoically, waiting for her cue. She was supposed to enter a quiet room, and serve Allen and Gregory a glass of wine and dust off the table in preparation for the homecoming of her railroad train-conductor husband Milo, based on the real-life character of Neal Cassady. Painter Larry Rivers was playing this role, wearing a ratty-looking conductor's uniform with a real train conductor's hat. Delphine was such a disciplined actress that she managed to make her entrance. She had to worm her way through Allen, who was hopping around the room, trying not to trip over his pants and underwear, while Gregory continued to somersault around the studio. They were joined by Peter Orlovsky, who made an unplanned entrance, wrapped in wet towels, brushing his teeth with one hand and waving a toilet plunger with the other.

"I'm here to clean up America!" he shouted over and over.

Every time Delphine would try to enter into the shot, Peter would unwrap a towel from his body with the hand he was holding the toothbrush in and dangle the towel in front of her.

"Perhaps this could be construed as a statement of trying to shield Delphine's character from the pain and humiliation of the poet's sense of rejection," said Alfred hopefully, as Robert kept filming.

Just as Delphine had run out of ways to try to enter into the shot, Larry Rivers made an unexpected entrance in his railroad conductor's outfit, honking on his alto saxophone, cheeks blown out, eyes staring wildly in different directions, while he did a waltz step punctuated with an occasional pirouette.

Finally, Delphine could no longer deal with the total chaos. "Alfred. *C'est impossible! Je ne peux pas travailler comme ça.*"

"I'm sorry, Delphine," said Alfred in a remarkably calm and soothing tone.

"Quoi?" she responded

"Oh, God, I forgot she doesn't speak any English. David, tell her in French she was *marvelous*, but we will probably do this scene again, and will have to lose some of the improvisory moments and remain more faithful to Jack's initial ideas. Still, I like the spirit Gregory, Allen, and Peter are bringing to all this. However, we don't want to peak too soon. We should save some of the excessive behavior till the *end* of the discussion about poetic form, to give the scene a more intimate and lyrical tone."

"Whaddya mean, Alfie?" said Gregory. "I was gettin' into it. That bit where I poured everything all over Allen. It's like King Kong being attacked by the bastards in uniform, before he falls off the Empire State Building. The individual being screwed by the state. It's the old 1930s social realism shot, Alfie. Ya got it? Oscar level material. Come on, man, you're supposed to be directin' a *movie*!"

"Gregory, I love your vitality and sense of the cinema, but perhaps if all of you are a little less creative *initially*, and stick a bit closer to Jack's outline, the improvisory sense can remain, although it must be couched in a slightly more structured framework," said Alfred.

"Let me wipe the wine and grease off my camera lens," said Robert Frank quietly, in his cultured Swiss accent. "Don't worry, Alfred. We'll find some moments."

"Dave," rasped Gregory. "Play 'A Night in Tunisia.' I wanna teach Delphine how to dance. Come over here to Gregory, Delphine baby. We gotta give this film some sex appeal."

Gregory lurched towards Delphine, who recoiled in horror.

"Don't be upset, Delphine," I said to her in French. "I know this is not what you expected, but none of us know what to expect. Gregory and Allen and Peter are just having fun by seeing how far they can go before Alfred and Robert go berserk. But Alfred and Robert will *never* go berserk, and when the whole film is done, they'll make it into something beautiful. I don't know how, but I know they will. Remember, Jack will narrate it when it's all put together. The more obnoxious they become, the more it justifies your eventual anger, culminating in throwing us all out of your house."

"Ahhh," said Delphine. *"Je comprends."*

"It's like 'The Mad Woman of Chaillot,' Delphine," I said in French. "Except you're the sane one."

"Bon. Ça va. Pas de problème," said Delphine, looking relieved.

"Did you tell her to stay calm, and that we love her?" asked Alfred.

"Kind of," I said.

"All right, everybody, now that we've embellished and improvised, let's try to do that first scene again." Alfred spoke as if he were addressing a meeting of aldermen at a Sunday church luncheon. Nothing any of us did seemed to faze him.

"Allen, if you could put your underwear and pants back on, we'll try to do this scene again. I think we can have a simply marvelous scene that we can do in one take. The less editing, the better. Peter, if you could return the towels and toilet plunger to the bathroom and put on your clothes, and Gregory, stay just as you are. The French fries and ketchup in your hair give the impression of a poet so obsessed by his work, that he has no concern whatsoever about his appearance to others. I know you will all do it brilliantly this time. Remember, you are poets discussing your work. Just remain calm and natural. Don't act. Be yourselves."

The room was quiet as Robert began to pan slowly towards Gregory, Allen, and Peter. Larry Rivers tightened the rubber bands holding some of his saxophone keys together, and Delphine Seyrig stood erect with her head bowed down, as if in prayer.

"Aheeee! Aheeee!" An earsplitting series of squeal-snarl-bark-howlings suddenly filled the room as Gregory Corso, screaming like a banshee, leaped on all fours across the studio, jumped up off the floor through the open window onto the metal fire escape attached to the side of the building, brandishing a Raggedy Ann doll that had been lying on the floor, and clambered down the fire escape to the street below.

Waving the doll over his head, he ran through the midday traffic into the middle of the street, shouting insults at the startled passengers. Most of the people in their cars locked their doors and looked the other way.

I ran outside into the cold January street to make sure Gregory would not get run over or freeze to death without a jacket. One young woman jammed on her brakes, stopping as Gregory was dodging traffic while shouting at the passing cars.

"What are you doing?" she asked incredulously. "Would you like a ride to Bellevue Hospital?"

"Nahh, Sweetheart. We're makin' a movie. See the camera up there?" He pointed to the open window of Alfred's studio, where Robert Frank was filming Gregory's antics.

"Can I be in it?" she said, suddenly opening her purse and putting on some lipstick.

"Sure," said Gregory. "Park your car and come on up to the studio."

"Are there any stars in it?" she asked, putting the final touches on her lips and opening her box of mascara.

"Yeah, baby, you and me," rasped Gregory.

"Who are you?" she said.

"I'm Fabian Fongool, the Roman heartthrob," said Gregory. "You can see all my films in the foreign language art houses. I just won Italy's equivalent of the Oscar, the Stu-gotz! I got it on me. I worked hard for this." He brandished the doll. The woman looked dumbfounded.

"Who's he?" she asked suspiciously, looking at me in my moth-eaten floppy gray sweater, as I tried to direct traffic while subtly attempting to pull Gregory back to the sidewalk to avoid his getting run over in the traffic jam he was causing.

"That's Dave. He looks after my daughter," he said, holding the doll up again to her window and patting the doll on its head. "Say hello to the nice lady," he cooed in the doll's ear.

"What?" she said incredulously.

"Well, on film shoots, Dave also doubles as my baby-sitter. The rest of the time he's my valet," said Gregory. "Hey, Dave, get my jacket pressed, roll another joint for me and one for my new co-star, and park her car. What's your name, baby? We make a beautiful couple."

"You're sick!" she responded, and with tires squealing, she drove off.

"She coulda had a great film career. She blew it!" Gregory yelled to Robert through cupped hands.

"Robert, Alfie, how was that? Was that the ultimate uncontrollable 'Lust for Life' shot or what? Print it. We're all going to be rich and famous!"

"Shut up, loudmouth!" screamed the owner of a nearby small shop as I gently led Gregory to the curb. "All you guys are frightening my customers. You've been partying and smoking the wacky weed up there all day. I woulda called the cops on you already, but Leslie's a good guy. How can he put up with you *schlemiels*? Don't any of you have jobs?"

"Yeah, I got a job. I'm working day and night starring in this film to send my daughter here to college. Say hello to the nice man, Sweetie," said Gregory, holding up the doll and waving its arm at the store owner.

"Ha ha. Very funny," said the store owner sarcastically. I noticed he was trying to suppress a real laugh as he turned to go back to his shop.

"I'm spreading the word," whispered Gregory confidentially to me as we entered the building to go back upstairs to Alfred's studio to continue filming. "Advance publicity. I'm revealing highlights of the film. It's the coming attractions shot."

We entered Alfred's studio, and Robert was already filming another scene with the young art gallery owner Richard Bellamy, who was playing the Bishop, clad in a black suit and overcoat, similar to the dress style of Orthodox Jews.

The painter, Alice Neal, was sitting in front of a squeaky pump organ, playing "The Old Rugged Cross." She was the

Bishop's wife in the film, dressed like the perfect, conservative, dutiful mate.

"Just in time, David," said Alfred. "You're a significant person in this scene. I'll cue you when you're supposed to make your entrance. Just carry your French horn in the case, don't take it out to play it yet. Say hello to everyone in the room and make them feel comfortable. The Bishop and his wife are having a dignified conversation with Delphine and drinking tea, after the Bishop's wife stops playing the organ. Then she and her daughter and the Bishop will be introduced to Allen, Gregory, and Peter Orlovsky, who will talk to them about their poetry."

I stood quietly next to Delphine Seyrig. "This is most bizarre," she said to me in French. "I know they won't do what they've been told to do."

"Well," I said. "I'm sure they'll try to calm down. Pretty soon, everybody will do what Alfred and Robert tell us to do."

Just as Alice Neal got up from the pump organ to rejoin her daughter, played by Sally Gross, who was sitting, prim and quiet, on the couch, drinking tea, Allen Ginsberg and Peter Orlovsky came charging into the studio from a tiny closet in the back, both stark naked, waving dried flowers, while Peter croaked his own atonal version of Cole Porter's "Love for Sale."

"That's a take!" shouted Gregory. "Print that. Adam and Eve in New York City. It's Oscar time!"

"They certainly are uninhibited," said Delphine to me in French.

"Your input as poets is invaluable," said Alfred graciously. "Nonetheless, I think we should try to stick to Jack's story line. Let's try to restrain ourselves. We're searching for a quiet moment."

"Keep the cameras rolling," said Gregory. "Alfie, you're the Cecil B. DeMille of the Beat Generation."

"Alfred, I think you'd better tell Jack to wait a few more days before he comes to see us making the film," said Robert, quietly.

"Out of all this, we will have some great moments. But so far, we have wandered a bit from his script."

"We don't need his script," said Gregory. "We need more wine!"

A week later, Jack called me and said he was going to come by to watch us film his work. By this time, Gregory, Allen, and Peter had influenced all the rest of us into group hysteria. Often Robert would laugh so hard that he could not hold on to his camera, as we celebrated what we all knew would be our final time as underground film stars. Often we would party for hours before we even started filming, and by the time Robert turned his camera on, we were too zonked to even know we were being filmed.

Robert and Alfred remained sober and committed. So did Delphine Seyrig. The rest of us succumbed to the temptations of wine and weed.

The afternoon that Jack arrived, we celebrated even longer than usual before filming. Jack looked bemused as he studied the shambles of Alfred's usually immaculate studio. The floor was now strewn with crushed beer cans, soda pop bottles, and empty gallon jugs of red Gallo wine sticking to dried-up puddles spilled by their sides. Discarded wax paper wrappers from half-eaten pastrami sandwiches moved ever-so-slightly as hordes of cockroaches feasted on their greasy remains. Ground-up donuts, stale French fries covered in crusted ketchup that were now hard as rocks, were surrounded by scraps of paper with poems and sketches that had been torn up. Old underwear, towels, and socks that stood up by themselves had fallen from the broken-down chair.

"Good God, Alfred, my shoes are stuck to the floor," said Jack, laughing. "Neal's house never looked this bad. Carolyn wouldn't have allowed it."

"It's effective, though, to show why Delphine, who is playing Carolyn, becomes so furious that she throws everyone out at the end," said Alfred.

Jack slumped quietly in a chair, viewing the madhouse surroundings. It was 3:30 in the afternoon, and it seemed like midnight at a New Year's Eve party at a mental institution where the patients had taken over. Alfred came over and knelt by Jack's chair.

"We have an excellent *esprit de corps* among our cast members," Alfred said in a soothing tone.

"So I've noticed," said Jack, as Larry, Peter, and Gregory tried to lead everyone in the room in an almost unrecognizable rendition of "Boulevard of Broken Dreams," while Allen did a herky-jerky ballet number, clad in a sheet, like a Roman senator swatting flies.

"They're getting in character, Jack," said Alfred, encouragingly.

"I hope they get *out* of character," said Jack, looking dismayed. "I want them to do something that relates to what I *wrote*."

Alfred paused, and responded with the classic filmmaker's response to anyone worried about a film they participate in.

"Don't worry, Jack. It will all be fixed in the editing."

"In that case, Alfred, *laissez les bons temps rouler*!" said Jack, getting up from his chair and doing an unsteady fox-trot with Delphine while Larry Rivers honked on his alto saxophone, accompanying the braying of the cast of *Pull My Daisy* as we all tried to sing "Lush Life." Two hours later, Jack returned to his chair and listened to Gregory and Peter give a long harangue about what they would do when they became elected as the new President and Vice President of the United States.

"When are they going to start filming?" asked Jack.

"The cast is not totally disciplined yet," said Alfred. "Don't worry, Jack."

"In many ways this is marvelous, Jack," said Robert enthusiastically. "Nothing is going as planned. We'll create an extraordinary film. This is a moment in time that can never be captured again."

"It's good you're here, Jack," I said. "We'll get started eventually."

At about 9 P.M. Alfred clapped his hands. "All right, everybody. Let me please have your attention. We've been here over six hours. I think we are prepared to shoot a scene and show Jack how much we respect his work. Let's all settle down."

"Settle down?" shouted Gregory. "Do you know what happens if you ever settle down? That's the Hollywood shot. Swimming pools and broads. Big business gets you to sell out and wear a tie and then POW! . . . in comes the Gestapo and blows your ass away. We gotta make a film like the one Picasso made that no one can stand watching. The heavy artsy avant-garde shot. We need you in the film, Jack. You play a football player who gets a concussion and starts to hallucinate. He thinks he's the king of France and marries Delphine, who he thinks is the sister of the Dauphin. But she's actually a transvestite named Herman. Ya got it Jack? It's like Shakespeare, where a man's a man and the women are, too." Gregory gave me a conspiratorial wink and pointed towards the tiny bathroom, signaling for me to go there. "Now Jack," said Gregory, "the subplot thickens. The sheriff comes to town and mows down the troublemakers. Then you dump Delphine and marry the sheriff."

"But Gregory," said Jack gently. "I don't want to be in the film. I just want to see what I wrote, portrayed by all of you just the way I wrote it. I have a plot."

"So what?" said Gregory. "Nobody in New York City pays any attention to the plot when they go see a flick. They're going to the movies to eat popcorn, get high, take a nap, try to cop a feel from their date, and get outta the house. All they wait for is the end of the movie, when the sheriff comes to town and mows down the troublemakers. Hey, Dave," he yelled. "I said to Jack that all they wait for is the end of the movie, when the sheriff comes to town, and mows down the troublemakers."

"*Mon dieu*. Jesus, save me from my friends," said Jack.

"Hey, Dave, wherever you are hiding, that was your entrance cue. Since you're supposed to be a hip musician and used to be a boxer and a gym teacher, you're supposed to have good timing. Your timing sucks!"

Gregory banged with both fists on the bathroom door and screamed at the top of his lungs.

"Again, Dave. *All they wait for is the end of the movie, when the sheriff comes to town, and mows down the troublemakers.*"

The door to Alfred's bathroom came crashing down off its hinges as I charged out of the tiny bathroom, having made a rapid change into a full cowboy suit and Stetson hat, firing two toy cap pistols at Allen, Gregory, and Peter, who rolled around on the floor, doing several death scenes apiece, while Richard Bellamy in his black bishop's outfit began an improvised stoned-out eulogy and Alice Neal sat down and played "Nearer My God to Thee" on the squeaky pump organ.

"How was that, Jack?" said Gregory. "The John Wayne heavy cowboy hero shot. But Dave messed up his timing."

"I'm sorry, Gregory. I heard my cue but I was making my costume change to surprise Jack and I couldn't unlock the bathroom door. I'm sorry, Alfie, I had to break it down."

"No excuses, Dave," said Gregory. "Your timing sucks. You'll never make it as an actor. Stick to music, and be prepared to go back to the part-time post office job you had. The theater needs performers with timing and charismatic personalities!"

As he completed the last two words of his sentence, he took a flying leap, making a perfect landing, arms outstretched like a ballet dancer, onto the lap of Kerouac, and whipped out an unopened bottle of Thunderbird wine from the side of his coat pocket.

"A little surprise bit we cooked up for you, Jack, to show you we love you, man. *A la santé,*" he said, opening the bottle and toasting Jack.

"If you love me, quit goofing and let Alfred and Robert finish the film," said Jack. "I want to see my ideas come to life off the page. This film is part of the story of my life."

Delphine Seyrig came over and put her arm on Jack's shoulder, who sat in the armchair, as Gregory ranted away. Gregory crawled off Jack's lap, rolled a corncob-sized super-joint of pot, lit up, and began another rambling monologue about his time in jail.

"I know he is strange, Jack," said Delphine soothingly in French. "But he loves you. We all do. We only want you to have some fun. You look so sad. You are the artist we all love and admire. Your books are exquisite. We only want you to laugh a little and find some joy in life. You are such a magnificent improviser. Don't worry. Whatever the film, if you can ever call it that, turns out to be, you can tie it together with your narration. I can't understand much English, but when you and David performed together, it sounded like angels singing. Don't worry. Let them be silly. Let them have fun. We'll salvage something beautiful out of all this to honor you. When you put your words to the film it will sing like the angels sing. You and David can do it. Robert and Alfred can do it. We can all do it. I don't know how, but I know we *will.*"

Jack smiled, and kissed Delphine's hand like an old Breton nobleman. *"On va voir,"* he said.

Jack called me the morning after his long day and night of watching our filmed psychodrama. "I'm not coming back to see any more goofing around. I'll watch whatever it ends up being, and narrate it like a jazz soloist. Just like Bird at Massey Hall, the live concert where Charlie Parker does everything live and it's all perfect. And whenever Bud Powell would play a chord that sounded wrong to the uninitiated listener, Bird would create something perfect to compliment it. I'm ready, Davey. *Je suis prêt!*"

A week later, we finished filming *Pull My Daisy*. We had a final all-night dusk-to-dawn cast party that was not that much different from the days and nights we were filming, except Alfred Leslie, and Robert Frank could relax. They no longer had to put up with us. Gregory handed out cigars to all of us. He, Peter, and Allen stopped clowning around for the first time in weeks and read us all some of their latest work. Delphine did a monologue in French. Jack and I played together. At dawn we all went home, exhausted. Our underground film careers were over at last. We still had to have the film edited, have Jack narrate it, and have me score the film and the title song, "Pull My Daisy." I explained to Jack that Robert had the monumental job of finding those moments he waited for with endless patience, and assembling a film that could resemble Jack's initial storyline in some way.

Jack went with me the night after our final cast blast-out party to a dress rehearsal at the Phoenix Theater. For weeks, I had been scuttling back and forth, from highly disciplined rehearsals with director Stewart Vaughan, whose productions were always done in exquisite taste, unlike the crazed madhouse of Alfred Leslie's studio.

Jack and I sat quietly as the actors gave a flawless performance.

"Quite a contrast from our *petit flic,*" said Jack as the final curtain went down.

"I'll tell you, Jack," I said, "I know our last three weeks were like the famous painting by Hieronymus Bosch, *Descent into the Mouth of Hell,* where all the hobgoblins and demons are racing down a gigantic tongue towards the hellfire of a giant stomach.

Still, we had something that will never happen again, and like Robert said, 'We can capture a moment in time.' A little bit of the old New York no one else would ever film or even care about. Your original three-page story outline was great."

"On va voir," said Jack. "We shall see what we shall see. Right now, I'd like to see that beautiful new waitress at the Figaro. She looks like the one to lead me to nirvana. I'm getting too old to keep getting brokenhearted. She's fine!"

We walked down Second Avenue before heading East to the Figaro. Jack started humming, and to my amazement, was humming the theme I had written for winds and strings. It was my music for the overture for the second act of the production that Jack had just seen an hour ago.

"You've got some ear there, Pops," I said.

"Naw," said Jack. "It stayed with me. I'd know it was yours without being told. The timbre of the woodwinds and string quartet. Like Poulenc or Satie. Like some of the music you wrote for *Twelfth Night* last summer for Shakespeare in the Park. I still have the acetate discs you gave me. We should use these kinds of sounds in our film. Jazz and Shakespeare. Bach and Kerouac. We'll enlighten these fashion-crazed New York snobs with our yin and yang. We'll show the cinéastes how one idiom flows naturally into the other, like two rivers when they meet and become one."

"That's what I hope we can do, Jack," I said. "I don't just want to jam through the whole film. We could make an LP recording someday of our poetry-music readings, but with a film, the music has to help tell the story of what you're seeing, and what you don't see. And sometimes you need *silence*. Just like the story about the two people listening to Miles. The band starts playing "Bye Bye Blackbird" and Miles puts his trumpet down and turns his back to the audience for ten minutes. One guy turns to the other and says Brother, I paid ten bucks to hear this cat blow his horn and he's strolling through the whole set. He ain't doing nothing. He hasn't played one note! His friend turns to him and says, 'It's not what he's playing, it's what he's *thinking*!'"

Jack laughed. "That's right. The magic beauty of a Colorado night with the stars not whispering a word to one another."

"Well, I don't know about that," I said. "But the film will definitely need the addition of something structured. No matter what Robert can come up with in editing all the craziness, it's never going to look like *Lassie Comes Home* or *Gone with the Wind*."

"I hope not," said Jack. "I want it to be like *us*! I want it to look and sound and feel like *us*!"

"It will, Jack," I said. For the first time in weeks I felt hopeful and optimistic about the film.

"I'll play for you like I always do when you narrate, but if you wear earphones and I'm far enough off mike, we'll hear each other and play off each other like we always do. Then, I'll compose some music to fit the narration and the film later on. I can finish writing the score in ten days. I'm on a health kick now. Yogurt and wheat germ and vegetables. My mind is clear. Alfred said we have just enough to pay union scale for a chamber ensemble and my jazz quartet. I can hardly wait."

"I'm not even going to see the film till it's time for us to do it," said Jack. "I want the narration to be natural, spontaneous, like Lester Young wailing with the Count Basie Band, like Roy Eldridge or Fats Navarro in a long-lost late-night jam session."

Jack started scat singing the melody and improvised choruses of Lester Young's classic recording "Lester Leaps In" as we walked the final blocks towards McDougal and Bleeker Street.

"Can you see the ghosts of O. Henry, Edna St. Vincent Millay, and Eugene O'Neill hovering above us?" asked Jack.

"I know I always feel something powerful when I get to this part of the Village," I said.

"Moi aussi," said Jack. "I feel a powerful desire to have the new waitress at the Figaro give up her dreary life in New York City and come with me to live on a little farm in the mountains, where I can write great novels dedicated to her, and you can find a Western gal and join us to write symphonies and serenade the birds with your mournful horn."

"Sounds like a good plan to me, Jack," I said. "But first we have to finish the words and music for the film."

"Then we can begin *On the Road,*" said Jack excitedly. "It's a natural movie adventure tale. You could write the music for a whole symphony, and play with your band in the film in the part where Neal and I are listening to the young musicians at the jam sessions, the children of the American bop night. And we could get Dizzy Gillespie, Thelonious Monk, Sonny Rollins, Max Roach, Jerry Mulligan, Al Cohn, Zoot Sims, Lee Wiley, and George Shearing to be in the film . . . *oh, mon dieu,* Davey. All the underground genius poets of music. Ramblin' Jack Elliot, the Brooklyn cowboy-saint. The mariachi bands and sanctified gospel singers. We can make a movie of *On the Road* and show the lost despairing souls who live in isolation, stranded in the lonely cities, a film about the America they dream of. *On the Road* can show all these people the beauty part that so few of them have ever seen. The movie can share the same energy that writers like Walt Whitman, Thomas Wolfe, John Dos Passos, John Steinbeck, James Baldwin, Carl Sandburg, and Carson McCullers celebrated. And we can let America hear her night-sounds. All the unsung late-night jazz heroes, singing through their saxophones and trumpets. The old songs written about the America that is vanishing. Oh-h man, I remember in the thirties listening to the radio in Lowell and hearing the big bands, as they traveled from town to town. And dreaming about cowboys cooking their meals on an open fire under late-night starry skies. And meeting Indians who could help me find the Indian past we have in our family's blood. I used to read books in French under the covers with a flashlight and dream someday of being a writer. Life is so short, Davey. I feel older each day. I feel my life is an hourglass where the sand has started running faster and faster, and I can only watch it flow to the bottom and pray to my precious Jesus that He will make me able to provide for my mother, so she never has to come home again, tired and aching in every bone from a torturous job in a factory. Even though I've made a little money from my books, she still thinks I'm a bum, her crazy son, the writer. I don't blame her. I want to get married again, and have a big family, and all of us can live together. Sweet Joyce knew she couldn't marry me. Dody Muller knows I want to marry her but she thinks I'm too crazy. Carolyn would never leave Neal to marry me. It would kill him. Maybe Dody will change her mind. If she doesn't, maybe the waitress I am about to meet will be unable to resist my charm. We could get married at City Hall, and move out to a cabin near the Crow Reservation in Montana and live off the land. You can stay with us and write symphonies and find a big Western gal who loves you. You can cook her those jazz omelets and she can bear you beautiful children. You can teach them the secrets of the universe: how to play music and baseball."

"I'm ready, Jack," I said. "Everything I own I can fit in two huge straw boxes, except my piano. I'm ready to roll."

"Well, let me check out this waitress," said Jack.

As we approached the Figaro, a block away, the lights on the east side of McDougal Street were all turned off. We were walking on the west side. Jack immediately crossed to the east side of McDougal Street, to walk the remaining block in total darkness. He huddled close to the buildings, and eased his way forward.

"Jack, let's get back on the sunny side of the street," I said. "We might fall through one of the open trap doors on the sidewalks. I can hardly see where I'm going."

"Nah-h-h," said Jack. "Stay on this side, Davey. A writer should always be in the shadow."

We eased our way through to the back room of the Figaro. It was jammed with young people, many wearing black berets, all black clothes, the young men sporting dark glasses and goatees, some carrying what appeared to be recently purchased knapsacks. Most of the young men and women were carrying books, whose covers they displayed as they spoke to one another. There were copies of *On the Road*, a poetry anthology of Dylan Thomas, and books by Jean-Paul Sartre and Albert Camus. Most of the young women wore black fishnet stockings, black skirts, and tight-fitting black sweaters. Many of the young men carried brand-new bongos, some with the price tags still dangling from the tuning keys.

"It's like Catholic school," said Jack. "Everyone's in uniform."

For a place packed with young people, the atmosphere was remarkably tense. I felt a knot slowly developing in my stomach. No one seemed to acknowledge anyone else. The old freewheeling atmosphere of the Figaro was another faded postcard in the scrapbook of New York memories. The enormous energy of two years ago now seemed as much of the past as O. Henry's nineteenth-century Greenwich Village.

"Strange," said Jack, smiling. "Look at the pictures on the wall, Davey. We're like tourists in a museum about ourselves."

On the wall was a montage of black-and-white photographs. There was one of Jack reading at the Gaslight. One of Miles Davis and Charlie Parker playing together on 52nd Street. A photo of Dizzy Gillespie and Thelonious Monk when both were very young, wearing goatees and berets, Dizzy with horn-rimmed glasses and Monk with dark shades. And a photo of Mingus and myself with his quintet from 1955 at the Cafe Bohemia. And a new photo by John Cohen of Gregory Corso, Larry Rivers, Allen Ginsberg, Jack, and myself at the diner next to Alfred's studio, taking a lunch break only three weeks ago when we were still filming *Pull My Daisy*.

Jack stood up, cupping his right hand over his eyes like an Indian scout, looking for the waitress who was to be his salvation.

"She's not here tonight, Jack," said the manager of the Figaro, working his way through the crowded room. "I know who you're looking for. Everybody comes looking for her. She took off to Kentucky with a bartender from uptown whose father has a horse farm. But she'll be back. He's a creep. Hey, it's good to see you guys. It's been a while. I just got John Cohen's picture of all of you making that underground film. What a bunch of weirdoes to all be in a film together. But, hey, with what these kids dig nowadays, the Beatnik ticket is hot. With all you guys together, it can't miss. No way."

"I dunno," said Jack, looking depressed. "I hope it will be okay." His face brightened. "How's Brooklyn Bernie, the saintly moving man?"

"He doesn't come here anymore," said the manager. "He tried reading 'Hiawatha' and all the kids started hissing him after the first four lines. The room sounded like all the steam pipes busting in the middle of winter. It was intense. He split. He knew he didn't fit. It's a new scene. The fun times are over. Business is booming all over the Village. More money than you would believe. Look at all these kids in their outfits. It's like a Shriner's convention. They all get dressed up and come down to the Village to be Beatniks. This is happening all over the country. You guys started a trend."

Jack's face darkened and he leaned forward, his eyes flashing, his voice tinged with hurt and melancholy.

"We didn't start anything. I'm an author who likes to read his work and Davey's a classical composer and jazz musician who likes to play for me. We have nothing to do with *this*. We do our readings with music for the joy of the moment. And always will."

"All of the kids know you, Jack," said the manager.

"But do they read my books? Do they hear what I'm saying? Do they want to open up their hearts and share true love and compassion with their brothers and sisters and join hands and sing old songs together and dance with joy at the miracle of seeing a sunrise on a crystal-clear autumn day?"

"Well, I'm not sure I'd go that far, Jack," said the manager, "but they're *definitely* into being Beatniks."

"That has nothing to do with me or my work," said Jack. "I'm a writer. I write books for people to read. I'm an author."

"You sure are, Jack. One of the best . . . Listen, fellas. Coffee and food on the house. Just one favor. For old time's sake, can you do one poem with music for me? Then I've got to take care of business. We've got two tourist buses coming in about fifteen minutes. I don't know where I'm going to squeeze them. They're coming to look at the Beatniks. It's incredible. We could stay open twenty-four hours a day. We almost do now. Let me hear that one about driving into Denver."

"Nah-h," said Jack, opening up his spiral notebook. "I have some I just wrote yesterday."

I unpacked my French horn and Krishna flute from India.

Jack began to read, and I closed my eyes and played. I opened them and saw the manager blow us a kiss as he worked his way towards the front door, where a huge tourist bus was pulling up.

We really got into it, and forgot that Jack had come here to meet with his new soul mate, the irresistible waitress. We forgot that we were going to plan to write a piece together using Jack's words for a chorus and symphony orchestra, and had come here to talk about that, and about the music for our film. We forgot about everything. I think we even forgot we were at the Figaro, which now resembled a costume party as a busload of tourists with cameras charged in, taking pictures of one another posing with dour-looking teenage suburbanites in their mandatory Beat wardrobes, holding up the books and bongo drums they had brought with them.

We kept on with words and music through all this, till Jack had read everything in his spiral notebook. Then he made up spontaneous verses, rolling out the phrases like a preacher. When he finally stopped to take a sip of the half-pint bottle of Wild Turkey he had concealed in the pocket of his lumber jacket, a young couple at an adjoining table got up to leave.

"What were you guys just doing?" the young man said testily. "Was that supposed to be jazz-poetry?"

"Oui, mon cher," said Jack.

"What?" barked the young man, sounding like a prosecuting attorney.

"You were correct," said Jack gently. "That was not only supposed to sound like jazz-poetry, better called poetry-music–music-poetry. It was what you thought it was. Your question was the perfect answer."

The young man looked perplexed.

"As a fledgling Zen Master, I want you to know I'm happy you were here," said Jack. "You blessed our poems and music with your gracious presence. We hope you and your lovely friend will take our work with you as a gift from us to hold forever in your hearts."

"What the hell does that mean? Who do you think you are?" snapped the young man.

"I think, therefore I am," said Jack. "Descartes said that before me, but before you and in the presence of your lovely companion, I want you to know I not only *think,* I *know* who I am. I'm Jack Kerouac. *Et voici,* my trusty comrade in the arms of the muses of music, David Amram."

"You're telling me you're Jack Kerouac and David Amram?"

said the young man, his voice rising. "Prove it," he barked. "Show me your driver's license."

"I don't drive," said Jack.

"Ah-h," snarled the young man, as his date, who had been watching us dispassionately with a somewhat stoic expression, suddenly gave us a sneer of contempt.

"Name dropper. What a phony. You two guys look like unemployed plumbers from Jersey City," he hissed. "See, baby," he said to his date. "I told you most old squares like these two cats will lie about anything and pretend to be anybody if it's Saturday night and they can't get laid. You guys are two lame-assed nobodies." They turned on their heels and stalked off.

"They are a charming couple but obviously not connoisseurs of the performing arts," said Jack, laughing. "I thought we sounded good."

"Yeah, but we don't look like Beatniks," I said.

"Remember, Davey, what Charlie Parker used to say, 'The hippest thing is to be a square'."

"Well, this scene is a little too hip for me. Let's split, Jack," I said, as my French horn case was knocked over by a middle-aged tourist, wearing Madras shorts, white knee-length socks, and a black beret and black horn-rimmed glasses with no lenses. He wore a paste-on goatee and was posing with a teen-age girl clad in mandatory black.

"Martha," he yelled to his wife. "Film me above my waist so they don't see my shorts. I wanna look like a real Beatnik. Wait till the fellas on the bowling team see this. Whatta riot!" He turned to Jack. "Well, old-timer, how you like this freaky scene?"

"It's not my scene," said Jack. "I'm thirty-seven. I'm too old."

"Me too," said the tourist. "But I can still have fun. Ya gotta learn to loosen up. Roll with the punches. Ya gotta learn to talk the Beatnik lingo. You gotta learn to be . . . like a real gone cool hep-cat man, you dig? Like groovy, you follow what I'm sayin'?"

"I understand you perceive the entire situation. I'm glad it brings you happiness," said Jack gently.

"You guys ought to get some new clothes, some real down threads, so you could fit in better," he said.

I noticed he had a copy of a mimeographed booklet, "How to Talk Like a Beatnik," that he was thumbing through, to enhance his vocabulary.

"Where did you get that?" I asked.

"In Elyria, Ohio," he said. "One of the fellas on the bowling team from Sandusky got me a copy. It's a riot. It shows how to have a cool pad, what to wear, how to score with chicks. But that leaves me out. I'm married to Martha. But we're havin' a Beatnik Halloween party this fall for the Lion's Club social. I'm going to get blow-ups of these photos here at the Figaro for the wall display back home. Pictures with all these freak weirdo Beatniks. Hey, Martha, let's take some more snapshots."

Jack and I left the Figaro. "Well," said Jack. "I guess all this is an extension of Eisenhower's warning about the perils of the military-industrial complex. This is the ignoramus-industrial complex. Taking kids' money and misinforming them at the same time. It just means we have to work harder."

"Jack, I'm going back to my apartment and write some more music," I said. "Come on over now and we'll hang out some more."

"Nah," said Jack. "Unless Dody throws me out, I'll spend the night with her. Maybe she'll decide to marry me after all. Man, I wish that waitress was still here. She was *fine*. How could she disappear before we shared a few precious moments of light and ecstasy? I've been dreaming about her. Well, go do your work and I'll do mine. Stay strong and stick to your guns. None of this," and Jack gestured, palms up with a despairing look at the army of tourists and nouveau-Beatniks surrounding us, "none of this will last. *Ars longa, vita brevis.* We must never give up. All our dreams will come true. We were born to share the holy light."

"I agree," I said. "But please walk on the well-lit side of MacDougal Street, on the way to Dody's apartment, so you don't fall through an open grate. Take your share of some of that holy streetlamp light."

Jack came back to town a week later and we went to Jerry Newman's studio to record the narration for *Pull My Daisy*. Robert

Frank and Alfred Leslie looked exhausted from endless hours of editing. Jerry Newman, Jack's old buddy, had his sound equipment all set up. Alfred had cleaned up the mounds of garbage from our invasion during the filming, and his studio was austere, immaculate, and remarkably peaceful. But we all felt Jerry's small sound studio would have better acoustics and no traffic sounds. Jack was cradling a bottle of Châteauneuf-du-Pape that Alfred had gotten him as a present. He was rocking back and forth, his eyes half-closed, as if in prayer.

"I think he'll do a more thoughtful and evocative narration with a fine French vintage wine, rather than if he drinks that rot-gut wine he seems to prefer when he visits the Bowery," Alfred said to me.

"A la santé," said Jack, toasting us all, and gurgling down a gulp from the half-empty bottle.

"Je . . . suis . . . prêt! I'm *ready*!"

"Calm down, Jack," said Jerry Newman. "We've got all night. Just imagine we're back with Dizzy at Minton's. Be mellow. Keep cool."

Jerry had gone with Jack to Minton's in Harlem in the forties and recorded Dizzy Gillespie's song written for Jack on his wire recorder one night. The tune was called "Kerouac." Dizzy loved Jack and let Jerry record it. When I played with Dizzy, he always asked for Jack. "How's the Frenchman? What's up with my man J.K.? That *On the Road* was a *bitch*, David. He was one of the first to understand what Bird and I were doing. And he can write his *ass* off!"

"Okay, Jack," said Jerry. "Get ready to wail."

"Je . . . suis . . . prêt!" Jack put down the nearly empty bottle of Châteauneuf-du-Pape, smacking his lips and straightening up his shoulders like a boxer about to leave his stool to begin round one. "I'm in a beatific state, Davey. Let's roll on down the highway," he said.

Robert Frank put the film in the projector, the light spilling back and reflecting on his three-day growth of beard. There were dark circles underneath his eyes, bloodshot from almost no sleep. Still,

Robert's level of concentration and determination made both Jack and me begin to tune into each other, before we had even made a sound. We sat in silence. Alfred stood, his arms folded, intense and full of energy, without saying a word. I felt at that moment like we were a group of test pilots about to attempt to break the sound barrier for the first time.

I put on a pair of earphones so I could hear Jack. Jack put on a pair of earphones so he could hear me. We had never even used a microphone in any of our performances before, much less earphones. We had never planned anything in advance, much less rehearsed. We knew from the first time we played together we were totally in tune with one another. We were confident we could do anything. Neither of us had seen one foot of the film, and no idea of what it was even about. Robert began to roll the film. The numbers 10-9-8-7 began to flicker on the screen. Jack took a deep breath, as if he were about to dive underwater. I sat at the piano, waiting.

The opening shot of New York early morning was so strikingly beautiful and evocative that I forgot to start playing, and I could ESP Jack's astonishment as well. Robert's genius as a photographer was transferred to film. The opening scene, all in black and white, reminded me of a Goya painting, stark and full of beauty.

"Early morning in the universe," intoned Jack. My mind clicked into gear, and I began to play, accompanying Jack's flowing phrases, as I watched the film.

"How in the hell did Robert Frank and Alfred Leslie ever do this?" I kept asking myself, as the film, counterpointed by Jack's spontaneous narration, unfolded.

Somehow, a story was being told, as if by magic, as if it had all been planned that way. Jack's voice complemented the grainy black-and-white scenes. All of the hours of insanity that occurred during the filming had been edited out, with the exception of a few moments to provide comic relief. Through all the madness, Alfred and Robert had been able to film what they needed, knowing Jack could tie it all together. It looked like it had all been planned ahead of time.

Delphine Seyrig was magnificent as the harried, long-suffering wife. Her grace and dignity as she moved through the filthy, cluttered kitchen of Alfred's studio, which we had mercilessly trashed in our endless partying, was like an anthropologist's dream come true. Robert had filmed a genuine example of mid-twentieth-century crash-pad culture, complete with authentic live cockroaches, gray grease from several nearby high-cholesterol New York diners, complemented by several socks that had grown so rigid and crusty that they stood on the floor as if they had been cast by some unknown twentieth-century foot-fetishist sculptor in speckled marble.

Jack was in top form, gesturing towards the screen, as he wailed with his improvised narration, rising to the challenge like Charlie Parker soloing with his string orchestra at Birdland. His words were like a great jazz solo, soaring above and weaving through the structure of the film, shaping it, teasing it, and telling a story-poem as if it were a familiar fable, a Charles Dickens tale, or a nursery rhyme. I played my best, wishing we could go on for hours.

Suddenly, the film was over. We all sat in silence, overwhelmed. None of us said anything. Jack rocked back and forth, cradling his now-empty bottle of wine, eyes closed, as if he were praying to himself.

Finally Alfred unfolded his arms, came over to Jack, and put his hands on Jack's shoulders.

"Jack," he said, obviously as moved as all of us were at his astounding narration that was one hundred percent ad-libbed but seemed to fit the film perfectly. "You're truly amazing. I think we have the makings of something truly extraordinary. What you just did was beyond belief. What you see on film is a far cry from your three-page outline we gave to the cast, but it will all work."

"Amazing, amazing," said Robert Frank. "But I'm scarcely surprised. I knew it would be. I knew it would happen. We've captured a moment in time. That's all one can do."

"I agree," said Alfred. "We have the makings of something totally different than what's being done in new American films. We must now think of how we can weave the story you originally were going to tell into what the picture is saying."

"I just did that. I'm done. *C'est ça! Fini!* Davey, let's sing a song for Alfred and Robert for their genius work. We're done. Let's celebrate!"

"Jack," moaned Alfred, looking horrified. "Do you mean to say you're going to stop narrating? After one take? We've just begun to explore the possibilities."

"Even in an imperfect world, anything is possible," said Jack. "But there is no possibility of my doing any more because I have told the tale. The deed is done. It's truthful one-time-only spoken-thought recorded. It will always remain spontaneous, every time it is repeated. We caught lightning in a bottle. If we open up the bottle to analyze it, and let the genie of spontaneity out of the bottle, he will fly away and never return again. Now all we need is Davey's music. Let's celebrate!"

"Jack, oh Jack," said Alfred despairingly. "We *have* to do several more takes. We're just getting *started.*"

"We're getting started on our *next* adventure," Jack said animatedly. "If Hollywood can't do *On the Road,* we can do it. We'll just hire some professional actors. Davey can do the music and I'll have a cameo playing one of the saintly old bums. We're now on to our next adventure. This one is completed. We sailed halfway around the world, and landed safely home in port, like Melville returning on a whaling ship. Play "Round about Midnight," Davey. Let's celebrate. I want more wine."

"Oh, Jack, my God, *please,*" said Alfred. "We've all worked so hard. We've tried desperately to make a film that tells a story and I think if we continue to search for a narration that . . . "

"I can't, Alfie," said Jack firmly, jutting out his lower jaw ever so slightly.

"Why, Jack? Why?" said Alfred.

"Because I believe in the sanctity and the purity of natural thoughts freely flowing, like a Mozart sonata or Slim Gailliard singing a tale of woe in some lonely midwest bar. It's what I spent my life trying to achieve as a writer. To get the first pure thoughts down on paper and I can never quite do it. Editors and critics still don't understand what I'm doing. I'm *speaking*. What we just did was what I try so hard as an author to achieve."

"I understand all that, Jack," said Alfred. "But you've never even seen the film before. How can you possibly think your first instinctive improvisation, as brilliant as it was, was the correct one?"

Jack put his empty bottle of wine on the floor, sat straight up, and stared at Alfred.

"Because I'm touched by the hand of God," he said quietly.

There was a long silence. I remember thinking, as modest as Jack was about all things concerning his work, that his assessment of his gifts was accurate. He was simply stating a fact. In 1982, I reminded Robert Frank of that moment. We were in Colorado, where Robert was filming many of us again at the twenty-fifth anniversary of *On the Road*'s publication. We both agreed that Jack was simply stating a fact. He was touched by the hand of God.

In 1997, I wrote the music for Alfred Leslie's play *The Cedar Bar*. As we sat together after the show with Dody Muller and many of the old cast members of *Pull My Daisy* who had come to see the reading of Alfred's play, I reminded him of that moment with Jack in 1959, thirty-eight years earlier.

"All of us were touched by the hand of God," said Alfred, smiling.

"But Jack never forgot it," I told Alfred.

Alfred wasn't smiling, however, that night in 1959. He sat with his head in his hands. Silence again filled the room, except for the sounds of Jerry Newman chewing on a pastrami and corned beef sandwich while he waited to see what we were planning to do next.

"Jack," I said. "Why don't we do what we did at our first reading at Circle in the Square, when the kid with the long beard and knapsack told us he'd come all the way from Wyoming, and wanted us to do the part about George Shearing from *On the Road*, and we had just played it before he got there. Remember? We did it again in the second half of the show, when you guys finally returned from your partying—a completely different version."

"We always do a different version each time we do one," said Jack, matter-of-factly.

"Well, let's do it again, Jack," I said. "Old Alfie had to put up with the crew of *Mutiny on the Bounty* for three weeks with all of us, and just about got evicted from all the commotion we caused in the neighborhood, and we trashed his studio. Let's do it again, man. It'll be even better. I enjoy hearing you over the earphones. It's like going to a drive-in movie."

"Aww-right. Okay, Davey. *Pourquoi pas?* Heavenly muses, fortify my journey with more *fine wine,* into the depth of Davey's deep dark Dharma as we pursue . . . *take two*!"

Alfred breathed a deep sigh of relief, Robert rewound the film, Jerry Newman put down his pastrami and corned beef sandwich, Jack opened a second bottle of Châteauneuf-du-Pape, I drained a can of Dr. Brown's Black Cherry Soda, and we did a second take of the narration. I started off playing differently, and Jack did a completely different version.

I remember that neither of us thought about what we were doing either time. All of our energies were focused on doing it at the moment. This was not a process that could be analyzed by a scientist, systematized by an anthropologist, or merchandised by a fake guru. We just did what came naturally.

Alfred and Robert both knew that the narrations were a work of art on their own, even without the film. And yet each narration fit the film in an uncanny way. Alfred and Robert ended up using some of each of the two narrations. Two weeks later, I was ready to record the score and the title song, "Pull My Daisy," with lyrics by Jack, Neal Cassady, and Allen Ginsberg. Unfortunately, the complete versions of both of Jack's narrations, with my original improvised accompaniment, as well as fifty hours of out-takes from *Pull My Daisy,* were all lost in a disastrous fire a few years later, at another studio of Alfred's. All Jerry Newman's original sound recordings also were lost, misplaced, or disappeared.

The night we finished Jack's narration, Jack and I stayed at Jerry Newman's studio till 5 A.M., after Alfred and Robert went home. We were celebrating the completion of Jack's narration. Jack played the piano, and I improvised lyrics and played French horn. Then I played piano, flutes, and horn, and Jack made up an incredible song about our 1958 trip on the subway to Brooklyn College, and the near disaster of performing there for a packed house of students who were furious at him for answering each of their questions with a question, like a New England crackpot Zen Master. Then he launched into a chillingly accurate parody of what it would be like someday when the sacred traditions of Eastern religions became mainstream. Like the Beatnik phenomenon, it would become turned around to the opposite of what it was all about, with hustlers and sleaze merchants cutting out the essential soul as they ripped off young people's money.

I wish we had a recording of that night. Jack predicted what would become known as the excesses of the '60s, and even his own eventual downfall, as a result of refusing to endorse behavior attributed to him that he found repugnant. He was like a reporter describing his own future.

All of this was rapped out spontaneously, with humor, musicality and zest. When Jerry Newman died, many of his tapes mysteriously disappeared. Still, what is left of the half-hour version of *Pull My Daisy* with the narration and the final music is an indication of what we did and were about. Most important, we always knew we could create something fresh each day, so when we gave it away and forgot about it, our only hope was that the energy we shared with others would inspire *them* to be creative. And we knew if our work or ideas were lost or stolen, we could always create something new.

I had two weeks after Jack completed the narration to compose all the music for *Pull My Daisy*. Portions of the score I improvised in one take, using earphones, listening to Jack, and watching the film, matching Jack's voice and inflections the way I always did.

The composed portions of the music were scored for alto saxophone, viola, English horn, bassoon, bass violin, and percussion, and I played piano, French horn, and percussion.

I had Sahib Shihab play alto sax. He had played with Dizzy, Monk, and the Oscar Pettiford band I was with for two years. I had been a member of Sahib Shihab's own short-lived band, The Composers, in 1956, with Kenny Burrell playing guitar. Sahib was a master musician, and I knew he could play accurately and beautifully during the scene in the film that showed Larry Rivers playing his saxophone, with no sound. Sahib did this all in one take.

"I never sounded *that* good," said Larry, when he watched the finished film, and heard Sahib's brilliant solos.

When Sahib and I played together with Oscar Pettiford's band in Birdland in 1957, I introduced him to Jack. Like all musicians, Sahib loved Jack as a person, as well as a writer.

"He's soul people to me," Sahib whispered in my ear, when we were recording the music for *Pull My Daisy*.

Jack was sitting blissfully in the control room, eyes closed, feeling the music as Sahib and I played with bassist Arthur Phipps and drummer Al Harewood.

"He's real people. He doesn't try to be hip. He has no white thing/black thing. He's just a regular cat. And he can write his ass off." (Exactly what Dizzy always said to me about Jack.) "I wish Bird had lived to get to read about himself in *On the Road*. Kerouac is the only cat who understood where our music is coming from. I remember seeing him up at Minton's when we were getting it all together. Jerry Newman too. They were there, before it ever came downtown. Jack was always cool. He's not white. He's not black. He's Kerouac. I just hope he looks after himself. I can see he's juicing a lot. That's no good, man. You've got to talk to him, Dave. Remind him God only gives you one body. Tell him to love himself. We need cats like him."

Sahib played perfectly, and all the other musicians were also able to play everything at sight and complete the score in the one three-hour session we had to record all my music.

"Hey, Dave. Get more time next time, for Christ sakes," said Midhat Serbagi, who was playing viola. My old buddy from 7th Army Symphony days used to come to Lucien Carr's jam sessions with Jack and me. Midhat would play and sing Lebanese music, as well as jazz. He became a member of the Metropolitan Opera Orchestra, but was always open to all music. He was from Boston and loved Jack's Lowell accent, which was similar to his own.

"Hey, Jack, your narration sounded good, man," said Midhat. "I could understand what you were saying. Maybe you could teach these New Yorkers some good diction, so we could know what the hell they're talking about. Let's all go up to the Cape this summer and sleep on the dunes in Provincetown. I wanna get the hell out of New York and go back home to Massachusetts."

"I'll be there, Midhat," said Jack. "Just don't drink up all the beer before I get there."

Hearing them talk reminded me of how much Jack treasured his roots. The musicality of the New England accent was part of Jack's magic as a speaker, narrator, and spontaneous rapper. You could hear the sound of Lowell in everything he did.

Anita Ellis sang the title song for the film. She was an old friend of Alfred's and agreed to record it as a favor to him. I had already recorded the accompaniment during our three-hour session, so Anita overdubbed the song in two takes.

"*C'est fini*," said Jack. "We have something for our grandchildren to look at someday. They'll see a glimpse of who we were. Maybe they'll want to make their own *petit flic*, and rejoice in the simple things of life.

"Man, I love that music you wrote when they show the cockroaches crawling in the sink. That's New York, captured on film. A thousand cockroaches, cruising under a leaky faucet over a pile of dirty dishes. I'm sorry they didn't use the part when you broke down the door in the bathroom and emerged in your cowboy suit to shoot Allen, Gregory, and Peter."

"That's okay, Jack," I said. "They can always scrape it off the cutting room floor and use it for the sequel, *Son of Pull My Daisy*, or submit it to the film library at the New York School of Bad Acting."

A short time after Anita Ellis had recorded the title song, the film was mixed and we had a screening of *Pull My Daisy*.

Afterward, we were all invited to a cast party, with a lot of other friends to celebrate the film's completion. After a few hours of merriment, Franz Kline stood up and raised his hands for silence. Everyone of us in the room that night, even the most incorrigible egomaniacs and hyperactive nut-cases, all paid attention. Franz was one of the people we all respected and admired.

"I want to say a few words to all of you. I congratulate all of you for making a film that brings us all together, and documents some precious moments of everyday life. It shows us as we really are as artists. Hanging on and hanging in and hanging tough. But I don't want to talk about the film. I want to talk about our lives. I'm older than almost all of you. Most of my life I barely got by. Recently, the art scene exploded and I've become a rich man. But my life is not built around fame and money. I was just as good an artist when I painted portraits for a dollar in the Village. Now those portraits are worth thousands. But they're no better or worse than when I drew them to be able to buy myself a meal. They're part of the body of my life's work, a document of my survival.

"My older landscapes of Pennsylvania are worth so much now that I have to hide them so I don't get put in an even higher tax bracket. For years, nobody would pay a dime for them. They're still the same paintings. They didn't get any better. I treasure them as much as the recent black-and-white abstracts that made me famous overnight. What I'm doing now made me a rich man, but all that is beyond my control, and has nothing to do with my work or my commitment. My dealer is furious. I've shown him my latest work. I'm returning to color. He tells me to ride it out and change when the fashions change. I told him *no*!"

We interrupted Franz with a spontaneous series of cheers.

"Yeah, Franz." "All right." "Right on."

"Sock it to that greedy sucker," shouted Gregory Corso.

"I told my art dealer, 'I paint each picture from my heart.' I've followed my heart all my life. I can't change *that*! And none of you should, either.

"Don't confuse fame and money with art. Rejoice in your fame if you get any. Spend your money if you get any. But don't ever forget what our job is. Don't forget we're in this for *life*!

"Now, Jack, as for your film about the Beat Generation, whatever that is, without you, none of this would have happened. We all know there is no Beat Generation or Beatniks. The *poseurs*, merchandisers, and mediocrities that adopt a label to sell what is worthless have a right to live. But let's not confuse fashion with fact. The fact is that *On the Road* is a great book that spoke to people where they live—in their hearts.

"Jack, I remember you and Amram performing at the Five Spot

and painters' lofts before *On the Road* came out. I remember you, Alfred, and Robert and Larry from years ago. I know almost all of you in this room.

"Let's all thank Jack. He has the cross to bear. He is recognized more for a false image created by a merchandising myth than he is for his true gifts—as an artist. I'm in the same position. I'm no spokesman for Abstract Expressionism, or any other ism. I'm Franz, from a small town in Pennsylvania. Anything people want to know about me they can see in my paintings or read in a library. So, Jack, thank you for making it possible for all of us to be together and make a little film about our lives. I like it. It's simple, fun, and unpretentious. And it's in black and white!

"Now in order for my wonderful philosophy and sociologic insights to be imprinted forever in your memories, I need a goddamn drink so I can toast you all." Robert poured Franz a tumbler full of Scotch whiskey.

"Here's to *Pull My Daisy*," said Franz, raising his glass. "Here's to Jack Kerouac. Here's to all of you here tonight. And here's to Jackson Pollock and Charlie Parker and Louis Armstrong, King Oliver, Bunk Johnson, Bessie Smith, Bela Bartok and all those now on the other side in that spirit world. You're in our hearts. You are part of us. Remember us poor bastards down here and know that we remember you. We're still all sinners, so put in a word for us so we can join you upstairs when our time comes. Here's to life!" Franz gulped down the entire tumbler, and walked over to Jack. He put his arm over Jack's shoulders.

"Jack," he said, "let's show these big-city sophisticates how to party."

As bedlam broke loose, with drinking, smoking, dancing, poetry being read, insults and jokes shouted, bongos, congas, pots and pans being banged, and the whole loft shaking with all of us carousing till dawn, I felt that we had reached the end of an era. I had no idea why, but I think all of us sensed that our underground network of friends, bound together by the desperation of our situation, bonds of mutual compassion and respect that were fragile at best, was now being demolished by changing times.

The 1950s were over. The company store had bought up our ideas and repackaged them into an image so specious that we realized we were no longer welcome unless we wanted to join the charade. I think Robert and Alfred knew better than Jack and I why *Pull My Daisy* should be made. As Robert said, with *Pull My Daisy* we captured a moment in time.

Sojourn with Dody Muller

Pull My Daisy created a lot of interest, to our amazement, and many members of the cast came in June of 1959 to hear the premiere of my "Autobiography for Strings," the first orchestral piece I ever wrote that used the principles Jack and I had discussed almost every time we got together. Jack couldn't come to the performance. He was in the process of selling his house on Gilbert Street in Northport.

When I heard the first rehearsal of "Autobiography for Strings," I knew I had accomplished what Jack and I were both passionate about achieving in our formal work. The diamonds in the sidewalk—in this case, the musical ones—sparkled with a life of their own. What I had heard in my head all these years could now be heard by others, and for all its complexities, it sounded natural. And spontaneous. It stood on its own as a piece of music without needing twelve pages of program notes to explain what it was.

I called Jack and told him I would get someone to make some kind of tape of the piece to send to him.

"I know you'll get to hear this played live, Jack," I said. "It's a little under nine minutes long, and all the elements fit together to make the string orchestra sound like a natural voice for all those poetic sounds of jazz, blues, Latin, and European soul music. It's a good piece."

"It better be," said Jack. "I wish my autobiography could take nine minutes to read. But think of this piece as the first chapter in a whole series of pieces that will reflect your whole life. Tell everyone in the orchestra and all the gang at the concert that I have them in my heart."

"I will," I said, "and we'll all be thinking about you and your mother. Have a beautiful trip to wherever you decide to go. I'll try to come see you in Northport when I'm out on the Island."

Just before the orchestra played "Autobiography for Strings," I told all the musicians to think about Jack, Charlie Parker, and Brahms, and they'd know what to go for. The hall at NYU was packed, which didn't happen too often. The conductor, Maurice Peress, chosen a few years later by Leonard Bernstein to become assistant conductor of the New York Philharmonic, was beaming.

I thought about Jack as the piece was being played. The same music, books, painting, and poets of the present and past, and the travels we had taken to many of the same places had inspired us both. And out of the panic, carefree good times, insecurity, and overwhelming desire to share our dreams with others, we had both found a way to somehow discipline ourselves to write our ideas down. We were both involved, like so many of our contemporaries, in trying to catch lightning in a bottle. I had a friend record the performance so I could send a copy to Jack. I wanted him to hear it, too.

One morning in the first week in October, 1959, I heard my phone ring faintly above the roar of automobile traffic, bus brake wheezes, braying horns of delivery trucks, fire engine and police sirens, the rumbling of the subway, and the shouting of the school kids from P.S. 41 through my back window. As I pulled myself out of bed, it kept ringing. I stumbled over piles of music, laundry, instruments, and discarded yogurt containers that littered the floor and went into the tiny triangular room to answer it.

"Davey, Lamont Cranston here." Lamont Cranston was the name of the Shadow, an imaginary invisible character whose deep bass voice was heard nationwide on a popular 1940s radio show. We all loved to listen to the weekly installments of *The Shadow* back then.

"Mr. Shadow, are you in your new house in Northport?" I asked.

"Nah," said Jack. "I'm moved in but I'm in the city visiting Dody again. She knows I've strayed but I'm here visiting to make amends for my romantic transgressions. I'm still a sinner but I know she'll forgive me, because I do love her. Come on over to her place right now. Put down your work. We want to see you. I want to show you something I'm doing. I know you'll dig it. *Viens tout de suite.*"

I hadn't had the chance to spend that much time alone with Dody and Jack since we had finished *Pull My Daisy*. She was a wonderful artist but a very private person. When Jack, Allen, and I went to her art opening, it was nearly impossible to talk to her for more than a few seconds in the mob scene. The situation was the same when we would go to other artist friends' openings or sit together at the Cedar Tavern and try to follow five conversations at the same time.

All of Jack's friends were happy that he had found such an extraordinary woman to be his soul mate. Dody was big-hearted, warm and down to earth, with a Texas smile that could break your heart. In addition to being such a fine artist, Dody was an unusually beautiful woman, with equal amounts of strength, grace, and dignity, who did not tolerate fools lightly. She was proud and independent. With her Native American background, she was often asked the most rude and insensitive questions, such as: "Please Dody. Tell us. What *is* your ethnic background?"

Dody would then sniff, stand up straight, and gaze directly into the eyes of her questioner.

"I'm an American, darlin'. *All* American. Mostly American Indian. When I'm asked this question by Europeans, we've usually had a conversation or two before the question is asked, and we've also usually known each other for quite a while. I would never dream of asking *you* this question. But since you're asking, I'll tell you. *Je suis un cocktail americain*. Does that answer your question?"

During this period, women were throwing themselves at Jack, not realizing he wanted a woman who was a soul mate as well as a bed mate. He often spoke of how he cared most about closeness and tenderness. Dody made him feel that closeness.

By the time Dody and Jack got together, she already had a life as an artist. She was someone we all respected. Dody Muller was her own person who didn't need anyone for support, either financial or psychological. She and Jack together created a whole energy field that crackled with excitement. Even when they were sitting in her apartment, just relaxing, you could feel that electricity. It made you feel happy being with them and seeing the harmony between them.

Like all of us, Jack needed someone who could help ground him and provide some semblance of a normal life. In the late '90s at Dody's seventieth birthday party, she told me that Jack was so emotional and operated on such an intense level of feelings, that she found she could relate to him as she would with a woman friend. She could talk to or listen to him without being buffeted by aggression or smothered by a wall of insensitivity—the typical 1950s male way of living life. Jack did not believe in some master plan. He lived for the moment, and except for his writing, was open to anything and anybody.

"Half the things he said he hoped we'd do . . . moving to the mountains, lying together in hammocks when we grew old together, creating art works together, having a family . . . I knew he meant them at the moment, but I knew they would never happen. I really loved him. But I knew it couldn't last. We all drank a lot back then but Jack had a problem. He couldn't handle being a public person. We had some fine times together. He discovered the visual artist that was within him. It was there. I'm glad he found an outlet for all that talent, in addition to his talent as a writer. If I helped him, I'm glad, but I didn't give him anything he didn't already have.

"He also was searching for his Indian heritage. I told him if he actually had any he would have to find that by himself. My blood was not Iroquois. He had to find his way and he knew it. He had to do that for himself. We all had to do that in our own way. I understood that part of him better than he ever did himself. He never did find proof of any Indian ancestry, but you don't need proof to feel it."

Dody was Jack's port in the storm. When he was with her in New York, women didn't start climbing all over him when they saw him with Dody. They sensed that she was no one to mess with, and they could see that Jack and Dody loved one another.

I was glad to hear Jack's voice on the phone.

"Come on over, Davey," he said.

"I'm on the way, Pops."

It was a perfect October fall day to walk to Dody's and enjoy the vibrant streets of 1959 Greenwich Village. Strolling through the Village always guaranteed you a front row seat to some form of street theater, twenty-four hours a day. Walking down 8th Street, you would see people dressed like Vikings, selling homemade paper flowers and radios with no batteries and sporting Che Guevara buttons. Young women in all kinds of outfits, like a perpetual Halloween party, swinging and swaying down the street. Young mothers with babies tucked in knapsacks, engaged in heated conversations about Fidel Castro and whether the New York Yankees would ever regain their glory. Street musicians playing everything from tenor saxophones held together with rubber bands to screechy mouth sirens held under the tongue that when played by three or four musicians sounded like flocks of exotic birds in the Amazon rain forest at feeding time. People reciting poetry to no one in particular. Serious-looking NYU students leaning against lamp posts reading copies of Albert Camus's *Caligula,* which had a brief run on Broadway a few months later (I wrote the incidental music for it, opening February 15, 1960, a few weeks after Camus's fatal car accident). Old Italian women in black shawls, looking as if they had never left the old country, oblivious to the manic madhouse surrounding them, out for their daily post-shopping stroll.

Young hustlers playing shell games and three-card monte, street magicians and jugglers, and one famous Village character who paraded up and down 8th Street like a living Picasso painting, dressed like a Harlequin clown on the left side of his body, and a Flemish burger about to have a portrait done of himself by Vermeer, on the entire right side of his body.

Cooks and busboys taking a break, sitting in the sun on splintered orange crates reading the sports page of the *Daily News,* and rapping with passersby. And a small army of guitar pickers in mangled Stetson hats, looking like concrete cowboys. Young jazz hopefuls, eyes fixed to some unknown place, listening intently to the music in their heads, ambling along the street at a certain bent angle, emulating their personal hip heroes of what now seemed to be a bygone era . . .

Greenwich Village, the magnet for us all.

Finally I crossed the line to what was called the northernmost part of the Lower East Side and zigzagged over to Tompkins Square Park, back again and further East to 319 E. 8th Street between Avenues B and C, for a look at my old sixth floor walk-up where I lived from 1955 to 1957.

Then I meandered some more, rapped with a few old neighbors, and finally arrived at Dody's. I rang the bell. Jack came to the door.

"I'm really hungover, man," he said. I noticed an occasional tremor as he spoke.

"Are you getting the shakes, Jack?" I asked.

"Nahh. Just a bad hangover. I'll be all right. Let me show you something."

"Are you doing more art work?" I asked.

"Of course. I have sketches you've never seen, and work in color, but that's not what I want to show you. Come back here."

We entered a darkened room. On the top shelf of an old brown dresser was a row of neatly stacked notebooks, binders, sketchbooks, and loose-leaf folders. In spite of the craziness of his life, Jack was always neat about organizing his papers. It was a reflection of his incredible inner discipline. Jack carefully withdrew a large notebook from a neatly stacked row of books, rearranged all the other books to close the gap, and pulled another chair next to him.

"Dig this, Davey," he said. He opened up the book and inside were lists of baseball teams, baseball scores, names of players, descriptions of various plays, league standings, and what looked like a possible script for a sports announcer.

"Is baseball holy?" I asked, quoting his famous line from *Pull My Daisy*. As crazy as it seems now, in 1959 this line had enraged many critics who felt that since Jack didn't write or live like Hemingway, he had no right to equate the manly sport of baseball with crazed poets and searchers of spirituality.

"You know it," said Jack. "Babe Ruth was some form of Buddha in the outfield. The Red Sox never should have traded him to the Yankees. New England will never recover from that. We goofed!"

"I see you have a Pawtucket team here. What is all this?" I asked.

"This is my own league," he answered. "I have games, batting averages, lineups, statistics . . . my own baseball dynasty."

"What made you decide to do this?" I asked.

"I miss football," he said. "You know that feeling. You were a gym teacher. You boxed a little in the Army. You miss it when it's gone. The sound of that crowd when they're behind you. . . . It's like the rush a great jazzman must feel when he plays a perfect solo and the crowd is there with him. He's playing them and they're playing him. I miss that.

"Now my books aren't even getting reviewed in many places. I'm being dismissed without even having my work read. They run the game. I can't review myself. But I can run *my* game. I can create a dynasty within a league. I can control the tempo of a game."

Jack rose from his chair and started walking around the room.

"Davey, wouldn't it be great to write a ballet or an opera, but use real ballplayers who suffered injuries, like I did, to appear in it? Satie wrote that great piece with the typewriter being played with the orchestra. He actually hired real secretaries to type along in time with the orchestra. We should do something like that about baseball."

"Wow, what an idea," I said. "We could have the conductor dressed up like an umpire, calling balls and strikes."

"Nahh, Davey, the *manager* of the home team should be the conductor of the orchestra. The umpire can be played by the local sportswriter. There is nothing more beautiful than seeing a double play perfectly executed."

"We could create a portrait of classic baseball plays through music," I said. "William Schuman wrote *Casey at the Bat*. It's a small operatic work."

"Yes, but that poem is just fantasy," said Jack. "We don't want to mythologize any particular player. The great players are already heroic in real life. This piece could be like a cantata, with real-life ex-athletes as part of it. *Pull My Daisy* was supposed to be based on a real situation before everyone started goofing around. We could do this the way I conceived it. If you're writing the music, everyone will be serious and not goof around.

"Remember, Davey, I'm a reporter too. Of our time, of our spirit. And of course I'm an author. This could be my tribute to our unknown minor league sports heroes."

"Maybe we could get a jazz group, a small orchestra, and a narrator," I said. "You could narrate the text, the dancers could carry out some of the action stylistically, and the orchestra and chorus could represent the crowd coming to the game, and create different moods for each team, with secondary themes for each team's players."

"That's an idea," said Jack.

"The problem would be how to get somebody to pay for all the musicians and the cost of getting all the music copied," I said.

"I'll suggest it to Sterling," said Jack. "He can do anything."

We spent about two hours leafing through his baseball book. I hummed along as I looked through endless pages of games and statistics, as neatly handwritten as if they had been hand-engraved by Byzantine monks.

"Have you finished composing the music for our new baseball masterpiece yet, Davey?" asked Jack, when we got to the last page. "You've been here over an hour. Is it done yet?"

"Well, Jack, writing music down on paper is different from improvising. I could do something spontaneous to accompany the whole book we just saw by improvising the whole thing myself. But if I was going to write a well-constructed piece, with every note a winner, for others to play, and make that whole two-hour piece *sound* natural . . . man, that's at least a year's work. You know that from your own writing. You *make* it sound natural. But each note, like each word, has to be perfect. But if you don't stay in touch with improvising and that creative atmosphere in which improvisation can flourish, you won't have a sense anymore of what natural music sounds like. That's why I'll never give up playing with and for musicians, poets, and anybody where we can exchange ideas on the spot. It keeps your sensibilities alive."

"That's why we have to get more chances to do reading and music together," said Jack. "I know we will. Those were great moments with Lamantia and Hart."

Jack paused, stared slowly at the floor and looked dejected. I saw his tremor start again.

"Maybe I'm getting too old, Davey, for even thinking about performing in public. Or even appearing in public except when I go shopping or go to the liquor store. I'm a middle-aged man, Davey. You caught me in the last days of my youth. You're about to turn thirty. You're in your prime. I'm getting old. That's what I said to Neal. We're both getting to be old men."

"Jack, you're just in first gear," I said. "Your best days are yet to come. You're only thirty-seven years old. The world missed the train, but you're still on schedule and on the case."

"I dunno, Davey," said Jack, casting his eyes downward again. "Lots of days I feel lost. When I'm not writing I feel lost. When I'm writing, I'm in the heat of battle. The spirit takes over and does the writing. The rest of the time, I'm lost. I love Dody. I loved Joyce. But I can't find my way anymore."

"Just write more and tune out everything else," I said. "Your work will save you. No one understands the gifts God gave us. Stravinsky said he was the vessel through which *The Rites of Spring* flowed."

"Same idea," said Jack, suddenly looking like his old energetic self. "But I have it all written down in my head before I write it. If we could do a baseball-music piece, we would have to make it seem natural, as if it were a great jam session epic, or a colossal Berlioz-styled work like his *Requiem*. We could perform it in Fenway Park with the Boston Symphony."

Jack started shaking again.

"Are you OK, man?" I asked.

"I just need a drink," said Jack. "But I'm trying to stop. You're lucky. You can stop. I want to, and I say prayers that someday I can turn the other cheek to all temptation. I think I'll just drink one beer and settle my stomach."

He went over to the icebox and took a six-pack of beer out and we opened up two cans.

"*Shlonshin, à la santé, Lecheyim.*"

"I'd like to have a count of all the times and all the people we've made toasts to," I said.

"Well, Davey, toasting is a part of communion. The neighborhood bars were like a second church to all of us in Lowell. That was our gathering place to commiserate. I miss that in New York. All the places we went to before *On the Road* came out have changed. The Kettle of Fish, the San Remo, the Cedar Tavern, the White Horse Tavern—even the Five Spot, all are different. There's no more intimacy. Even the coffeehouses are caricatures of some kind of bohemian way of life that's distorted. Beat meets bohemian, becomes bestial. I'm getting too old to go on the road to find that place of tranquility. We should all go together and live in the mountains on a farm."

Jack began one of his innumerable variations about his dream of all of his friends living together in a familial bucolic paradise.

After about a twenty-minute priceless rap, he ended his latest version of communal domestic bliss for us all by singing, "It seems to me I've heard that song before," and scatting new lyrics. We took out some saucepans from the kitchen cupboard and began accompanying ourselves.

"Well boys, I see you're hard at work on a new musical venture," said Dody, walking in with a bag of groceries and a bottle of wine. "Who is the party being given for?"

"You," said Jack. "We're serenading you with my undying love."

"Who's in first place in your pennant race?" asked Dody, looking at the baseball book sitting open on the kitchen table.

"The game's still in progress. I'll let you know," said Jack. "I just told Davey about my idea of making a musical work about baseball."

"How about calling it *Three Strikes and You're Out*?" said Dody, "That would keep us all on our toes. And make sure we always paid our rent on time."

"You can design the sets," I said.

"A holy trinity," said Jack.

"The three stooges," said Dody.

"Let's have a glass of wine to celebrate your new work."

Dody got a corkscrew and opened up the bottle of red wine. We toasted each other, a host of friends, and Jack and I slurp-chugga-lugged ours while Dody sipped hers.

"This isn't Thunderbird, for God's sake," she said. "Enjoy it. Don't be so frantic. You guys are always in such a rush to do everything and go everywhere. That's the sure way to do nothing and go nowhere. Take your time."

"You're a real artist," said Jack. "I'm just a beginner at painting, but with writing and music it's different. My way of writing and Dave's music celebrate the *moment* and captures *now*! We have to move with the speed of light. Like Charlie Parker, creating the masterpiece at the moment, with no going back!"

"Like capturing lightning in a bottle," I added, looking at Dody hopefully for approval.

"Wrong," said Dody. "That's how you are when you're hanging out, but your books aren't that way Jack, and you know it. They're put together so well that they *seem* effortless. I've heard your compositions, David. Jack's played me that acetate recording of *Autobiography for Strings* that you did last June over and over. You're not an avant-garde composer that lets anybody do anything they want to do and then says you've written it yourself. Your music is beautiful and disciplined."

"You're like Berlioz and bebop," said Jack, pouring himself some more red wine.

"People judge all abstract artists by that stupid Canadian movie where an artist is shown hurling cans of paint against a huge canvas which is then sawed up into separate pieces and taken off in a seaplane to be sold for a fortune to some ignorant collectors. It may be funny to some. It's a horrible cliché," said Dody.

"It's like the Beat thing. Or the Marlon Brando stereotype of him scratching himself and grunting in his undershirt as though justifying the idea that every member of the Actors Studio is a mumbler who can't act or complete a sentence. Or the image of the bebop moronic musician.

"The painters don't have it any easier. All of us in the art world who are creating our own styles are lumped together as Abstract Expressionists and then dismissed, regardless of what we're actually doing.

"This drove Pollock crazy. He studied with Benton. He loved Indian sand painting. That's why I never talk about my Indian blood. I don't want to hear a lot of foolish Indian jokes that don't have the slightest thing to do with what being an Indian is.

"Our culture is defined by clichés and stereotypes, and we have to waste valuable energy overcoming all of that. We have to create our own destiny. We have to be responsible for our actions. People only judge what they're able to see happening. So *slow down*. Go at a painterly speed. I'm speaking to you too, David. You're too frantic. You're worse than Jack. Take a day off and go to the park and don't talk to *anybody*. Just listen to the birds."

"*Les Oiseaux Exotiques* by Messiaen," said Jack. "All bird calls. That's what you need to do, Davey. Write a piece like Messian with bird calls. You can put bird sounds in the baseball piece. Show the team in spring training in Orlando, Florida, and open up with bird calls. We used to hear the birds there every day."

"Whatever you do, take your time," said Dody. "I remember when Franz Kline told you you had enough ideas for a thousand symphonies, and to simplify."

"Like Richard Strauss's final songs or Matisse's final paintings," said Jack, downing another glass of wine in three gulps. "The New York intellectuals all said they were childlike."

"They weren't childlike," said Dody. "It took him his whole life to get to that level of sophistication and mastery. They're brilliant."

"Well, Davey, we've got to do something together," said Jack. "Brando never answered my letter about *On the Road*. He said one time he wanted to star in it. I know you're going to be writing the music for Kazan's *Splendor in the Grass* next summer. Maybe Kazan could talk to Marlon and they could do it together. You told me in 1958 when you first worked with Kazan on J.B. how much he loved my work."

"He does, Jack," I said. "But I don't think he and Brando are speaking since the House of Un-American Activities hearings."

"What a bunch of crap," said Jack. "All those crooked right wing politicians on TV, waving the flag, as if they cared about America. All they care about is lining their pockets with graft and payoffs. And all the Hollywood weekend Communists in their chauffeured limousines thinking that they're representing all the poor and suffering people of the world. They deserve each other, the right wing fanatics and the self-righteous weekend revolutionaries. None of them care about anything but themselves. Jesus walked among the poor and gave tender love and mercy. All those political fanatics should be forced to read Franz Fanon's *Wretched of the Earth* and then do penance and be forced to put their principles into practice."

"Well Jack, you have to respect Marlon's feelings about the blacklist in Hollywood and those hearings that ruined so many lives. Senator Joe McCarthy was a national disgrace and an enemy of freedom," I said.

"I know he was," said Jack. "And so was Joseph Stalin. All politicians make me sick."

"I'll drink to that," said Dody.

"Me too," I said.

"Here's to unconditional love and the teachings of Buddha, Jesus, Mohammed, Lao Tse, Moses, Sitting Bull, and all forgotten heroes," said Jack.

"And don't forget John, the bartender at the Cedar Tavern," said Dody. "We're supposed to meet there tonight with Franz. John will have his philosophy of art and life ready for us to hear for the hundredth time."

"Do you tink desse guys are really any good?" asked Jack, in a perfect imitation of John the bartender's voice. "Dis is my painting of a fish. Ya know what da hell you're lookin' at, when ya see my stuff. How ya like it?"

"I wish you could do that for John," said Dody, laughing.

"I wouldn't dare," said Jack. "He'd eighty-six me from the Cedar Tavern or punch my lights out. Or both."

"Well, David, if you want to come drink with us tonight, you're more than welcome. We'll be there about 9 P.M. We'll save you a space in our booth."

"OK," I said. "It's 12:30 now, so I'll walk home and start writing music and quit at 8:45 and walk over."

"Are you still with that pretty gal from upstate New York?" asked Dody.

"Yes," I said. "She's great."

"Well, bring her with you. She'll have fun and she and I can talk when you guys start to monopolize the conversation."

"Don't forget we must begin our next collaboration," said Jack. "If we do our baseball music-drama it will be as if Abner Doubleday, the founder of modern baseball, meets Richard Wagner. This could be a milestone in twentieth-century American culture."

"Jack, you need a cup of coffee," said Dody. "You've had too much wine and too little sleep."

"Don't listen to her, Davey," said Jack. "I can see it all as a great musical work."

"Well, Jack," I said, "I know we'll definitely do something."

"*Ça va,*" said Jack. "As long as we burn with Pater's hard and gemlike flame."

"Go home and write some music, David," said Dody. "I'll see if I can get our Jack settled down."

"I'll never settle down," said Jack. "I was born to be a wanderer, a crazed solitary mystic in the lost American continent."

"Well, you're here right now with me, Jack," said Dody.

"I'm found!" said Jack. "I've been saved!"

"Hallelujah!" I said. "See you both tonight."

I left Dody's apartment and took a more direct route back to my apartment. I thought about what Dody had said. Jack and most of us were always told we were too frantic. We were always in a hurry. Most of us were so involved in what we were doing that we forgot to eat, sleep, pick things off the floor, go to the laundromat, or anything that didn't have to do with what we were working on at the moment or planning to do in the future. We were so accustomed to our high-energy group of friends in all the different fields of art that we didn't notice how bizarre we appeared to be with our heated discussions that no one else could understand. We used each other as sounding boards for our jaunts into the future.

Jack had the ability to be a part of something before it even happened, and to make you feel you were right there with him. Because of his gifts as an improviser and a genius-level writer of words, his monologues were always a preview of a new novel. He told me many times how he often had the whole essence of a book in his head before he sat down to write it.

He always spoke of his books as being part of one huge work, a legend of his family. In his fiction he used the surname Duluoz, but they were Kerouac in every detail. His plan for his masterwork was as open-ended as the life he lived from day to day. We were free spirits, and I wanted to tell Dody that we couldn't change, and I wanted to tell her, too, that she and Jack's mother were the two stabilizing forces in his life that kept him from spinning off into space.

Walking home I said to myself,"I'd better go back to drinking ginger ale again."

I kept thinking about seeing Jack with those tremors. I wished there was some way I could help him stop drinking. It was more obvious than ever that it was out of control.

The rest of the year was so full of activity that I don't think I had a day off. I was working around the clock, writing my violin sonata. When Jack went on the Steve Allen show on November 16, a group of us got together and watched. Now America had the chance to see and hear what Jack was all about. We all agreed it was the perfect way to end the decade.

The Sixties

As the new decade arrived, Jack was settled in his place in Northport and while the critics were starting to tear him to pieces, more and more people were reading his books. Jack would make his field trips into the city and often sleep on the couch in my 6th Avenue apartment, or crash out on one of my sleeping bags. I never knew when he was going to come or when he was going to leave, but I was always glad to see him. We would play music together. He would read me new writing and often have me play while he read. I would pound out what I was composing on my piano, trying to sing all the parts at the same time. We would take walks around the Village and the Lower East Side and bump into old friends and meet new people.

Jack was struggling, assaulted on all sides by critics of his work. It was not an easy period for him and he was showing the strain.

"They can put you down but they can't stop you from writing," I said one night as we were walking up 3rd Avenue, after eating stuffed derma and rapping in French with some students from Quebec.

"I'll never stop writing," said Jack. "I couldn't if I tried. I have to do it and I want people to *read my books*. My best days are yet to come. We'll do some work together to bear witness to the great musicians who left us too soon. All the great ones, from Bartok to Bird."

"You're our reporter, Jack," I said.

"*Merci*," said Jack. "I've got to give this stuffed derma a bad review in my next food column. I'm amazed at what you can eat. Your stomach's so strong, you'll live to be a hundred."

"So will you, Jack," I said. "You've got a lot more reporting to do."

"We've both got a lot of work to do, Davey," said Jack. "I'm going to try to stop drinking. I have a new book I'm writing. There might be something in these stories that could be an opera or an oratorio or even some art songs like the ones by Schubert or Richard Strauss. You could could set them the way you did for the song Anita Ellis sang, the theme for *Pull My Daisy* with neoclassical overtones and jazz harmonies, the Amramian Church style music that you innovated: Berlioz and bebop."

"I'd like to read them," I said.

"You will," said Jack. "I'm going to start soon. I'll make my detractors seethe with envy, but then when I see them, I'll bathe their feet because I practice compassion as Jesus did. That's why I will never succumb. I'll turn the other cheek and write another *chef-d'oeuvre*!"

During that period, I wrote Jack a note scribbled in haste from the Arts Foods Delicatessen, after making myself my customary enormous sandwich, and managed to mail it without obliterating the address on the envelope with horseradish sauce, mayonnaise, ketchup, and spilled coffee before the concert in April of 1960. John Sampas was kind enough to send me a copy of it in June of 2001:

Dear Jack,

I hope that you come. It should be a wonderful concert. The String Orchestra piece is like *On The Road*, my style with all the wild beautiful sounds that we have here going.

Call me OR 5-8456 if you want to come and I'll leave you two seats at the box office or I'll mail them out. Take care and cheers! The movie narration was a gas. Also read in Esquire

last issue about the death of Thomas Wolfe.
Keep your spirits high,

UP!

Dave

Jack called and said he wasn't able to come, but wanted to get a tape of the pieces to be performed at the concert.

Copying My Kaddish with Kerouac

Jack called up one night in early 1961, about 11 P.M., and said, "Davey, come on over, I'm with my friend who's a carpenter. We're discussing the future of the universe."

"Jack, I'd love to," I said. "But I'm just finishing recopying the last seven pages of my 'Kaddish' for my Sacred Service. The chorus and cantor are performing the whole composition in Newark this spring, and I'm adding the Kaddish to the original version. I'm on a real deadline. You know how much I want to come and hang out."

"Bring the music and copy it here, Davey. I'll inspire you with psalms, smokes, and Thunderbird wine."

"Okay, Jack. I'll walk over. I'm going to bring my friend Yaffe. She's a great person, and she loves your writing."

"*Viens tout de suite*, Davey. *À bientôt*."

Jack hung up and I packed up my music paper, ink, pens, and ruler. I turned to Yaffe, had been reading in bed while listening to us rap on the phone. I could tell from her smile she knew which Jack I was speaking to. She had a natural psychic ability to see situations before they actually occurred.

"Don't bother to explain," she said softly. "I know you guys will be up all night, trading scat songs, fractured French proverbs, and travelogues. I love Jack's work more than any living writer. And I'm sure he's really sweet. But I have to be at my desk by 9 A.M. and *function*! Don't feel guilty. I know how much fun you are for one another. He comes and goes. See him while you have the chance. I know you'll be up till dawn. Come back so we can have breakfast before I go to work."

"It would be great if you could come along," I said sheepishly.

"No, it wouldn't," she said. "I'd be dead for the week. I'll spend time with you guys when I can sleep the following day. I don't know how you both do it. You never sleep! Have fun."

I gave Yaffe a hug and a kiss and walked out into the humming streets of Greenwich Village, heading west to the loft on Hudson Street where Jack was staying. When I arrived, Jack was singing the Lester Young solo from "Jumping with Symphony Sid," and making up lyrics to the classic blues variations Lester had created. Then Jack greeted me by launching into a perfect basso-profundo imitation of Symphony Sid himself, mimicking the jazz disc jockey's New York stoned-out late-night vocal style, as if Symphony Sid were greeting me walking into his radio studio.

"Well, jazz fans, that was "Jumpin with Symphony Sid" by the immortal Prez himself, Lester Young, the president of the tenor saxophone. You know that Prez wrote and dedicated that song to me and my show. Every time I go fishing, I look beneath the shimmering surface of the pristine waters and I see, beneath the flashing of the minnows, a vision of the beatific face of Prez in the waters, wearing his pork pie hat, filling the world with his Buddha-like saxophone-song-stories. And guess who just walked into the studio tonight, without his French horn? He's loaded down, like a great Talmudic scholar, with pens, inks, and music paper. Is it the ghost of Erik Satie or Poulenc? *Mais non, mes copains*. It's the mad Mezz McGillicuddy, of *Pull My Daisy* fame. Mezz is here gracing the studio with his august presence to write us an on-the-air symphony, composed on the spot from themes that you sing to me over the phone to ease the pain and frustrations of all the lost New Yorkers out there who dream of having their holy early morning philosophic discourses set to music."

Jack interrupted his monologue to take an enormous drag on a roach of marijuana that was lying in a nearby ashtray.

"Ah-h-h-h. . . . Davey . . . *Bienvenue*. It's good to see you, man. Every time I come to New York, I open up my arms to embrace the city, and it smacks me in the kisser. Let's go to the mountains, lie in hammocks and pick our teeth, and write a cantata together. We'll set my unpublished works to music. The critics can't annihilate my work if it's set for chorus and symphonic orchestra. We can take our 1957 New York jazz-poetry readings one step further. It's a drag we can't go out together and perform whenever and wherever the spirit moves us. I have to hide now, unless I come to your apartment, or visit Lucien Carr's for our subterranean jam sessions. I miss our spontaneous music-poetry numbers at the Figaro and Kettle of Fish and Washington Square Park. The Beatnik craze eliminated us from being ourselves in public. I have to hide out. Fame is a real drag. People who haven't ever read any of my books come up and bug me, expecting me to be Neal Cassady.

His dark eyes suddenly drooped, and I saw the sadness that had grown in him in the years since *On the Road* was published. He was slowly retreating into his own private place.

"You should have brought your sweetheart with you, Davey. I can't find anybody who understands my situation. I want to provide for my mother and live a simple life, but all the women I meet want me to be a madman. I'm getting old. I want a family and a simple life, but I'm trapped. It's my fault, *bien sûr*. But we must dwell on the positive. Copy your music. I realize without a Kaddish, your sacred service has no resolution. Mourning for the dead can be joyous. We shed tears of joy in Bach's B Minor Mass when *Crucifixus* is followed by *Et Resurrexit*. Be sure your Kaddish captures the mystical feelings of dialogues with the dear departed souls. All the soul people—Moses, Jesus, Mohammed, Buddha . . . They were all saintly goofs that understood there *is* no understanding, only accepting of the mystery of life, and the great darkness of the hereafter."

Jack poured himself a glass of port wine, and rolled a joint of hashish mixed with some fine Mexican bright green pot.

"*Viens, viens, cher* Davey," he said, lighting up and offering me a toke from the joint and a drink from his glass. "This is our communion, Davey, to soar above the brutal venality of New York's cruel cement penitentiary of the soul."

"I can't, Jack. I hate to sound like a Puritan father, but I've got to keep my brain cells clear so I can finish copying these last seven pages by tomorrow morning. The cantor, chorus, and organist have to read it for the first rehearsal. Go ahead and rap. What I'm doing is ninety-nine percent mechanical. It's super-neat copying and last-minute changes of dynamics and phrasing. I've already composed every note, so all I have to do is slowly write it all out."

I began copying the music, and Jack eased into an armchair.

"Davey, you're a Zen-like Jewish medieval monk, slowly writing the scriptures in painstaking calligraphy that is a work of art in itself. I won't bug you, man. You copy the music, and I'll smoke and drink for both of us. *A la santé*."

Jack drank two toasts and smoked the rest of the joint. "Ah-h-h-hhh. I feel the cherubic silence of midnight in Auld Manhattoes. Let me tell you about the French soldiers *contretemps* with the Arabs, meeting in the army barracks at 3 A.M., smoking kif, drinking mint tea, and telling stories. There were supposed to be mortal enemies, but they were all joined for brotherly understanding, playing music and sharing stories when the French authorities were asleep."

Jack continued to talk for hours, telling me about his adventures with the French and the Arabs, imitating their voices and their body language. As I continued copying my music, I listened to Jack, buoyed by the torrent of words, so musical, like a great jazz solo, always spontaneous and yet logical. Finally, I completed the final bar of the Kaddish. I looked up at Jack's face, animated as he continued his Homeric rap. I noticed it was light outside. Jack continued, completing his monologue with a story about his search for his French roots from the lost history of the Kerouac family journeys from Europe to Canada to New England, and his own journeys from Lowell to New York and around the world, in search of enlightenment.

"Oh, man," I said, putting down my pen and closing up the ink well. "That's the most incredible rap I ever heard in my life. Even Lord Buckley never had a monologue that long or detailed. Every side street you visited became part of the whole journey. You never got derailed. That was a *five-hour-long* perfect story. I wish I'd brought a tape recorder. You could have transcribed it verbatim and have a complete fact-fiction novella with no editing. It was out of state, Pops!"

"*Merci*," said Jack, wearily. "You know, I try to write that way, just to have it sound as if I were speaking directly to the reader. To make my writing flow in a natural way, to go for it, like a Charlie Parker solo, straight from the heart, through the horn and out into the entire universe. That's all I'm trying to do in all my work. The critics hate me for it. They think it's sloppy writing and accuse me of having no discipline. My thoughts come from the experiences I've lived through, inspired by the hundreds of books I've read, and the sweetness of Haydn string quartets and Bartok concertos, the poetry of Céline, Baudelaire, Whitman, and Dylan Thomas I've studied. My voice is the voice of the genius hobos, cowboys, musicians, and wanderers I've been with whose natural way of talking is the greatest poetry of all. You remember when we did those readings together in '57 and '58? How we dreamed that all America would attend the wedding of the spontaneous and the formal? But the critics and the snobs of the New York literary world dismissed me as the ignorant football player Canuck lumberjack, typing reams of stream-of-consciousness confessionals. They dismissed me and they now ignore me. They won't even review my books."

"They didn't appreciate Bartok or Charlie Parker either at first," I said. "A few did, but most couldn't handle the directness and honesty, the lyricism and soulfulness, without posturing or frills. Nuthin' but the truth. All musicians love your work. Dizzy Gillespie always asks me about you, and remembers you from your days in Harlem, when he wrote 'Kerouac' for you at Minton's. All the painters and actors I know, and all the kids I see when I play high school and college concerts, are crazy about your books. Your writing proves what Duke Ellington said about music and life. It don't mean a thing, if it ain't got that swing!"

"Ah-h-h, Davey. I hope you're right. I just want peace, to write and tell my story. Someday when we're old men, we'll sit and laugh together as our grandchildren read my books and listen to your symphonies. We'll sit in our rocking chairs, watching the rivers flow by, drinking tea and looking back on our life journeys. I hope your Kaddish is beautiful. Send me a tape if I can't come to the synagogue in Newark hear it. I'm tired, Davey. I don't want any more hassles in my life."

I got up to leave. We hugged each other goodbye.

"Get some sleep, Jack. Don't ever let anyone hassle you. Your detractors will all fade away, and your work is here to stay forever. Don't even give it a thought. Remember this gem of Talmudic knowledge from the Catskill Mountains stand-up comics on how to handle a heckler. 'Avoid arguments with *shlemiels*. If you let a *shlemiel* draw you into a debate, when a passerby sees the two of you argue about something inconsequential, he won't know which one of you is the *shlemiel*'."

"Amen," said Jack. "Shalom, Davey. We'll go to Mass together when I get back to the city."

Composing "A Year In Our Land": Words and Music

In 1964 I received a call from Harold Aks, a gifted conductor, dedicated teacher, and free spirit, who was able to survive teaching at an established university where his gentleness and love of music was appreciated. He asked me if I had any ideas for a cantata.

"Yes," I said. "For a few years now, Jack Kerouac and I have talked about doing something together, based on Vivaldi's *Four Seasons,* but having it set with the four seasons in America. I want to have some of Jack's writings and other authors' as well."

"That sounds like a marvelous idea," said Harold Aks. "Do you think you can have it ready to premiere next year? Our concert is at Town Hall next May. Can you get it done in time?"

"Yes!" I said.

Jack was in town and I told him I had a surprise.

"Come over to the bar on the block next to the old Five Spot," he said. "Charlie Mills and I are are here having a cocktail and seeing his fans from the film *On the Bowery* that he wrote the score for. He's singing everybody the themes from his *Crazy Horse Symphony*. Bring your French horn. He needs some help."

"I'm on my way," I said.

I grabbed my horn and walked over to 3rd Avenue and listened to Charles Mills sing excerpts of his score. I had taken a few lessons from him in 1955 and he was a great teacher and brilliant composer who also loved jazz and American Indian music. Jack always enjoyed spending time with him, as we all did.

"I've been asked to write a new piece for the Interracial Chorale," I said breathlessly to Jack and Charlie.

"Buy the kid a drink," said the man standing next to Charlie and Jack. "Buy him a double Black and White with a Johnny Walker Red chaser. That's an interracial drink."

There were a few appreciative chuckles

"Chug-a-lug-it, boy!" said my newfound patron.

I downed both drinks and could feel the alcohol searing my innards like Drano being poured down a clogged-up kitchen sink, and then it began to take me in its seductive caresses and guide me to a new secure place where I would feel no urgency to continue my frantic pace. Suddenly the bar looked like a Charles Dickens Christmas tableau, even though it was May of 1964. Jack gave me a knowing wink and downed a tumbler of Scotch. I could imagine staying there and getting wasted and finally sleeping on the street on this balmy spring night with all the winos and never having to do anything the rest of my life but get high.

"You look wonderful, David," said Charles, staring at me with his enormous brown bloodshot eyes. "It's good to see you having something to drink besides ginger ale. Have another."

"No, Charlie. Thanks, but no thanks. Let's go out and walk around before I pass out."

I grabbed my French horn to help balance me and staggered out to the sidewalk. The May evening air, combined with the carbon monoxide fumes from the passing cars and trucks, restored my equilibrium. We started walking south towards Hong Fat's in Chinatown, which was one of New York's great late-night hang-outology centers and a good place to sober up, because the waiters would always come with their ammonia-soaked mops at 4 A.M. and slap them down in front of you as a combination instant detox treatment and cue to exit and go home.

"I like that name, the Interracial Chorale," said Jack. "At first it sounds bizarre, but look at the text for Beethoven's 9th Symphony, 'Ode to Joy'. All about the world's people holding hands."

"When Mitropoulos conducted my symphony in New York," said Charlie, "I had to show my identification to get in to hear the premiere of my own piece. He had left me two tickets, but since I don't even own a necktie, and looked a little raggedy, the people at the box office at Carnegie Hall couldn't believe I was actually Charles Mills, the composer of the new work being debuted there that night."

"That's because they think serious composers have to wear a white wig, like Mozart did," said Jack. "I admire Mozart for his clarity and elegance and humor, not for his wardrobe. After *On the Road* came out, it was assumed that I would wear a brown tweed coat with patches on the sleeves, smoke a pipe, become a tenured professor of literature at a prestigious ivy league college, disassociate myself from all my old friends, and start seeing a psychiatrist to cure my newfound writer's block."

"That's not the course you seem to have taken," said Charles, chuckling as he passed us a bottle of Taylor port wine he had in his ever-present briefcase that served as a wine cellar as well as a repository for his manuscripts.

"No," said Jack. "Exclusivity is death. But I'll promise to wear a tie when the New York Philharmonic plays your next piece and I'll do the same for you, Davey."

We walked along, crossing Canal Street, and I thought about how much talent was wasted in our community of European-based classical music.

"It's all going to change," I said.

"It has to," said Jack. "We have to be patient, and turn the other cheek. The Philistines are doomed to becoming ensconced in the tomb of their own mediocrity."

"All we can do is keep doing our work, and never lose sight of why we are doing this for our life's work," said Charles Mills. "It will have to change. The whole world is changing. We're right on time. Our music is right on time. Your books are right on the money, Jack. When our society catches up with us in twenty years and understands what we're doing right now in 1964, it will be 1984. But it won't be like George Orwell's 1984. It will be our 1984. A whole new bunch of young cats will be out there with something new and meaningful. And we'll be leaning on our canes and cheering them on. It's only the insecurity of people born in this country who are trained to feel that anything indigenous has to be second rate. We have to learn to love ourselves and then to love one another. Our artists should be a source of national pride."

"I understand. It's snobbism as much as racism," said Jack. "When I was invited to literary soirees after *On the Road* came out, my Lowell accent put my hosts into a state of frenzy. And when I spoke in French they were horrified by my Quebecois accent. They made me feel subhuman, like a cartoon of the French-Canadian logger, the Canuck redneck . . . They didn't know they were in the presence of a *classicist* that read more literature than they ever knew existed. Those snobs. They tried to make me feel miserable, but *they* were *Les Miserables*. I'm sure they never read Langston Hughes or Fanon or Ralph Ellison or Alice Dunbar-Nelson or all the other great black writers, any more than they read my books. They probably haven't read most of the great white writers either.

"You've got to start writing this new piece tonight, Davey. Whatever you choose for the texts, whether it includes my writings or not, it should reflect the genius of Charlie Parker and Louis Armstrong and Bessie Smith and Billie Holiday. You've played with the greats. You have to maintain that spirit and the spontaneous feeling we share when we give our little soirees together. It should sing, like Walt Whitman's poetry, and be as moving as Dylan Thomas reading his 'Child's Christmas in Wales'."

Jack lifted the near-empty bottle of Taylor port wine that we were passing back and forth, and took a giant gulp. "You can extend Bach's *Coffee Cantata,* Brahm's Requiem, Shubert's Mass, and Berlioz's Requiem with today's writers and today's music that's being supressed the way my books are being supressed. What are you going to call it? *Amram Ariseth*? *Davey's Dark Descent to Doom*? *Mezz McGillicuddy's Midnight Mass? The Bopman's Big Borscht Breakthrough?* Only the Shadow knows . . . " Jack handed the bottle back to me.

"There's one *petite goutte* left to drink," he said, "and then we'll toast your new masterpiece with some vintage Ripple wine purchased last night right here on the Bowery." Jack pulled out a bottle from his rucksack and unscrewed the metal top.

"That's my favorite midnight pick-me-upper," said Charlie enthusiastically.

"Charlie, you are a man of *bon goût*," said Jack. "It's not necessary to smell the cork for this vintage because it has no cork. It has a distinctive American bouquet, of old hobos sleeping in burlap sacks underneath bridges on sad Saturday nights, as we plot the overthrow of the concert halls of the world with the fresh new sounds that sing about the sacred joys of America."

"Hip hip hipster, hooray," said Charlie. "That's the kind of music we've got to hear more of."

"Well, actually I had something like that in mind," I said. "I told you about this before, Jack. I want to use the idea that Vivaldi had in his *Four Seasons*, only I want to have the texts describe the four seasons in America and have each season represented in a different part of the country."

"*Fantastique*, Davey. Have a taste of this inspirational Ripple," said Jack, his face brightening. "It sounds like you're ready to begin composing it right now. What other texts are you using to set to music?"

"I want to use something of Jimmy Baldwin. He's given me all his books when we meet at San Remo's. He's got all my music. I've got all his books."

"Excellent," said Jack. "He is one of our unsung sherried heroes."

"I'd also love to set something of yours."

"I want you to, Davey," said Jack. "Except for *Pull My Daisy*, everything we did together is up in the air and in the memories of those sainted few who attended our *moments musicaux*."

"Do you have any suggestions?" I asked.

Jack then proceeded to list the authors and poets, the names of their books, described what they had written, interspersed with quotes that flowed as naturally as his own improvisation, as a result of his incredible memory. After about twenty minutes, he paused.

"Is that enough?" he said.

"Jack, that's enough for several lifetimes," I said.

We headed toward the Figaro, where we had gone so many times. It was a cloudy night and I already knew I could start composing my new cantata, *A Year in Our Land*. Jack, like Johnny Appleseed and Walt Whitman, had spread the seeds and set the stage. He always practiced what the Buddhist philosophy emphasized as the best way to help others to find answers. Jack always said you guided others by showing them how to ask the question and search within themselves and then you would be ready to search the world outside yourself.

"You're a Zen master one more time, Pops," I said as we walked by the Village Gate on the way to the Figaro.

"Right now, I'm dreaming of a waitress at the Figaro who may become my bride if she's still there and hasn't become someone else's. I dunno. I was too old for Joyce, Dody thought I was too crazy, all the beauties I meet want me to be myself as I was in 1947 when Neal and I started our adventures, and this is 1964. I'm getting old, Davey, I'm getting tired. I have to stop drinking."

He pulled a fresh bottle of Thunderbird wine from his rucksack as Charlie drained the remains of the Ripple wine.

"Here's to your new cantata. Here's to Howard Hart and Philip Lamantia and you and me. This was our sacramental wine before our jazz-poetry forays at the Brata Gallery and Circle in the Square and Brooklyn College. 1957 was such a good time. Lamantia warned me about the literary scene. He told me to be careful. He was right. They idolized me and then they turned on me."

"Your place is secure Jack," I said.

"America has a history of killing all its lyric artists," he said. "But we'll outfox the Philistines. Stick to your guns. Be pure. Smile sweetly in the face of adversity like Jesus with his crown of thorns. And when we get to the Figaro, see if you can get that other waitress's phone number. She's best friends with the apple of my eye, and now works the night shift with her. They'll both be there tonight. Play her some Wagnerian excerpts on your French horn when we get there. She loves musicians."

"Then she'll love me, too," said Charles. "If she has a friend, we can stay up all night and go down to city hall in the morning and have a triple wedding ceremony."

When we got to the Figaro, Charlie saw an old flame and after a few minutes walked off with her, arm in arm.

"*Adios, muchachos,*" said Charlie over his shoulder. "God has smiled on me. Being meek and humble has paid off again."

The Figaro was packed with people, and we didn't see anybody we knew. Just as we were about to squeeze into a tiny table in the back room, a familiar voice greeted us.

"Hey, Jack," said Brooklyn Bernie the moving man. "What you been up to? I don't read about you much anymore. Are you still writing? Whatever happened to the Beat Generation?"

"It never existed," said Jack. "Davey and I are creating a cantata. Maybe you can be in it."

"You guys know the only shtick I got is the *Rime of the Ancient Mariner* and I bombed out with that every time. I'm saving up some money and gonna study acting with Uta Hagen."

"Well," said Jack, "the New York theater will rise again."

We sat down and the owner bought us food and snuck us some drinks, and while Jack was partying, I took out some manuscript paper and began setting the epilogue, 'Walt Whitman Take My Leaves America,' to music. Jack met up with the waitress he had wanted to see and they went off together. I stayed in the back room of the Figaro, drinking coffee and sketching the setting of the finale of the cantata, using the lines from Whitman I had thought about for years. When I looked up at the clock on the wall, it was 4:30 A.M. I knew I had to get home, crash, get up, and write music.

I finally had the chance to begin to write a piece I dreamed about doing. I knew my new cantata, *A Year in Our Land,* would get performed with a fine chorus, excellent soloists, a great orchestra, and a conductor who loved my music. I knew I would have the chance to set some of our most important authors' words to music and I could honor Jack's words in a formal written-down thoroughly composed orchestral work.

When I woke up the next morning I was full of energy and called up Jack.

"Oh *mon dieu,* what a hangover I've got. What time is it?" asked Jack.

"Time to start writing my cantata," I said. "Where is your new true love?"

"She had to go to her day job," he said. "She is really beautiful. Sensitive and compassionate. I think I'm in love. Tell me what your new *chef d'oeuvre* is going to be about again, in detail."

I recounted to Jack what I had told him the night before. I explained that my cantata, *A Year in Our Land,* would celebrate the four seasons in America, and that each of the four seasons would be set in a different part of the country. Jack again suggested about fifty books to read, and I painstakingly wrote the names of all of them down. I told him how I knew that this would happen someday when I left Dody's apartment after visiting him there nearly five years ago in 1959. I reminded him of the idea of the baseball opera and how that triggered my imagination.

"We'll still do that someday," said Jack. "And then I'll make you the assistant manager of the Pawtucket team. Now get to work, Davey . . ."

For two weeks, I read and took notes, like looking for a needle in a haystack (or diamonds in the sidewalk).

I thought of Jack as I composed the cantata. All the conversations about our respective travels, all the adventures, dreams, flavors, smells, sounds, and people he met and wrote about, and all the places I had been and people I had played with and for inspired me. I thought about the great times we had together as I composed and orchestrated the cantata. Sometimes, when Jack would visit, I would sit at the piano, pounding away and croaking out as best I could the passages for the chorus and soloists and try to sing some of the virtuosic interludes composed for the orchestra alone. Occasionally, after a few drinks, he would join in. He had such a remarkable ear he could remember portions that I had sung to him over the phone or played in a previous visit, and sing them with me, even though I could only play a rough outline of what these portions of the cantata would sound like. His phenomenal memory of conversations extended to his encyclopedic knowledge of music. Anything he heard once could be instantly recalled.

We always had a great time together and always had fun. Jack remained a purist and an idealist all of his life. Even though we always ended up laughing, I could see and feel the pain he was experiencing. This was the fall of 1964. The new pop culture had become a colossus that seemed intent on simultaneously rewriting history while making a fortune for a handful of entrepreneurs. According to the New Order, no one over thirty was to be trusted. We were informed that jazz was dead, and that novels, symphonies, operas, and acoustic folk music of the world were now all irrelevant. Ironically, Jack was accused of being responsible for all of this, while being called a red-necked reactionary conservative because he refused to go along with it. At the same time, he was reviled by the literary establishment as some kind of a Cro-Magnon Philistine, whose only talent was his ability as a speed demon at the typewriter. As the deposed King of the Beat Generation (a title he abhorred), he was held responsible for the self-indulgent excesses of the 1960s.

"I love America, Davey," he used to say. "Our country created jazz. It gives a place to come to for the wretched of the earth to seek a haven. All of our families came here to join the Indian people in their great circle. Our lost continent, from Canada to Mexico, is precious. I know what's wrong with America. But how can they blame this self-hatred and the exploitation of innocent kids by greedy merchants on Jack Kerouac? Didn't anyone ever *read my books?*"

He felt betrayed by some of his old friends who, because of his refusal to join the tune-in, turn-on, drop-out LSD Brigade, or because of their jealousy of his past success or their own craziness, were no longer able to support his needs: to be appreciated, respected, and loved for the generosity of his spirit, and the enduring value of his work. He felt they were no longer concerned with his vulnerability and the hurt he felt by critical rejection of the most important thing in his life, his writing.

I loved his work. All musicians I knew felt the same way. He was the towering figure of our so-called Beat Generation. All of us knew that. And he didn't need a Beat Generation to justify his work. He was as eloquent and original a voice in American letters as Mark Twain, Walt Whitman, Carson McCullers, Ernest Hemingway, William Faulkner, or F. Scott Fitzgerald.

We had long since stopped reading and jamming together in public. It was too stressful for Jack. We would go to Lucien Carr's home and play music till dawn, or sneak to the back of the Figaro in the darkest part of the café and do a little impromptu improvisation for college kids who thought we were two over-the-hill Greenwich Village nut-cases, or play at my place.

I could always cheer him up, but I knew his road was a long one, and it would be years before America would appreciate what a treasure he was to the world. I feared he would not live long enough to see his greatness appreciated. Even though I was eight years younger, I was not sure in my heart of hearts that I would be around to see Jack get his due. But I knew then that I was with someone whose work would endure forever. It had nothing to do with fame. Jack was unknown in 1956 when we first got together. It was not about celebrity or fashion. It had to do with being in the presence of greatness that was as pure and simple and brilliant as a bright, cloudless summer day at the beach, when you look at the perfect blue of the ocean and the sun's glitter on a wave in the distance almost knocks you over with the power of its reflection.

In the late fall of 1964, as I was completing my cantata *A Year in Our Land,* I had put it aside for four months. I knew I could finish it easily because I had it in my head. I would only need three weeks of uninterrupted time in March of 1965 to finish and orchestrate the rest of the cantata to have it ready for its premiere in May.

I had been called by ABC television to compose *The Final Ingredient,* an opera of the Holocaust, that was to be a one-act opera that was only fifty-six minutes in length for a network television premiere in April of 1965. I got a place in New City, New York, in an empty cabin next to a twenty-acre field with horses. My only company was a nest of rats that served as a cleanup crew for any leftovers from my homemade dinners.

I worked around the clock, setting the libretto by Arnold Weinstein to music. *The Final Ingredient* was based on a true story of a group of prisoners in a concentration camp in World War II who held a clandestine Passover service while being held captive by their Nazi guards. It was a heartbreaking story. Arnold Weinstein somehow managed to create a libretto that made this horrendous experience uplifting. It made me reevaluate my own family's struggle to escape persecution in the mid-nineteenth century, and escape to come to live on this continent.

When I spoke to Jack about the opera, he told me he would say some prayers for me and all who had perished. He also loved Arnold Weinstein's play *Dynamite Tonight* and Arnold's poetry. We all did. Along with Delmore Schwartz and Joel Oppenheimer, Arnold Weinstein was an icon in the Greenwich Village and Lower East Side community of artists. The three of them were fortunate that, like the children of Israel, they were left unlabeled when the plague of the Beatnik Myth tarred and feathered so many of us. It was as if they were beneficiaries of a Passover dispensed by a somewhat just higher power. Delmore, Joel, and Arnold all loved Jack's work, and we were all friends.

I told Jack I would get him a reel-to-reel tape of the opera when it was performed in April to add to his collection of my "underground vegetarian hits," as I affectionately called them.

"All your stuff will be recorded someday," he said to me. "Remember what you said Jimmy Baldwin told you. 'Always keep a carbon copy.' Never throw away anything you wrote. If it's beautiful, it will stay beautiful. I *still* can't get *Visions of Cody* published. Just stick to your guns. Keep working. *Burn* with that hard and gemlike flame."

I mailed Jack a recording of a live performance of *Dirge and Variations* by the Marlboro Trio that he had seen broadcast on a Sunday morning TV show. He loved chamber music as much as he loved jazz. Jack called and told me that he liked it and I sent him more recordings of my symphonic music and some great jazz sessions from my score for the *Manchurian Candidate* that were never used in the film that featured tenor saxophonist Harold Land. I also sent him my score to Arthur Miller's play *After the Fall,* for which I had composed the music a year ago.

In late February, he wrote me a short one-page letter from Florida.

Feb. 27 '65

Dear Davey: -

Playing the tapes - Neat - Who is the alto? - Nice drums, bass too - Glad to see from N.Y. Times you getting along in yr. career (opera for Israeli motif) -

See you sometime this Spring in Auld Manhattoes

Yours, Jack

Real Yiddish name : - Jean-Louis Lebris de Kérouac

(I'll call you before I interrupt your Poulanc-and-Satie-like musical meditations on Sixth Ave.) Nutty Jack
(So little to say in letters anymore, as one grows older)

While I was finishing work on the cantata, I completed rehearsals for the *Final Ingredient,* due to be broadcast nationally Sunday, April 11, 1965.

I called Jack and told him he could watch it on ABC network television. He sounded worn out and told me he had been punched out in a bar and that he was going to have to cut back on his drinking, but that he would watch the broadcast. We talked a week later, and he asked me to tell Arnold Weinstein, who wrote the libretto, that he thought he had done a great job with an almost impossible challenge and that we would all have to get together in New York when he came to pay a visit.

Jack wasn't able to hear the world premiere of *A Year in Our Land* at Town Hall on May 14, 1965. When he came to visit, I read him the enthusiastic review in the *New York Herald Tribune*.

"*Fantastique*," said Jack. "There's no way they can fit this into the Beat Generation dungeon. We'll get there yet. Let's plan a baseball and football oratorio."

San Francisco Reunion

In the fall of 1965 I finished my cantata *Let Us Remember*, with a text by Langston Hughes. He was a poet who, along with Dylan Thomas, was a favorite of all musicians, because of his flowing style that made you want to read him aloud. Like Dylan Thomas, you always knew what he was talking about, and he wrote from his own life experiences and made you feel what it was like to be part of them. And like Jack, he was shunned by many of New York's ever-changing fashion-conscious arbiters, who were only concerned with who was in and who was out. Fortunately, Langston knew, as Jack knew, that he was writing for a worldwide audience. Neither of them ever forgot their roots or the love they felt for their people and the love of sharing that keen poetic sense with others.

Langston knew of the friendship I had with Jack and also understood what Jack was going through.

"Once they say they love you, you have to be prepared to deal with what it's like when they hate you," said Langston. "I learned a long time ago that when I'm referred to as a historic figure of the Harlem Renaissance who now is reduced to writing a newspaper column, that means I'm supposed to accept my demise. Fortunately, my physician agrees with me that I'm still very much alive. Here in Harlem, I'm bearing witness to what we did a long time ago. All the young kids working for me understand I'm an artist first and foremost who loves his people and loves this country that we helped to build. Our blood and tears are part of everyone's life.

Without us, where would music, dance, poetry, sports, and a major part of our way of speaking English be?

"Like Jack, I am a reporter of my time and place. He will always pay his dues for maintaining his French-Canadian identity and his love of the Catholic Church. He refuses to be a white Uncle Tom for the New York literary establishment, and he also understands the destructive nature of well-meaning people who fancy themselves as revolutionaries and are handing over the country to oppressive people by glorifying drugs and irresponsibility.

"I'm criticized by many for not being militant enough, after spending my whole life working to open up the doors of understanding among all of us. It seems that any of us selected to be spokesmen are expected to be entertainers to an elite group who wish to keep us divided. Jack comes from the Whitman tradition of embracing and yea saying.

"His work embraces all of the Continent and he really writes about jazz with an understanding that is rare. He loves our music and seems to understand it because he feels it. You can sense that in his writing. And he draws on his European roots.

"When you speak to Jack next, tell him to persevere and remember to keep his eyes on the prize. He must not allow himself to succumb to despair. We have to be strong to stay in this business. We have an obligation to fulfill. We have to be strong. Tell him to dig deep."

In late October of 1965 I called up Jack in St. Petersburg and told him I was flying to San Francisco to attend rehearsals of the cantata and would look up old friends.

"Tell them Jack is still writing and that I love and miss them all, and that I will be back when I can. Try and see Lamantia and Howard Hart if they are around and tell them we need a reunion to show how music-poetry should be done. Call Ferlinghetti and find out how Neal and Carolyn and the kids are doing. I know Neal still visits her to see them. He needs to get away as I'm trying to, from all the illiterates who have no idea of who we are. When I saw him last summer, he was with a group of hangers-on that treated him like a monkey on a string. I know Carolyn will survive. She's strong. But Neal is lost." He paused, and I could feel his sadness across the many miles that separated us. "Try to see someone," he said. "I miss all the good times."

"I'll try, Jack," I said. "I miss them too. I don't think I'll have much of a chance to find everybody because we have a lot of rehearsals and I want to make sure Langston's text and my music come off the way they should. Langston sends his love to you and says to stay strong."

"Tell him I will and that I'll turn the other cheek to the Philistines," said Jack, laughing as he always did when he said this to me and others. "Tell Langston to stick to his guns and I'll stick to mine and tell everyone there I haven't had a drink in a week. I may visit Lowell while you're in San Francisco and if I do I'll go to Mass and say a special prayer for you, for Langston and for your new work. Maybe they will do *A Year in Our Land,* and my portion of *The Lonesome Traveler* that you set to music will be heard west of the Rockies."

"Someday I know it will," I said.

"That's our secret weapon, to circumvent our detractors," said Jack. "We can be spontaneous and throw it away and keep the same spontaneity as we *write* it down, so that the reader and the listener feel us talking directly to them. One genre compliments the other. Bach improvised fugues as well as writing them down. Homer scatted the *Iliad* and the *Odyssey;* someone else wrote it down for him."

"That's great, Jack," I said. "I'm going to write that down."

"Be sure to remember that Jean-Louis Libre de Kérouac told you this to inform the illiterate of what we are about," said Jack, chuckling.

I ripped out a scribbled page of my torn address book and wrote it down.

"I've got it, Jack," I said.

"If you encounter an army of Beatniks and *poseurs* at your concert, tell them to please read my books and listen to your music and then look inside themselves to find their own beauty and that LSD and the whole barbarian trip is a charade leading to a dead end. At least tell them to read Shakespeare and the Bible and listen to Bach and Charlie Parker."

"That's a promise, Jack," I said. "I always do that anyway."

"I'm tired, Davey," said Jack. "I have to stay here for my mother's sake. The climate is good for her. Say hello to her. She loves to hear you speak French."

I talked to Gabrielle in French and made her laugh as I always did. She told me that she was feeling better and that Jack was being a good boy but that he should tell all the people who came by day and night banging at the door to leave them alone in peace. I explained to her that this was nothing that Jack could help and that he was a great artist who was misunderstood. She told me how women were trying to take him away from her and that she was afraid he would run off with some tramp and leave her all alone.

"Jamais," I told her. "Never."

"Bon. Tu est un vrai ami," she said.

She asked me about Lenny Gross, whom she loved. He was the curly-headed boy-wonder editor whom Jack and I met in 1958 at Brooklyn College at our last public reading with Howard Hart and Philip Lamantia. He had visited their home in Northrop, and like everyone else who ever met him, Gabrielle was crazy about him. *"Le petit Lenny. Il est adorable.* When are *you* getting married?" she asked, suddenly breaking into English. "When will you find yourself a nice Jewish girl and have a family? You're not getting any younger."

"Soon, I hope," I said sheepishly.

"Maybe you'll find a wife in San Francisco," she said. "There's a lot of single women out there. But don't marry a tramp."

" I won't. I promise."

Jack got back on the phone.

"Tell your mother I promise I won't marry a tramp," I said.

"If you do, I know she'll soon become a sainted angel," whispered Jack.

I could hear Jack's mother screaming at him in French wanting to know what he was saying to me that she couldn't hear.

"J'ai dit que Davey va trouver une ange." (I said that Davey will find himself an angel.)

"I'll be looking." I said.

"God will provide you with one," said Jack. "Have a great trip. I'll pray for you."

"I'll pray for you too," I said.

I arrived in San Francisco and met Paul Kresh, who had put together a whole program that included a concert performance of the ballet score of *Judith* by William Schuman, a work for narrator and orchestra with Edward G. Robinson as the soloist, and another world premiere of a short evocative piece for trumpet and orchestra by Charles Morrow. The featured piece was the world premiere of my cantata *Let Us Remember.*

During a break in rehearsals I became friendly with a spaced-out-looking violinist. We talked about music for nearly an hour and then I said, "I told Jack Kerouac I was going to try to look up a bunch of people but I have no idea where they live anymore. Herb Gold is the only one I know who stays in the same place and pays his rent. Everyone else is floating. I have a friend I'd like to see who is a fine composer, Morton Sobotnick, and I found his address somehow in my jumble of papers and don't know where this street is in San Francisco."

I showed Paul Kresh the address. "It's in Haight Ashbury," he said. "A lot of Polish people live there but it's becoming the new North Beach. You can score a lot of dope and meet a lot of wild chicks there. They're running around all over the place."

I thanked him and took off to find Morton. When I finally found the building and rang the bell, there was no answer. I noticed quite a few young people dressed in homemade costumes that looked like they were auditioning as extras for a Civil War movie or a pirate film epic.

Many of the women had long jackets and skirts that looked like they were made out of homemade velvet curtains, with open blouses that made it difficult to look away. Many had long hair flowing down their backs with their hair parted neatly in the middle, offset by flowers neatly placed over their heads like members of a water ballet in an old Esther William's movie musical. Some were wearing thin rimmed wire glasses. They seemed happy and content.

Many of the young men had open-neck shirts and bandannas, like the old Errol Flynn costume movies and some were sporting eye patches. They had long hair and were smiling and surprisingly cheerful. I sensed that the old Beatnik stereotype of what we were supposed to have been like was no longer a universally accepted fashion statement—at least not in this neighborhood. What a relief, I thought to myself. I'll have to call Jack and tell him that there are finally some young people who are not trying to look like Beatniks.

I could smell the aroma of pot being smoked out on the street. I suddenly saw what looked like my old basement apartment on 16th Street in Washington, D.C. from 1949 to 1952, only this present incarnation seemed to be some kind of old bar and grill. I had no idea where I was at this point, having walked from Morton's apartment building for a half an hour, soaking up the sights, sounds, and ever-present pot fumes. For some reason, I felt drawn to the bar. I walked down a few steps into its dimly lit interior, squinting my eyes for focus.

"Well, look what washed up on shore. Mezz McGillicuddy," shouted a voice that could only be Gregory Corso.

I squinted my eyes and saw Gregory, Peter Orlofsky, Allen Ginsberg, jazz pianist Freddie Redd, and actor Gary Goodrow, both in the cast of *The Connection* in New York and friends of mine from the first few weeks in the city in 1955. I saw a tall brooding figure gazing at me, bobbing his head and laughing.

"Of course with your busy schedule trying to keep jazz alive and bringing Berlioz, Bach, and Bird to the uninitiated masses, you probably don't have time to search your once promising mind to activate the remaining brain cells not destroyed by your youthful excesses and nights spent in ecstatic embrace with all those fine chicks that used to fill whole cities before the heathen began their deprogramming of America's youth and leaving us high and dry but never high enough to forget those golden days of big bands and open hearts and warm embraces that you certainly are in need of giving as I am in need of receiving, so give old Neal a brotherly bebop hug."

"My God!" I said. "Cassady!" We gave each other a hug. Then I gave everybody at the bar a hug.

"This is like a bar mitzvah," said Gary Goodrow. "Did you bring me a gift?"

"Dave brought himself," said Freddie Redd. "He brought the gift of himself. I'm playing a gig here in San Francisco later this week. His ESP told him I needed a French horn player to sit in with me, so here you are, David, right on time. Did you pack your ax?"—a musician's lingo for "bring your instrument."

"Always do," I said. "Tell me where and I'll be there. I only have one night I'm busy."

I told them I had just spoken to Jack a few days ago, and asked them why they were all here at three P.M. in an empty bar on a sunny day.

"We were driving around San Francisco with Neal at the wheel and suddenly we decided to come here," said Allen. "We hadn't been here in twelve years. This is a place we used to come to with Jack when we weren't in the Mission District or North Beach. We ran into Freddie and Gary and invited them along. We just were drawn to this place for a kind of sentimental return to a time long gone."

"Like our man Marcel Proust's *Remembrance of Things Past,*" said Neal. "But we're not lying in a cork-lined room in Gay Paree, we're here in San Francisco with an army of young gals waiting to be swept off their feet by the brilliance of our collective intellects and manly charms if we can get off our keesters and go back to the van and let me drive to pick up two angels of the night who happen to be waiting just for me to fill their lives with love and sensual satisfaction."

"Good," said Allen. "We'll pick up Neal's two young friends and drive them over to Fisherman's Wharf where we're having a poetry reading tonight. You can play for us, David."

"It's the cast of *Pull My Daisy* revisited six years later," said Peter Orlofsky in a stentorian bass voice, like an opera singer. "Bring on the broads."

"How 'bout some ladies for Gregory?" said Corso to Neal. "Don't they know I can immortalize them?"

"Just be sure to keep yourself mortalized," said Gary Goodrow. "None of us are in a rush to be immortalized yet."

"I'll drink to that," said Freddie Redd.

"I will too," I said. "But first I want to drink to Jack."

I ordered seven ginger ales from the bartender and we all raised our glasses.

"I'll drink to Jack, too," said the bartender, pouring himself a tumbler full of Courvoisier brandy. "The new generation you see out on the street smoking all that reefer killed the bar business, but I'll join in your ginger ale toast to Jack. Kerouac has held up a mirror for Americans to make us see ourselves so that we can learn to love each other again. He's a drinking man with a big heart."

"To Jack and all of us," I said. "To Langston Hughes, who brought me here, and to all of you for being here."

We drank our ginger ales.

"Time to go," said Allen. "I wish I could see Jack. He is angry with me. I can't get him to understand the new consciousness and political implications of what he started. He could make a fortune if he went out on the college circuit with us, and we all held hands with the new revolutionary spirit that's sweeping the country. He could be a real star. He could be an icon. He could be like a rock star."

"He just wants to be respected as a writer," I said.

"Of course. We all want that," said Allen, somewhat testily. "But that's not enough. This is a media culture. Marshall McCluhan and Timothy Leary are leading the way to a new consciousness. He has to let his old ways of thinking go and be part of what's happening *now*."

"Jack will always be part of what's happening now, Allen," said Neal. "He is the chosen one. He is the voice that will always be with us. He is a classic writer."

"Well, his books are going out of print," said Allen. "It's not enough just to sit at home looking after your mother and writing in a vacuum."

"Jack will never write in a vacuum," said Neal. "His voice will always be heard. His words will be here when we are all gone."

"Well, we're still here now, so let's get moving," said Freddie Redd. "Let's see how much Neal remembers about the jazz scene that all the rest of you forgot about, if you ever dug it in the first place. Neal, you and Dave do some scat singing. Gary and I will be the rhythm section."

"See you in twelve years, boys," said the bartender. "Every twelve years I expect a reunion. Next time bring Jack. Drive carefully, Neal. The cops are getting mean. San Francisco's not what it used to be."

"Nothing ever is," said Allen. "That's the definition of change. Things move on."

We left the bar and climbed into the van. It was a classic pre-Hippiemobile, the kind that became so popular a few months later. Neal got behind the wheel. As if on cue, two stunning young women, classic California beauties with rich manes of natural blonde hair, tapped on the door of the van.

"We're here, Neal. Let us in," said the taller of the two.

Neal opened the door and ushered both of the women into the empty front seat. He introduced them to us, mimicking W. C. Fields as a train conductor announcing different stations.

"Gals, I'd like to introduce you to everyone here that you don't already know. In addition to Allen, Gregory, and Peter, who of course you have met innumerable times before today's special journey, we have Mr. Freddie Redd, a legendary master of jazz piano who has not only played with all the greats, but is considered by his peers to be one of the greats himself. You certainly all know Gary Goodrow, who can improvise a whole play on the spot from suggestions from the audience in the same way as our special visitor Dave Amram sitting right here on the seat behind you directly to the left side of the aisle of our little limo. Dave, as I'm sure you have heard, can make up scat poems anywhere, anytime, as he did after intermission when he did the first jazz-poetry readings in New York with Kerouac, because when the poets would disappear during the break, leaving him hanging hopelessly in front of an angry mob of New York heathen waiting for the troops to return from their poetry off-duty break, which of course as I'm sure you gals know was led by old Jack himself, along with Phil Lamantia and Howard Hart, who were unable to stop their street-side wine guzzling and women-chasing with their newfound fans and return to bail out Dave by reading their latest masterpieces, which forced poor ol' Dave to make up scat parables with rhymes at the piano so that the audience who still remained wouldn't attack him physically as well as abuse him verbally, possibly destroying his French horn chops and stifling his creativity forever. So, darlings, please make yourselves at home on our little journey and tour of the Bay Area and everyone say hello to Tiffany and Mary, as we leave on our way headed towards Columbus Avenue and the joys of San Francisco's many pleasures, before arriving at 6:45 at our final destination at Fisherman's Wharf for a sound check prior to tonight's poetry reading. Tiffany, do you have a few words to say to all of us assembled here?"

"Hello, everyone," said Tiffany, gently putting her arms around Neal's chest and shoulders as he continued rapping away, driving, and talking over his shoulder.

"Of course," said Neal "our trip is made complete by the holy hale and hearty most divine Miss Mary, who is gracing us with her presence this afternoon."

"Hi," said Mary. She took Neal's right hand and began massaging it as he drove with his left hand on the wheel, continuing his tour guide monologue. "Nice to be with all you fellows."

"Yeah, I'm sure it is," said Gregory in a sullen tone.

Neal began talking to me as Gregory and Allen started one of their endless arguments. He continued driving with one hand, managing to somehow steer the van through the traffic and respond to Mary's hand massages and Tiffany's neck rubs with moans of approval while carrying on a conversation with me.

"Dave, can you believe how there is now a new army of young kids who no longer call themselves Beatniks but think that somehow we are responsible for their wanting to drop out of life instead of meeting it head on? They never heard a note of jazz, never read a book beyond its cover, never hitched a ride, or lay out in a field somewhere at night with their true love to talk about ecstasy here on Earth. They think I am a living legend and that Jack is their father figure and most of them never read a word he wrote. They have no idea of who we are and how we got to be the way we are. Allen can deal with this. He's a master of change and fashion. I'm not. I'm stuck in the middle of the stream, up shit's creek without a paddle. I'm derailed. The train left without me. I'm in the caboose, all alone with my saxophone. . . . Hey girls, do you want to to hear something Dave and Jack and I grew up with? It's a railroad song."

Neal started singing "Chattanooga Choochoo" and after completing the chorus and the bridge, he made up lyrics with rhymes, snapping the fingers of his right hand, which he temporarily freed from Mary's hand, on the second and fourth beats while Tiffany was now patting and massaging his head and kissing his neck as if he were her exotic lapdog.

Neal scatted four perfectly constructed bars, conducting an imaginary orchestra with his right hand without missing a finger snap, while continuing to drive with his left, like a crazed ambidextrous race car driver symphony conductor, watching the traffic, smiling at both Tiffany and Mary, flashing occasional fleeting glances over his shoulder at each of us in the van, while making up scat verses. He began to sing.

> *"You gals think you love me, but you*
> *don't understand*
> *You got to pay your dues before you*
> *sit in with this band."*

Neal continued scat singing as all of us in the van responded with laughter, verses of our own, whoops of approval or insults.

"You're so . . . bizarre, like . . . oh man, you're so . . . like . . . a real Beat *trip*! Tee hee . . . " squealed Tiffany, bursting into uncontrollable giggles.

"That was amazing, Neal," said Allen, in a professorial tone of voice.

"That really sucked," rasped Gregory. "Get out of the poetry scene. That scat doggerel is for morons!"

"Oh, like *really* . . . like don't you know, Gregory?" said Tiffany, throwing her arms around Neal's neck as if to protect him. "Neal is a genius. Jack never would have written *On the Road* if it hadn't been for him. He's the real Dean Moriarty."

"You don't have to educate me, sweetheart. Educate yourself. Finish junior high school so you can read something beside comic books," snarled Gregory, like Humphrey Bogart in a gangster movie.

"Oh, you're just jealous," said Mary, kissing Neal's ear and rumpling his hair. "No one ever wrote a book about you!"

"No one ever has to," said Gregory. "I write my own books."

During this exchange, Neal kept on singing softly and like a seasoned tap dancer, came right in on cue.

"Girls and boys, let's not fight
Scat with me
till you get it right
I'll never become
a rock and roll slave
Hip these kids to the
message, Dave"

I began scatting about meeting Dizzy Gillespie in my basement apartment in Washington, D.C., in 1951, how Charlie Parker came there in 1952 two times, how my mentor, the great conductor Dimitri Mitropoulos, inspired me to dare to continue being a composer of concert music as well as a jazz musician and was a man who loved literature, jazz, art, and mountain climbing and was devoutly religious like Jack, how Jack and I had first met in '56 and how I wished Jack could become the new brakeman for the Chattanooga Choochoo and ride the rails back to San Francisco to be with all of us to hang out and hear the new cantata.

Neal and I then sang the final lyrics to "Chattanooga Choochoo."

"Whoa!" exclaimed Neal.

"I think I can get you a booking at the National Association of Schizophrenics and Manic Depressives Annual Convention," said Gary. "There might be an opening."

"I wish we could do something like what we just did now at your concert at the Opera House," said Neal.

"You wouldn't have to worry about the concert going into overtime," said Gregory. "You'd empty out the house before you finished the first five minutes. Get out of the poetry scene. It's not your game."

"We're not in the poetry scene, Gregory," I said. "We're just having fun."

"Well, I'm not," said Gregory. "All these beautiful girls keep walking down the street and I'll never see them again."

"Wait till your poetry reading tonight," said Allen. "If you show your loving side, you'll find someone to share your love with."

"I don't want to hear any more Buddhist crap, Allen. I want some *action*!" shouted Gregory. *"Right now!"*

"I remember Jack telling me about how much he dug working with you on that cantata, *A Year in Our Land*," said Neal softly, as if Gregory, who had now opened up the window and was shouting at startled passersby, weren't even there. We all knew that Gregory had a heart of gold and felt obliged to be outrageous in order to feel comfortable with other people. Like the comedian Don Rickles, he displayed affection by insulting people, only if he felt it wouldn't hurt them.

"Old Jack should be here for this," said Neal. "He loves Langston's poetry. Have you gals heard of the great Langston Hughes?"

"Well, we have now!' said Mary enthusiastically.

"Oh . . . em-m-m . . . er . . . ah . . . like hold it there . . . did he play guitar with the band that opened for Screamin' Jay Hawkins? He was like . . . so . . . well . . . he had such a . . . hee-hee . . . firm little *butt*!" said Tiffany.

"No, darlin'," said Neal. "He's a great poet that Jack and all of us admired. He was part of the Harlem Renaissance."

"You mean he actually lived up there in . . . Harlem?" said Tiffany. "Wasn't he frightened? You know, like being around all those . . . you know . . . like . . . all those . . . different types of people. Like those Puerto Rican Mexican types that can't speak English and those black people and the Jewish-Italian gangsters."

"No," said Neal wearily, rolling his bloodshot eyes in despair. "He wasn't afraid at all. He and Countee Cullen, Duke Ellington, and a whole lot of other visionaries set the stage for the whole world that Jack and Dave and I grew up in. Our best music, art, theater, and poetry would never have come about the way it did without the Harlem Renaissance."

"Well said, Neal," murmured Allen.

"I've heard of the Harlem Globetrotters," said Mary.

"Fuh-*get* about it," rasped Gregory. "These dumb chicks don't get it and never will."

"You're just jealous," cooed Mary. "Neal's a living legend. You know we'll never go out with you. You're not famous. You're just along for the ride."

"Just a minute, young ladies," said Allen, suddenly becoming angry, the way he used to be in the '50s when he would fall into fits of rage at the drop of a hat, before his recent trips to India cooled him out. "Gregory Corso is a great lyric poet. I prefer his work to mine. Jack really respects his work, in spite of their differences. Have you read Gregory's poetry, Tiffany? Have you read his work, Mary?"

"I don't read much of anything," said Mary. "I dig people, not books about people."

"I'm with you on that," said Freddie Redd, from the back seat.

"I . . . like . . . well . . . no!" said Tiffany. "I know that Jack is beautiful. I read *On the Road* four times, and *The Subterraneans*."

"I read them too," said Mary. "Those books are real. You don't have to be a college professor to understand what he's saying. Neal got us to read Franz Kafka too. He's weird!"

"You guys think we're stupid because we've never been to New York," said Tiffany. "Well, let me tell you something. This is a big country, and your small-minded attitude makes you all mental midgets. That's why we all love Jack and Neal. They are for real. Mary and I wish we could meet Jack. We feel like we know him from reading his books. When we met Neal, it was like he was part of our family."

"I can't believe you completed a sentence," said Gregory.

"Oh shut up!" said Tiffany. "Save all your insults for those pathetic women that go to hear you read your poems."

"They're not pathetic," said Gregory. "They're intelligent.

They're sensitive. They want meaning and romance in their lives. I'm like Jack. I come from the classic tradition of literature. I'm self taught. I went to libraries like Jack did. I read all the time when I was in jail. Jack read when he was out at sea. We were both naturals. Neal is a natural. Dave is a natural. So are Gary and Freddie. That's why we're all friends. We're all drifting down the same stream."

"Without a paddle, gals," said Neal. "Understand that. Society wouldn't let us on board their train, so we built our own canoes and now they've taken away our paddles, but we're cool because we know how to improvise."

"How 'bout Jack?" said Tiffany, in a different tone of voice than we had heard since she had gotten on the bus. Suddenly she wasn't playing the dumb blonde role. "Where's he going? What is he doing with his life?"

"Dave is in touch with him more than any of us right now," said Neal. "But he still has his typewriter. He can still write about *anything,* and make it all meaningful and interesting to anybody and everybody. He remembers *everything.* He wrote my greatest books for me. I want to write about what he left out, about the parts of my life that are left over. But, gals, let us not become morbid as we remember the words of that old standard, with my improved additional lyrics . . . You're so young, and I'm so beautiful . . . "

Neal began singing, making up a song based on the old classic, and Mary and Tiffany went back to their party mode. Neal began a long monologue about all the big bands from Chick Webb, Lucky Millender, the great territory bands of the Southwest and Midwest, the golden days of Kansas City when Mary Lou Williams, Jay McShann, Charlie Parker, Buddy Tate, and Roy Eldridge all played at jam sessions there and when Count Basie set the stage for Coleman Hawkins and then Lester Young to pursue their own stylistic innovations for all the music that lit up the world and vocalists like Billie Holiday changed the way we looked at music forever. Like Jack, Neal was a true scholar of the streets who knew jazz as an observer but understood the language and had the heart and soul of a true musician. Like Jack, he had a natural rapport with musicians. Like Jack, he had a deep respect for the geniuses, known and unknown, who all helped create the body of work that helped move all of America, as well as the whole world of music, forward.

"Gals," said Neal. "We're dealing with more than show business here, when we talk about jazz. This is the music that both Martin Luther King and Malcolm X grew up with. The sanctified church is the foundation of most of what we hear. Jazz will always be the voice of our innermost dreams that we dare not utter and that these musicians articulate for us. Jazz tells us we can dare to keep on dreaming."

"That sounds like the Sigmund Freud shot," said Gregory testily.

"Sigmund Freud was a coke head," said Neal. "He was so self-centered, he never got laid. That's why he appeals to people with a poor self-image. He couldn't dig himself, so he couldn't dig others."

"Well, we dig you, Neal," said Mary, "because you're the coolest. Let's stop here for a minute and go up to my apartment with Tiffany. I'll take a bath and you can tell us more about Edgar Cayce."

"All reet-o-roonio," said Neal, winking at me. "I'll be right back, fellahs. Mary, Tiffany, and I are going to go deep sea diving in her bathtub and see if we can find Edgar Cayce's lost Isle of Atlantis."

Neal parked the van. Tiffany and Mary got out on the passenger side and Neal leaped from the driver's seat, ran around the front of the van, and bounded up the stairs of the small apartment house ahead of Tiffany and Mary.

"Hey," yelled Gregory. "Let me come too. I need a bath. I'll tell you all about Keats and Shelley and Lord Byron and about drowning at sea."

"Forget it, short stuff," said Mary over her shoulder as she climbed the stairs behind Neal and Tiffany. "You're too mean to be a playmate of ours."

"I keep telling you, Gregory, that you have to let your natural sweetness and inner beauty flow outwards," said Allen gently.

"I don't need to hear the Hare Krishna shot, Allen. Save that for your act with the college students. I just want some *action*."

"Yes," said Allen. "But those girls have feelings. You can't talk to women like that anymore. They are people too. Neal and Jack have compassion for the women they are with."

"Agh!" groaned Gregory. "Another lecture about compassion. Dave, how does it feel to be hearing all this crap? Is this the set of *Pull My Daisy* revisited six years later? Is this the old nostalgia shot? Is this the Beat version of the Elks Club Shriners Convention Hadassah Sons of Italy Knights of Columbus Beat football team's high school reunion? Why isn't Jack here?"

"He is," I said. "I can hear him laughing and writing it all down on his notepad and in his head."

We knew Neal and the two ladies were going to be upstairs for a while, so we all kept rapping, talking about all the things that were happening around the country with all of our old friends and their struggles to survive, and how the Vietnam War was like a silent nightmare that wouldn't go away, and seemed to be dividing the whole country.

"I don't understand what's happened to Jack. He's become a warmonger," said Allen.

"I don't think so, Allen," I said. "He loves his country. He was on a merchant ship in World War II that went down right after he sailed on it, and all aboard were killed. He had a lot of friends on board."

"I know all that," said Allen. "But can't he see what our government is doing to the world?"

"That's beside the point," I said. "He doesn't trust the opportunists who are creating a youth culture designed to make money off young people by immobilizing them and handing the whole country over to the right wing and that's what is happening. The whole drug culture is a form of genocide too, and he feels betrayed by feeling forced to join something he feels is jive. He feels the military industrial complex is now joined by the antiwar industrial complex. Progressive politics is being taken over by the entertainment industry and handing over the country to the Philistines. It's jive."

"I'd say jive *ass*," said Freddie Redd from the back seat. "You think all that dope that comes to Harlem gets there by accident? Do you think high school kids should be encouraged by the entertainment industry to drop acid? This is genocide. Jazz brought black and white people together and people all over the world to a higher level, so the music business tolerated heroin, to get rid of us. The airwaves are controlled by gangsters and big business. The Vietnam War is a waste. So are the hustlers who are ripping off the kids who are against it. That's what you should be dealing with," said Freddie. "You don't see any gurus in limos running around Harlem. We'd throw their jive asses out!"

"Jack feels betrayed," I said. "He tells me that he feels isolated. His forebears came here from French Canada for a better life. He loves this country and the whole American continent. He always tells me about wanting to find his Indian heritage that he feels was part of his Canadian family's past. He thinks he has Iroquois ancestry. He tells me how he can feel that coming through him, and how so many Indians here and in Mexico tell him they see that in him. That's some heavy stuff. He's very humbled by that. That's got nothing to do with politics."

"That's got everything to do with politics," said Allen. "The corporations are destroying the planet. If you endorse this war, you are not only a warmonger, you are a corporate oppressor."

"Well, if Dave is a corporate oppressor, he should buy some more expensive clothes and move out of that rent-controlled rat hole on 6th Avenue and stop going out with waitresses who want to be opera singers and give me a million dollars!" said Gregory, suddenly becoming animated. "How 'bout it, Dave? Can you sell one of those tanks you manufacture and give me the money? I'll dedicate another poem to you. The Thanksgiving poem I dedicated to you in 1957 was a gift but it was short! Give me a million warmongered corporate dollars and I'll write you a whole book of poems. And then I'll turn you on to some of my leftover ladies."

"Thank you Gregory," I said. "I'm cool the way I am. I just want to get this new cantata played right. I'm glad you can all come to the concert."

"I just want to see you dressed up like the Penguin in *Batman*," said Gregory. "Mezz McGillicuddy puts on the dog."

"I'll be interested to see how you set Langston Hughes verses to music," said Allen.

"I used the same approach I did when I set Jack's words to the *Lonesome Traveler* and the words of Steinbeck, Whitman, Thomas Wolfe, James Baldwin, and Dos Passos," I said. "I tried to honor the natural musicality of what was already there and enhance it. Just like when I spontaneously accompany Jack or you guys, I try to *listen*, to *feel* what it is about."

"Well frankly, David," said Allen, "you must realize that you are living to a large extent in the past. Why don't you play rock music? Jazz is dead. Classical music is dead. Kids want to hear simple songs that they can hum back after one hearing. You could make millions of dollars. Television commercials are changing the world. America is sinking to its knees. Don't allow yourself to become passé."

"Allen, what's beautiful stays beautiful. Charlie Parker, Dylan Thomas, Ralph Ellison, Carson McCullers, Dizzy Gillespie, George Gershwin, Jackson Pollock, Joan Mitchell and Franz Kline, Odetta and Patsy Kline . . . they'll *never* be passé. They'll *always* be hip. Bach, Shakespeare, and Hector Berlioz will always be hip."

Gary Goodrow started to sing 'It Seems to Me I've Heard That Song Before.' "David," he said, "you're still on the same soapbox as the one you were standing on when I met you at my old loft on the Bowery ten years ago. If you stick to your principles long enough, you can successfully avoid being fashionable for the rest of your life."

"Hang in there, Mezz," said Gregory. "There's money to be made from giving it the masochist's shot. The uneducated *nouveaux riches* boobs that speculate in the art market think Van Gogh was great because he cut his ear off. To a certain type of snob, nothing succeeds like being a failure. That's how you get yourself a patron."

"I'll always work to pay my rent, Gregory," I said. "Dizzy told me one night that as long as there is one black man left on Earth who can sing the blues, jazz will never die. Jack says every time you speak to him, 'Stick to your guns. Turn the other cheek. Think of Jesus and his crown of thorns, and how he drove the money chansgers from the temple with his whip'."

"All right, all right, enough of all that," said Gregory. "Let's get going to our poetry reading at Fisherman's Wharf."

Gregory crawled over the top seats of the van and started honking the horn.

A window opened on the third floor. Neal, shirtless and beaming like a schoolboy, leaned out the window with bare shouldered Tiffany and Mary.

"We just found Atlantis. It was right at the bottom of Mary's bathtub."

A few minutes later, Neal came down with the ladies and drove us all to Fisherman's Wharf and we had a great open-air reading. I sat in and played with almost everybody.

"You played with Kerouac. Can you play with me? What's he doing now? Is he OK? He's my favorite writer. He's why I'm writing."

These were the kind of comments I heard in some form over and over, not only from the people whom I accompanied in their readings that night, but from young people in the audience and from musicians and other people in the arts who attended. It was refreshing to see all ages, from old San Francisco bohemians with white hair to babies dancing.

This was a few weeks before Haight-Ashbury and the whole of America exploded with a new fashionable merchandizing trend, replacing Beatniks with Hippies. The warm, communal feelings were in the air because San Francisco always had and still has a special feeling that nothing, not even earthquakes, could ever destroy. We hung out after the readings were over.

"These kids are here, but they only see this minute. They don't know where all this came from. They have no background, so they'll never move forward till they do," said Neal. "When I talk, they listen, but they don't *hear* what I'm saying. I'm trying to hip them to the happenings from Chaucer and Palestrina and Van Eyk to Proust and Bartok and Jackson Pollock and they think I'm a stoned-out relic, chasing young gals and speed-freaking them out with inconsequential meanderings of a mind that has been destroyed before they were born. They think anything and anybody before the Beatles and Elvis Presley are like fossils in a petrified forest. They can't *hear* Charlie Parker. They don't *read* Walt Whitman. They can't *hear* or *see* America singing. I'm glad for those younger poets that you played with them all tonight. That's beautiful. But they don't know who you are or what you've done. They just know you played with Jack and were in *Pull My Daisy*. We're raising a generation of middle-class barbarians. They get high just to sit around and indulge in sad-ass small talk. They don't see smoking weed as a sacramental rite and a gateway to a higher spiritual plane. Man, I'm getting too old and feeling older than I am. I don't have anyone to talk to. I'm treated like a clown. Like Pagliacci, who really had cause to sing the blues. You know the aria." Neal started singing "Vesti la Giubba," made famous by Caruso.

"Check that out, gals," said Neal, between phrases of the aria. "Vesti la giubba from the one-act killer opera *I Pagliacci* composed by the ineffibly groovy and soulfully swinging Ruggiero Leoncavallo, one of the most outta sight cats to ever grace the world of nineteenth-century lyric operatic stylings. Dig the rest of it."

Neal resumed singing as if he were auditioning for the role in an upcoming production at the San Francisco Opera House.

"Oh. Dig that. He thinks he's Elvis," said Tiffany.

"He sings *better,*" said Mary.

"Neal should be a rock and roll star. Look how good he looks in those pants when he moves around. He's so yummy."

"Whaddya think he is, a chocolate soldier?" growled Gregory. "Ya ever listen to what he's sayin'? He's brilliant. You broads are so stupid, it makes me sick."

"Well, we're smart enough to know who to be with, and it's not *you*, you loser," said Tiffany.

Neal stopped singing.

"Now, now, girls," he said gently, wagging his forefinger the way Jack did, a gesture later adapted by Allen in the '80s when he gave his readings. "Let's not be vicious or hurtful to old Gregory. He is one of America's great lyric poets and a treasure to be guarded and nurtured by us all. Without lyric poets, no society can survive. He's like Keats and Shelley. Without Keats and Shelley, England would have reverted back to being a primitive society again. Lord Byron, Blake . . . "

"Ever heard of them, girls?" rasped Gregory. "D'ya know who Keats is? D'ya know *one* poem he wrote?"

"Sure," said Tiffany. "By the shores of Gitchie Goomey . . . you know . . . Hiawatha!"

"Yeah, that figures," said Gregory. "Ya got the 'high' part right. Why don't you stop getting loaded all the time and do something with your lives?"

"Look who's talking!" said Mary.

"Now, now, now," said Neal. "If Jack were here, we'd all be mellowed out. Let's be loving to one another."

"How can I be loving?" asked Gregory. "You've got two chicks all over you and I'm all alone. You're bathing in love and I'm like a shipwrecked sailor cast ashore on a desert island, thirsty and hungry for love."

We all got back in the van. Mary sat next to me. I could feel myself start to get dizzy when she leaned against me to whisper in my ear. Her womanliness was like some kind of otherworldly energy generating right through me as she brushed her mane of slightly scented hair against my cheek and snuggled up next to me. I tried to concentrate on what she was murmuring in my ear.

"I actually like Gregory's poetry. He just needs to be kept in line. *Gasoline* is a great book. I love *Big Sur*. Jack really captured San Francisco's special aura. I really like your music. I like you.

"Neal is so lonely. He wants to be back with family. He's a real family man and he's so lost. Come stay with me. Hotels are so impersonal."

At that moment, Neal turned almost directly around as we were sitting behind him and gave me a knowing wink, a flicker of a smile, and a thumbs-up.

Mary was fantastic. I thought about never going back to New York. Her apartment was full of books, reproductions of paintings and prints, she had her own watercolors on the walls, and some

Alexander Calder–style mobiles she had made, hanging from the ceiling. She also played classical guitar and worked as a private nurse. She knew Jack's work and had a real appreciation of his use of jazz phrasing in his prose. When she was alone and dropped her party act, she was a completely different person.

I thought about jumping up on the stage after my cantata and when taking my bow, motioning for Mary to come up from the audience and propose to her on stage, and get married right there. With over a thousand rabbis in the audience, we would start off in the bosom of Abraham and walk hand in hand down the highway of life.

I called up Jack and told him all that had happened.

"The old gang. I miss them," said Jack. "Tell Neal to keep writing. Is Langston there?"

"No," I said. "He's in New York. I think he'll watch the part of our cantata that's broadcast on TV."

"I might be in Lowell when it's broadcast," said Jack. "I'll try to watch it. At least get me a tape to add to my Amramian church collection."

"I will, Jack," I said. "We all miss you."

"I miss all of you," said Jack. "It's lonely here. It's so hard to do my work. People keep coming by at all hours and bugging me. Tell Neal to stick to his guns. If you marry that fine young woman you just met, bring her back and you'll make my mother smile. She asks me why you haven't gotten married. She says you are *très gentil.*"

"I'm trying to be, Jack," I said. "It's a daily struggle not to become a creep."

"Keep struggling," said Jack. "We've got to spread the holy light. I'll say a prayer for you."

The concert was thrilling. All of the gang came. Freddie Redd wore a huge bow tie made out of some kind of velveteen material.

"Getting dap for the symphonic scene," said Freddie. "This is a step up from Gary Goodrow and Carlyle McBeth's loft on the Bowery."

"Ya look like a penguin," said Gregory, who was wearing torn sneakers, khakis with one knee ripped open like a castaway on an island, with an oversized red velvet smoking jacket that his date took from her ex-husband's closet when she was over visiting her child that afternoon. He also had a huge scarf wrapped around his neck, like a Basque shepherd. Neal came with two other breathtakingly beautiful young women. He was wearing a kind of Western outfit, like a Texas oilman, and came over to talk to me.

"I'm happy you're getting your music out there," he said. "So many cats never do. I wish Jack were here with us."

"I spoke to him last night," I said. "He sends his love. He misses everybody."

"Not as much as I miss him," said Neal. "He and Carolyn. They are my heart. I've lost them. The train's left without me. I'm stranded in the station."

Allen and Peter Orlovsky had on the same clothes they had been wearing all week and were both reading books, which they continued to do during the whole concert, somehow deciphering the words under the dim light that was left on in the back of the auditorium where we were seated. My piece was played and was the kind of performance composers rarely get. The soloists and chorus were beautifully prepared. The orchestra, under the direction of Gerhardt Samuels, balanced perfectly with one another and the soloists and chorus. Langston's words stood out and shined like jewels surrounded by the music.

There was a standing ovation, and the energy field created by an audience of over 1,000 rabbis with their wives from all over the country, transformed the San Francisco Opera House for the moment into a gigantic bar mitzvah, Labor Day weekend, family cookout, block party, wedding atmosphere. I was called up to take a bow. I saw Mary, radiant like a shining star in the galaxy, smiling from the audience. I bowed, and when everybody kept applauding and stamping their feet, I blew her a kiss.

"What a *mensch*. He's honoring his mother," shouted a woman in the front row, not seeing that the honoree was fifteen years younger than I was.

After the concert was over, people in the audience surrounded me. Instead of the usual formal stiff comments that were made, like, "That was most interesting" or "Quite unusual," people were grabbing me.

"You're wife's a *doll*!"

"It sounded so *Jewish*!"

"You did *good*. You're a real *yeshiva bucher* (a true scholar)."

"Those pants are too short. Can't you get your wife to fix them?"

"How can you write music for all those people?"

"Are your parents here?"

"I'm David's cousin, Dr. Goodrow," said Gary. "I'm a proctologist. If you have a problem, call me. *Machta leben* (you gotta make a living)."

We all went backstage and I thanked all the musicians and soloists and the chorus. Gary Goodrow was intent on seeing Edward G. Robinson. Finally his chance came, as Edward G. Robinson walked slowly towards the exit, still in a blissful state after his moving performance as the evening's narrator.

"Mr. Robinson, Mr. Robinson," yelled Gary, running up to him.

"Yes," said Edward G. Robinson, giving Gary a baleful glare.

"Mr. Robinson, I'm Father Francis O'Farrell." Gary lifted a miniature rubber squeaky Madonna doll up, like someone giving a hex sign at eye level, and pushing as rapidly as possible, filled the backstage area with a series of squeaks that sounded like a Mickey Mouse soundtrack.

"Mr. Robinson," Gary intoned in a perfect Irish brogue. "I demand equal time."

Edward G. Robinson broke into his famous Little Caesar snarl, and hunched over, instantly recapturing his immortal screen persona of the legendary gangster of the '30s.

"Very funny," he crowed in the bone-chilling voice we all grew up hearing of Hollywood's most feared fictitious gangster.

Robinson turned on his heel, still in character, and walked out the stage door exit to greet his fans, and everyone backstage applauded.

After the concert, we went to Enrico's to celebrate, and Herb Gold held court with his wit. Everybody was talking to anybody who walked by. Neal came over to say goodbye.

"Tell Jack to take care of his health. He needs to find himself a good woman and hold on to her. We're getting old, Dave. It was great to hear your piece. I could hear Bird and Berlioz and Bach, and most of all, you yourself. I'm going to try to do some more writing. Take care of Mary. She's a fine young lady, and I see she digs you."

"I wish she lived back East," I said.

"Take her with you. Drive her there. Or stay here. It's not like New York. Tell Jack I think about him."

"I will, Neal," I said. "He always talks about you."

"Tell him to cut back on the booze."

"I'll try," I said.

"David," said Herb later on in the evening, when everyone had wandered off, "you have a new fan base. One thousand rabbis can't be wrong."

"Don't forget me," said Mary. "I'm not David's rabbi, I'm his ra*bette*."

I never did forget Mary. I had to go back to New York and we talked on the phone and I tried to see if I could get work in the Bay Area. I was ready to go back out. I had dreams about her. Three weeks later, she wrote and told me she decided to grow up and was getting married to a doctor she went to school with. I called Jack.

"How did it go?" he asked.

"It was incredible," I said. "Everybody asked for you. Neal sends his love. So do Allen and Gregory and hundreds of others whose names I can't even remember. And let me read you this review from the *Oakland Tribune*. Langston was thrilled."

Expression of Faith

I cleared my throat and began: " 'Historic occasions call for historic achievements, and the Opera House in San Francisco provided them in abundance last night.

" 'A special musical program to demonstrate how the arts reflect religious faith was masterfully assembled and brilliantly performed for the three thousand delegates of the Union of American Hebrew Congregations.

" 'Foremost among the lavish achievements was the stunning world premiere of David Amram's all-embracing choral memoriam for all men that have died to preserve freedom, *Let Us Remember.*

" 'Amram's neoromantic, six-part work spoke an eloquent language from the very poetic pen of Langston Hughes. The universal message set to music from the traditional Yiskor is a work of moving profundity, of nobility, of compassion, and of sincerity, all in a direct style somewhere in the general neighborhoods of Honegger and Bernstein. A unifying musical motif bound the sections together with both subtlety and variety in this half-hour long outpouring of unadorned emotions.

" 'Hughes' English text formed a requiem pyramid, enveloped by a theme verse and topped by the deep memory of past oppression: Auschwitz, Dachau, Buchenwald . . . Montgomery, Selma, Savannah . . . as well as hopes for a future: A new world rises from the muck becoming a thousand roots, buds, a billion leaves . . ."

" 'Performing with great distinction, four vocal soloists were backed by the virtually complete Oakland Symphony, in its first Opera House concert, and the Oakland Chorus, along with a dazzling guest choir made up almost exclusively of leading Bay Area soloists.

" 'The enthusiastic reception called out to the stage the thirty-five-year-old Amram, who seemed as overwhelmed by the enormous impact of this colorful, yet forceful melodic work as anyone.

" 'This is a very listenable piece, with a universal theme and a musical integrity that nowhere sacrifices the vocal theme for orchestral effect. It performs what Casale's *El Pessebre* and Milhaud's *Pacem in Terris* set out to do with considerably greater success, musically speaking.' "

When I finished reading the review, Jack said, "That's great, Davey. Send Langston my congratulations. Now we have to get them to play *A Year in Our Land* out there. Imagine hearing my section of the cantata. The excerpt from *The Lonesome Traveler* where I wrote about being up in my shack in the mountains out west. Imagine that being played at the San Francisco Opera House! How's the fabulous Miss Mary?"

"She went on to greener pastures. She's marrying a doctor who keeps regular hours," I said. "She was so fantastic. I think about her every day. She was truly lovely in every way."

"Don't despair, Davey. There are oceans filled with fish and forests full of trees. Remember what my mother told you, Davey. There's a lot of single women out there. Just don't marry a tramp."

"I should have married her right away," I said.

"You can marry her later," said Jack. "She'll get bored with the doctor. He'll always be home on time for dinner, but he won't take her on those flights of the spirit to the ever unfolding series of rooms in Paradise, and then play her mournful ditties from the previous world on his piccolo. We'll both find ourselves fine wives, unless they find us first. Down here in St. Petersburg, all the good gals are taken. It's good for my mother's health, but there's no culture. There's no romance. I had a wild time in Lowell. I never got to see your piece on TV. I was out drinking. Send me an acetate or a tape. I want to hear how you set Langston's words. Maybe we could write a Jewish-Catholic choral piece to create new texts and music using the old prayers. We'll do more, Davey. My best days are yet to come. I'm tired but I'm still strong. I'm a writer. I always will be. An artist must burn . . . say it with me, brother."

And we both intoned together, "with a hard and gemlike flame."

In 1966 I was chosen by Leonard Bernstein to become the New York Philharmonic's first-ever composer in residence. Suddenly, I was part of the music establishment. I met composers, conductors, soloists, and musicians from all over the world. I was interviewed almost daily and was the subject of a three-page feature story in *Life* magazine. When I reiterated the philosophy that Jack and I shared and put into practice of celebrating spontaneity and formality and a love of all the beauty that our society ignores, overlooks, or discards, many at the Philharmonic thought I was somewhat deranged.

Leonard Bernstein, though, loved it. "You were speaking from your heart and spreading a very important message. I try to do the same thing, and the critics try to annihilate me."

Jack and I would see each other whenever he came to New York and we still had a good time together, although he became increasingly saddened by many of his old friends, who now seemed to have abandoned him when he needed them the most.

In 1999 I found a carbon copy of the letter I sent to Jack in 1968. This is what I wrote:

461 Sixth Avenue
New York, NY 10011
July 17, 1968

Dear Jack,
This is just a note to thank you for the nice card that you sent my editor about my book. [My book *Vibrations* was recently published.] Any word or encouragement from you means a tremendous amount to me personally, first of all. I

Robert Frank and Amram Reunion, the night before Gregory Corso's Funeral. Fall 2000 (Courtesy of Chris Felver)

Floyd Red Crow Westerman, Amram and Rambling Jack Elliot at De Jong Museum in San Francisco for the Whitney traveling Beat show, celebrating Kerouac with music. 1996 (Courtesy of Chris Felver)

Amram at his concert with Billy Taylor and Clark Terry, before performing "Pull My Daisy." 2000 (Courtesy of Chris Felver)

Amram and Kerouac at Dody Müller's art show at the Hansa Gallery in New York City. March 16, 1959 (© Fred W. McDarrah)

Early Beat: During a break in the filming of the historic beat film, "Pull My Daisy", featuring an original music score by David Amram, who also appeared in the film, the composer (top right, hand to mouth) shares ideas with some of his collaborators, including (left to right): poet Gregory Corso (back to camera), artist Larry Rivers, author Jack Kerouac and poet Allen Ginsberg. "Pull My Daisy" features Jack Kerouac's narration and a title song by David Amram, with lyrics by Jack Kerouac, Neal Cassady and Allen Ginsberg. 1959 (John Cohen)

Kerouac and Amram, at the filming of "Pull My Daisy" at Alfred Leslie's studio. February 1959 (John Cohen)

Amram, Ginsberg and Kerouac celebrating the completion of filming of "Pull My Daisy" at Dody Müller's art opening at Hansa Gallery. March 16, 1959 (© Fred W. McDarrah)

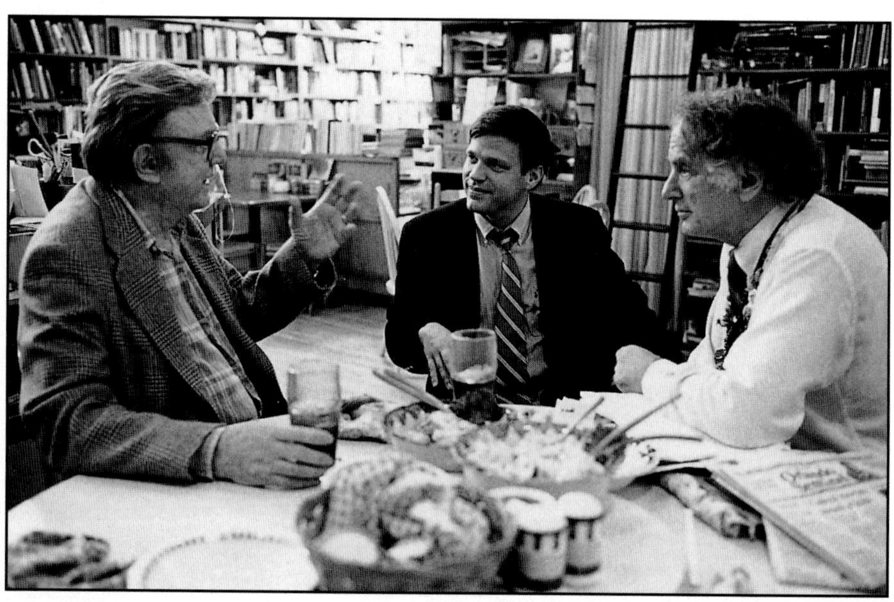

Steve Allen, Douglas Brinkly and Amram at Chapters Books, prior to their benefit concert for Kerouac Writers' Residence in Orlando, Florida. This was Steve Allen's final concert. 2000 (Courtesy of Chris Felver)

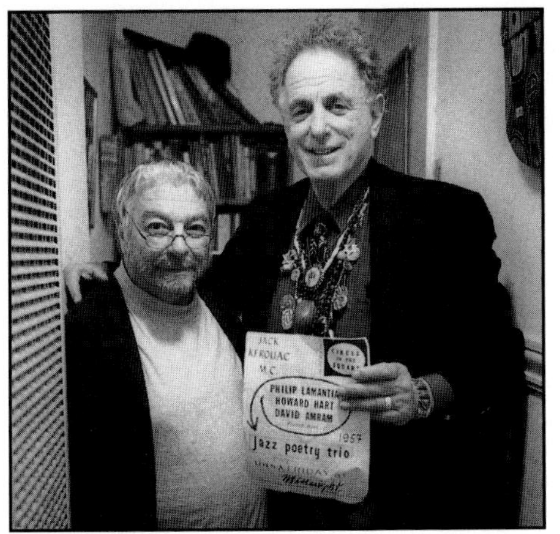

Philip Lamantia and Amram in San Francisco 44 years after their 1957 historic collaboration with Kerouac at New York City's first-ever jazz poetry readings, at the Brata Art Gallery. 2001 (Courtesy of Chris Felver)

Amram and Patti Smith performing at Gregory Corso's funeral at Our Lady of Pompeii in Greenwich Village, New York City. 2001 (Courtesy of Chris Felver)

Amram and Odetta before performing at a concert for the New York Folk Museum celebrating American felt roots of all the arts. 2000 (Courtesy of Chris Felver)

Amram and friends performing "This Song's for You, Jack" at Kerrville Music Festival, Kennville, Texas. May of 1992 (Collection of David Amram)

Conducting rehearsal with National Symphony Orchestra at Kennedy Center in concert with E.G. Marshal narrating, Amram's "A Little Rebellion: Thomas Jefferson" and passages from On the Road *with orchestral accompaniment.* October 1995

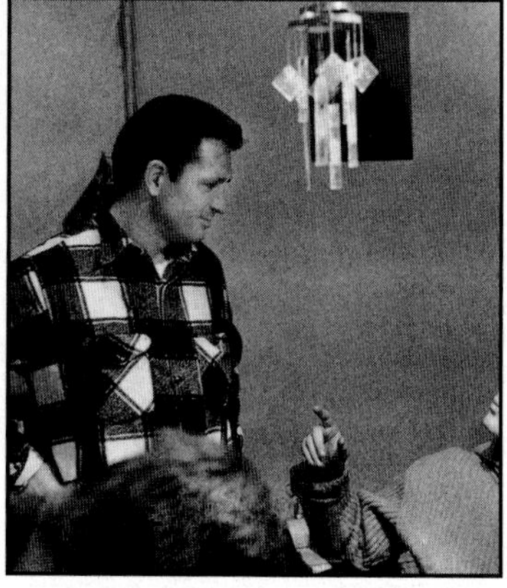

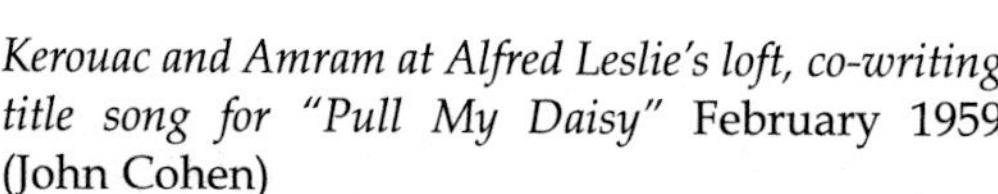

Kerouac and Amram at Alfred Leslie's loft, co-writing title song for "Pull My Daisy" February 1959 (John Cohen)

Amram, Percy Heath and Dizzy Gillespie performing at a Thelonious Monk celebration at Constitution Hall, Washington D.C. Gillespie and Heath both knew Jack and admired his writing about jazz. (Michael Wilderman)

Amram, dressed as cowboy, Gregory Corso and Alfred Leslie, preparing for a scene that was later mercifully cut from the film "Pull My Daisy." 1959 (John Cohen)

Amram at Jack's old house in Orlando, now the Kerouac Writers' Residence. October 2001 (Courtesy of Chris Felver)

David, Willie Nelson, and Native American dancers performing at Farm Aid, 1999, Nissan Center, Manassas, Virginia. (© Ebet Roberts)

Recording Amram's score for Kerouac's On the Road *for Rykodisc, 1998. Amram at piano, Jerry Dodgion, Johnny Almendra, Vic Juris, Victor Venegas, Candido, and producer Jim Sampas.* (© Ebet Roberts)

hope you could see from what I wrote about you in the book that I really dig you as much as I said I did. Also, I don't think that you have any idea of how many young people in their teens and twenties are reading your books and love them. I was picked up when my car broke down and driven out to Patchogue by a young kid who told me he thought you were the greatest American writer he ever read and had read five or six of your books, and when I told him I knew you, he spent a whole hour and a half asking me questions about you and about *Pull My Daisy* and about some of the things that we had done, about your work and your other books. At all the colleges I've been lecturing, people ask about you when they find out I ever knew you. You should be proud because you have a whole following now of a generation. None of the schmucks write about it because critics of any kind never know what is happening, but your work has more effect now than it did during your first boom in 1956–67.

I have been working my ass off and finished my opera and now I am starting with some more pieces and I am out at Fire Island. Lenny Gross and I miss you and so does everybody else out around Northport. I saw Yeseult about two months ago and Allen a few months ago. Also Gregory and a few other people. I've been working so hard. I usually just go out at night when I am in town to Casey's Bar and play the horn. Otherwise I'm working until midnight every day. I would really love to see you again and I have your last book, which I am going to read as soon as my opera is over this August 15th. I have two weeks aside just to read it.

If my book does all right, I think it will be a big help to getting my music performed, and maybe they'll play that cantata where I've set that piece of yours to music, and if they do, I'll try to get you a better tape of it. I hope you and your wife are well and if you ever do get to New York and you get a minute, call me because I really miss you and would like to see you even for a little while. Keep wailing as only you can do and I'll see you telepathically, if not any other way soon.
Cheers and blessings like always . . .

David

In the fall, I was thrilled to hear that members of the Houston Symphony were going to give a special concert of my symphonic music where I would conduct my own works, including *A Year in Our Land,* and also have my jazz quartet perform independently where during the course of the evening I would be a composer-conductor and a performer in my own jazz ensemble. Nothing like this had ever been done before, but thanks to Andre Previn, who could do the same thing so brilliantly himself, I was given the opportunity to fulfill a dream that Jack and I always talked about. Formality and spontaneity were appearing hand in hand in Texas, and I was at the helm.

When I got to Houston to start rehearsing all of my music, which included the cantata *A Year in Our Land,* I saw my old friend Jim Tankersley from the Seventh Army Symphony. Jim had helped coordinate members of the Houston Symphony and found a great chorus from Southern Methodist University, prepared by Ruthabelle Rollins, to sing the cantata. There were also four excellent soloists.

The Houston Symphony was a full-time ensemble, where each player in their respective sections of the orchestra played together year in and year out. Since the Cantata was structured to feature each section of the orchestra in the four principal movements, the difference in the playing was like the difference of the infield, the outfield, the pitcher, and the catcher of a major league baseball team, all having a great built-in rapport, as opposed to a pickup game where a team was thrown together.

The freelance orchestra that had played the New York City premiere was terrific, but they only had one rehearsal, and some of the players had never even met one another, much less played "Summer in the West." The wind players of the Houston Symphony, who had their music in advance, tore it up.

"I wish Jack were here to hear this," I said to Margot Pace, who had organized the concert.

"I wish he were too," she said. "I love his books. He has such a big following in Texas. He writes from the heart. You can feel him talking to you. He's not showing off in his writing—he's talking to you."

"Did he really sit on top of that mountain for a month?" asked Tankersley. "Didn't he miss drinking wine and seeing women?"

"Jack loved those solitary moments," I said. "And he loved the idea of meditation, reflective hours spent alone, to offset the wild times. It was only after *On the Road* came out that he felt trapped by having to act like Neal acted so many years ago. All of that wore him out. He told me how hard it was when he went to Lawrence Ferlingetti's cabin to cool out by himself in Big Sur, but still how much he wanted to recapture that feeling he had when he was lying in his bunk on a merchant ship, reading and writing, out in the middle of the Atlantic Ocean. He felt he could have been a monk or priest in another lifetime."

One of the members of the chorus came up to me after the rehearsal. "Mr. Amram, you said you knew Jack Kerouac. Is he still around, writing anything? You ever hear from him? Seems he kinda disappeared on us."

"He's still with us," I said. "He just wrote *Vanity of Duluoz,* all about his early life. It's a beautiful book. He read me parts of it on the phone. It shows where he came from and what he was about. All about Lowell and his family and his struggles to find himself and follow his dreams."

"I thought he was the leader of a Beatnik movement," said the young man, frowning and looking uncomfortable.

"That had nothing to do with him except to help ruin his life," I said. "He was, is, and, always will be a writer. He would have been just as great if he'd never come to New York. We were all lucky to get to know him. He is not only a great poet-prose innovator, he's a great commentator of our time, writing about what is overlooked or ignored in our society. He's our reporter."

"Well, if you say so," said the young man.

"The only Beatnik I ever saw or knew was Maynard G. Krebs on TV, and he was just a caricature," I said. "I'm what I've always been, and I'm trying hard every day to improve on that."

"Aw*right*," said the young man, bursting into a sunny smile. "You keep on improvin'. You got a good attitude. And you tell Kerouac he's got some readers down here. I always dug how he wrote about Charlie Parker and Monk and Dizzy. He seems to understand our music. You cats are all right."

I thought about this during the party after the concert.

"You look worried, Dave," said Margot.

"I'm OK," I said. "The concert was great. I can never thank you enough. I was just thinking about Jack. I know his health is bad. And he's lonely."

"I thought he'd get married again," said Margot.

"He did," I said. "He told me his wife Stella is saving his life and looking after his mother. But even with her, he can't get over the hurt. He feels his old friends have deserted him, and that worst of all, he's already being forgotten about as a writer. I just wrote him a letter about all of this. Young people love his work, even if they have to steal the out-of-print copies of his books from libraries to share with their friends."

Requiem: Jack's Final Days

In the spring of 1969 about 3:30 A.M. one morning, my phone rang. I jumped out of bed and staggered over to the phone in the tiny kitchen to answer to it. My place was in chaos. Papers and proofs were everywhere. I figured it was Terry Southern on the phone, and he must be at the 55 Bar hanging out with the boys and probably wanted me to come over for a nightcap.

I didn't want to bum out Melanie, who lay in bed glaring at me. She was a sweetheart and we had so much fun. I didn't want to ruin our romance by inflicting my craziest of all my night-owl friends on her, even though Terry always made her laugh for days after his unexpected late-night visits.

I picked up the phone on what was probably its fortieth ring.

"*Alors, Terry, Quelles sont les nouvelles, mon vieux?*"

"*C'est n'est pas Terry. C'est Jacky.*"

"Jack," I said. "Are you okay?"

"Nah-h-h," he said. "I'll never be okay. I never was okay. I'm just me. A poor boy from Massachusetts, stuck down here in Florida."

I heard him coughing as he put down the phone. I could hear him slurping down a drink after his coughing had stopped.

"Here's to you and your music, Davey. How are all the beautiful gals in New York? Do you ever see Joyce or Dody or Yseult? I miss New York. Man, I miss our soirees. We have to get together with Lamantia and Hart and do a concert again. Do you think anyone would come?"

"You'd pack 'em in, Jack," I said. "There's a whole new audience for your work out there."

"Tell the goddamn publishers that," said Jack. "They're remaindering all my books here in America. Overseas they're doing fine. I'm an American writer. *Don't they read my books*?"

"We all do," I said. "You've got to take care of yourself. Your work is here to stay. You've got to ride out the storm. Like Langston said, keep your eyes on the prize."

"Your letter was nice," said Jack. "I know you haven't forgotten me. I feel like one of those old washed-up boxers who go to bars and wait for someone to say, 'didn't you used to be . . . ?' before being bought a drink. Are you sure it's me those kids you wrote about in your letter are reading? Are you sure it's not Jack London?"

We both laughed.

"Tell Terry Southern to bring me a bagel, a regular coffee, and not to tell any of his filthy sexist jokes unless I haven't heard them before," said Melanie, who had risen from bed and was now standing behind me in her flowered nightgown, all sweetness and good cheer. "Let me speak to that old coot."

"It's not Terry, Melanie. It's Jack Kerouac, calling from Florida."

"Oh," said Melanie. "There goes my breakfast and bagel. Tell him I said hi. Maybe he can come up and visit us. We could drive him out to Northport. Send his wife and mother my best. I'd love to meet them all. I'm going back to sleep. Be sure and set the alarm."

"Melanie sends her love to you, Stella, and Gabrielle," I said.

"That's your new true love you told me about," said Jack. "Without the love of women, there's nothing but death."

"How are Stella and Gabrielle?" I asked.

"Stella is a saint," said Jack. "I got in a fight, got busted up, and she is helping me to type till I get better. Mamère is sick. Stella is keeping us all alive. We have to play together and show all those lost kids about the sunny side of the street."

Jack began to scat sing 'Sunny Side of the Street,' based on the song, but stopped after a few seconds.

"I can't do it, Davey. I'm sick."

I heard him put down the phone, cough, and heard the familiar sound of slurping down a drink, followed by a thunderous belch.

"Ah-h-h-h . . . Davey, get your horn and play me something over the phone."

I walked into the other room, crawled under the piano and took out my horn, and began playing into the phone.

"Ah-h . . . Davey. Sweet sounds from Auld Manhattoes. Have you seen Dizzy? Does he remember The Frenchman, as he so elegantly referred to the *écrivain distingué, moi-même?* He must be playing better than ever."

"I saw him a month ago. He's still carrying his message around the world. He'll never stop, either. He knows the world didn't pass him by. He's still waiting for the world to catch up with him."

"How's the TV documentary they're doing about you coming along? Did they edit all of the cantata, *A Year in Our Land,* that you did with the Houston Symphony? Did they sing the selections from *The Lonesome Traveler* OK?"

"It was fantastic, Jack," I said. "The chorus, orchestra, and soloists were smoking! They love you in Texas."

"That's good. *C'est bon*. I hope they show it down here in St. Pete. How is *Vibrations* doing?"

"It got fantastic reviews," I said. "I almost feel guilty, since I'm not a writer."

"*Everyone*'s a writer who's got a story to tell and knows how to tell it," said Jack. "I'm working on a new book now. I think it will be a breakthrough, and maybe even a movie. It's called *Pic*. Maybe *Visions of Cody* will finally get published, and my remaindered books will get reissued. Maybe I'll be judged by my words on the page, instead of comparing me to Beatnik *poseurs*, and dooming me as the fallen King of the Beat Generation. I wish I'd never used that goddam expression. I'm an *author*! I'm a *writer*. By your works ye shall be known!"

"Amen," I said.

"Been to Mass?" said Jack.

"Not since I went with you," I said.

"I'll say some prayers for you, Davey. I'll pray for you to have a family, and for us to all get a farm up in the mountains and sit someday with our children and we'll lie in hammocks and Neal and Carolyn will get back together and bring their children . . ." His voice trailed off. I heard him start coughing again, followed by more slurping sounds, terminated by a series of explosive belches.

"Oh, my goddam ribs. I feel like a football player again. Davey, do you believe Neal is dead? I know he's putting everybody on. I keep waiting for him to show up at the door. Davey, play me 'Pull My Daisy' on the piano, and we'll sing some four-bar duets."

I yanked the phone with its huge extension cord into the other room, tucked the phone between my chin and collarbone, and began playing and singing 'Pull My Daisy.'

"Good God, David, when will you become secure enough to stop auditioning for the whole world?" said Melanie, rising wearily from her pillow. "My family's right. I should leave you. You're completely insane."

"I'm playing for Jack," I mouthed to her, as I continued playing and singing into the phone.

"What?" she said.

"This is for Jack Kerouac," I yelled.

"Oh," said Melanie. "All right. Don't forget to wake me."

"Of course this is for Jack Kerouac," bellowed Jack over the phone, almost knocking the receiver out of my ear. "I'm the co-author, with Neal and Allen and you. Play it, Davey."

I continued playing, and began singing, and Jack joined in.

When we finally finished, he said, "I'm going to get well and finish *Pic*, my new book. It will bring me back. I'll show the world old Jack is not passé. My honor will be restored. I still have my pride. I know the value of my work. I'll stick to my guns. We're lyric artists, Davey. We're here for the duration."

"Give my love to Stella and Gabrielle. Tell your mother I said Lenny Gross is happily married and that I will be someday soon, I hope, and I'll keep my promise to her that I'll never marry a tramp."

"I'll come to the wedding, Davey," said Jack. "Our best days are yet to come. I'm going to get healed up and stop drinking and the world will change. I keep having dreams of moving back to Lowell and seeing everybody happy again, and coming to visit in New

York and having parties at Lucien's house and having all of us together again. Lucien, the kids, Dody, Joyce, Bob Donlin, Holmes, Giroux, Sterling . . ."

His voice trailed off. He began coughing again. This time, there were no more slurping sounds.

"One more thing, Davey. Why I called, other than to be sure you and your new sweetheart were still loving each other every day. When I get back on my feet, you have to set those parts of *On the Road* for narrator and orchestra. You can conduct the symphony and I'll narrate and we can go around the world. Some of the passages could be accompanied by you playing spontaneously on piano and then jumping back on the podium and conducting what you've written down. The spontaneous and the formal. Spontaneous and formal. Maybe we could start a duo using that name for our act and end up as two saintly old men with canes and tour the world. Laurel and Hardy, Jack and Jill, Abbott and Costello, Adam and Eve, Dizzy and Bird, Spontaneous and Formal. All the world's a stage, and all its players . . . ah-h . . . You know what I mean. I need a drink. Davey, are you still there?"

"Yes, Jack, I was just thinking about what you just said. That would be great, setting *On the Road* with orchestra, like Copeland did with the Lincoln Portrait."

"Promise me you'll do it," said Jack. "We'll get some great gigs. I'll buy a set of tails and we'll have the world premiere with the Boston Symphony. All my old friends from Lowell can come to the opening and we'll bring Boston back to the hallowed days of the Boston Tea Party. We'll bring some fine tea we can smoke in the lobby during intermission after our triumphant debut performance and, when Boston's dowager-patronesses are transported into the raptures of sweet Mary Jane's marijuana ecstasy, we can give them recipes for all the Quebecois delicacies like moose pie, old Lowell High School football buddy's family recipes for fried squid, and our famous baked beans. Even though I will have stopped drinking I'll give the editor of the *Boston Globe* a hit of Thunderbird wine since he never experienced the poetry of a night on Moody Street when Lowell was in flower and the jazz greats graced the evenings with sweet music to the ear . . . We can do it, Davey. We can write an opera together. We can do readings together again."

"I know we can, Jack," I said.

"Don't let what we started die, Davey."

"I won't, Jack. No way."

"Turn the other cheek," he said.

"Always have. Always will."

"Davey, are you ever going to spend three days just lying in a hammock, picking your teeth and doing nothing but meditating to cleanse your mind for your next masterpiece?"

"I don't think so, Jack," I said. "I don't have time for that."

"Me neither," said Jack. "I was just checking. I'll see you this summer. We'll go to Northport to Gunther's Bar with Stanley Twardowicz and find Adolph the Clammer and go out on his boat and shock the New York intelligentsia when they see the new Jack Kerouac drinking ginger ale like his old compatriot Davey, and we'll storm New York. We'll go to the Figaro. We'll ask about where to find an old farm in the mountains where we can all be together."

"Sounds like a perfect plan to me, Jack," I said.

"I always plan perfectly," said Jack. "Sometimes, the plans don't pan out. Without the love of women there's nothing but Death. Give Melanie a kiss and be good to her."

"*A bientôt*, Jack."

I hung up the phone.

"God, you and Jack have such long conversations," said Melanie, now awake for the day. "He must be terribly lonely, down there in Florida, away from all his old friends."

"He is," I said. "Any of us would be. He's looking after his mother and trying to find peace in his life with Stella so that he can write more. He's never gotten over the death of Neal. I can hear pain in his voice that was never there before. He has to stop drinking, but that's the only way he can stop the pain, and it's killing him. I don't know what to do."

"All you can do is make him know you love him," said Melanie. "You can take care of your*self*. Don't kill yourself. Don't be self-destructive. All you guys are so desperate to prove to the world that you are right about what you believe in. Stop trying to prove so much. Just do your work, enjoy simple things, and learn how to relax. Let yourself be loved. I've got to go to work. Good luck finishing your Horn Concerto. Let's go to Casey's tonight for dinner when I get back, and you can bring your horn and sit in with Freddie Redd and we'll get home early and both get a good night's sleep."

"Okay, Melanie," I said. "I love you. You're really understanding."

"There's not much to understand," she said. "All you guys just need to calm down and grow up. If I wanted to be with a dentist, I wouldn't have chosen you. I'm glad you and Jack talked. I know how much you love each other, and how much you worry about him. Aren't you glad you spoke and played music on the phone? You're the most positive person I ever met in my life. Why do you look so sad? You guys will get together soon."

"I hope so," I said. "But I don't know. He didn't sound right."

"He'll be fine. All those ex-football players live forever. I'll see you tonight and we'll go to Casey's for dinner."

A few weeks later, I climbed the stairs of my 6th Avenue apartment and sat down with my lox, cream cheese, tuna fish, onion, Swiss cheese, capers, and horseradish sauce breakfast-lunch special giant sandwich on rye bread that Igor Sudarsky of the Arts Foods Delicatessen let me go behind the counter each day and make for myself. I had three cups of coffee and before starting work, I turned on the answering machine.

"Dave, Ted Jones here. No number right now. Did you hear about Jack? I heard early this morning that Jack died. Have you heard anything?"

I didn't bother to check my other messages. I called the wire service where Lucien Carr had been working for years. Surely he would know what happened, but I couldn't get through. I didn't want to call any of Jack's friends, in case it was a mistake.

I sat down at the piano and played. I prayed for his soul and said a Kaddish and kissed an old Mass card he had given me in 1957. I could hear his voice fill the room. He always retained the music of his Lowell, Massachusetts accent whenever he spoke. The special sounds of Lowell's Little Canada, a sound that still speaks to my heart every day.

The phone rang and I answered.

"David, this is Richard Bellamy. I guess you heard the news. He's left us."

Richard was the Bishop in *Pull My Daisy* and had a small art gallery in real life and was a great friend to all of us.

"I imagine they will have a funeral up in Lowell at the church he was a member of as a boy. I'd go up with you, but I'm afraid it will become a public circus, one of those orgies of self-promotion that seems to be the dynamic of the '60s. Can you drive up?"

"I don't know, Richard," I said. "I have a concert in Washington. If it's the same day I could fly up and fly back afterwards, but I don't know if I want to go either, especially if it becomes a Beatniks versus the locals confrontation. Jack was a devout Catholic. He would want a traditional service."

"That's why I'm not going," said Richard. "I don't want to be there to see people leap in front of the cameras and have a Beatnik circus. I feel a terrible loss and compassion for his wife and all those who truly loved him through his life. Lucien and Carolyn, Joyce and Dody must be devastated. Let's all pray for him and keep his memory alive. Now that he's gone, he'll begin to be really appreciated for what he left us. I never knew anyone like him."

"Thank you for calling, Richard. You've really helped me to deal with this."

I hung up and the phone rang again. Old friends from all over the country, Canada, and some from Europe called all day and all that night. Many were crying. I had to cheer them up by telling them the wonderful things in his life that he had done for countless others and of the fun we'd had together.

Reporters also called up from around the world. Usually the first questions were: "Are you the David Amram who played with Jack Kerouac and wrote music for the Beatnik film *Pull My Daisy* and did compositions with him? Do you think he died from an overdose of drugs? I know this must be a difficult time for you to talk. Can you tell my readers about his Beatnik philosophy?"

"Are you the Beat Generation composer named David Amram

who worked with Jack Kerouac? If so, why do you think he killed himself? You have my sincere condolences. Could you give us your thoughts?"

I was brought up to be respectful to every human being who walks the earth, so I gritted my teeth when the words Beatnik and Beat Generation came before Jack's name. I tried to answer each person in the best way I could. Since each reporter asked me for a statement, I wrote one down to read to them:

"I was lucky enough to know him, to be his friend, to work with him, and maintain my friendship with him from the time we met and he will always be in my heart. He was one of the great writers of the English language and is yet to be fully appreciated. He will return to rest in his hometown of Lowell, which he always loved and never forgot. Musicians, poets, painters, actors, and everyday people now have a more inclusive and compassionate world to live in because of what he left us all, in his books and in his actions towards other people."

Every single reporter then asked me in some form or another one of the following questions:

1. Are you still a Beatnik?
2. Why was he no longer the King of the Beat Generation?
3. Do all you Beatniks still advocate free love, drugs, and flag burning?
4. Who will be the new King of the Beat Generation?

I knew if I uttered one curse word or said one sentence that sounded abusive, that would be what ended up in any articles or obituaries.

"May I read you my statement again slowly?" I asked, "Perhaps some part of it might be useful in some way, and answer some of your questions. I understand you have a job to do and are restricted by a deadline."

"That won't be necessary" was the universal response.

Then the same questions were asked again! I knew that not one word of what I said would be used by any of them. They heard what they wanted to hear.

Melanie came home about 6:30 and hugged me for about five minutes.

"I'm sorry, sweetie. But at least he's not in pain anymore. And look at the gift he left the world. Let's watch the news."

Melanie turned on my old black-and-white TV set with the clothes hanger arial wrapped in tinfoil and we flipped channels and saw the reports. Somehow, it made Jack's death seem more final.

The phone kept ringing, and I kept reading my statement and then trying to be polite to the interviewers who needed a few lines to reinforce the hideous slant that their editors were forcing them to pursue to guide their stories.

Finally at 9 P.M. Melanie said, "Turn on the answering machine. Let's go to Casey's and celebrate Jack's life. None of these reporters can possibly use anything you're saying. They want blood and guts. Beatniks with berets and bongos. Now that the so-called Hippie Revolution has turned out to be a disaster and is no longer in fashion, they have to find something else to dump on."

"Maybe they'll start reading Jack's books," I said. "That's all he ever wanted."

The next afternoon, I got a phone call from someone who claimed to be an assistant to an editor of a major corporate-type publication that was supposed to support the Revolution. It was sponsored entirely by record companies.

"Mr. Amram, we would like to know if we could photograph you at the funeral services of Jack Kerouac playing the French horn next to his open casket. The editor would like you to wear a beret and possibly sandals, to make it look authentic for our readers. If this is agreeable, we will do a follow-up feature article about you, even though you are currently not with any major record label. When are you planning to be at the service in Lowell?"

"I'm not going to be there," I said.

"But I understand you were very close. I can't believe you won't be there. Could you tell me why?

"You just talked me out of it," I said, and I hung up the phone.

At my orchestral and chamber music concert in Washington at the Corcoran Art Gallery, Ken Pasmanick, my friend from 1947, played in my trio for tenor sax, French horn, and bassoon. I had written it in 1958 when living on Christopher Street. Much of it was written when Jack was there, crashing out with Father Rover, Lamantia, and Howard Hart on my floor.

I told Ken I would dedicate the concert and this piece to him and his family.

"That's beautiful, David," said Ken. "I remember meeting Charlie Parker with you and how we played for him in your basement apartment in 1952 down here. I feel like I almost knew Kerouac from all you've told me about him. Now you're back in Washington and we're playing for him. He may be gone now, but what he wrote will outlive us all. I'll give your trio some extra *neshuma* (Yiddish for soul) when we play tonight, just for him."

I dedicated the concert to Jack and a few days later, Barney Rossett called me up.

"David, *Evergreen Review* wants a memorial tribute for Jack. We would like you to write it. You stayed friends with him till the end. I know he would have wanted you to do it. Just be yourself. Don't try to be literary. Just do it the way you speak, and tell the readers about him. It's devastating what happened to him and so many of our great American writers of this century. We have to keep his memory alive, till all his books are back in print."

Barney was one of the lights of the second half of the twentieth century in American publishing. Grove Press made history, not only in breaking the bonds of censorship, but in publishing Jack's *Pull My Daisy*, works by Genet, and vast numbers of great writers before they were discovered by the public at large.

His ex-wife, Joan Mitchell, was an outstanding artist and mentor of mine in Paris in 1954, and when I first arrived in New York. They both loved Jack and his work. I would have done anything for either one of them.

"I can just pay you fifty dollars, enough to cover the costs of one of those enormous sandwiches you make at Igor's Arts Foods Delicatessen each day, and dinner for you and Melanie at Casey's, but I'd be grateful if you could do it, and Jack's family would be as well. When can you get it to me?"

"Tomorrow," I said. "I'll stay up all night and write it, and if

Melanie digs it, I'll meet you at Arts Foods Deli tomorrow at lunch and you'll have it."

When Melanie came in and saw me typing, she looked over my shoulder.

"Stay right there, David. Don't move. I'll get you supper, a midnight snack, and breakfast. Turn off the phone. Who is it for?"

"Barney Rossett," I said.

"Perfect," she said. "He'll expect the best you can possibly do, and appreciate it."

I wrote and rewrote, took catnaps, and kept changing little things throughout the night. I wanted to get it right. This wasn't about me. It was about Jack, from one of the few people who stayed close to him, from before *On the Road* came out until his death.

I had purposely avoided going to the funeral in Lowell because I didn't want to add to the growing sea of misinformation, mythology and inaccurate representation of what so many of us were about, formed during the rich artistic era of the late '40s and '50s. I didn't have time to write another 465-page book like *Vibrations* in one night, so I had to telescope all that Jack meant to me in a few pages

I finished it at 3 A.M. and fell asleep in Melanie's arms.

"I'm taking off work today, and going to the Arts Foods Deli with you and Barney and we'll go to Casey's tonight to celebrate. Your fifty-dollar payment for writing the tribute will be well spent. It's beautiful, honey."

Melanie and I went to lunch with Barney and while I went back behind the counter to make one of my colossal two-thousand-calorie health sandwiches, Barney read the tribute.

"David," he said. "It's perfect. It will be published in our January 1970 issue *exactly* the way you wrote it. Maybe you can give me some of your sandwich-making recipes so that I can suggest a special diet to all my authors to give them the energy to get their work to me *ahead* of time."

We ate and talked about Jack.

"Let's go to a movie, David," said Melanie. "Don't go upstairs and write music. Let's take one day off this year like normal people.

We went to 42nd Street and saw two old Humphrey Bogart movies, and then went to Casey's.

"David, you're a special guest tonight," said Casey. "I don't want you running home and getting your horn and sitting in with Freddie Redd, at least not till 11 P.M. We have a table for you and Melanie."

Casey had been an old buddy of mine since 1960, and I always sat at the musicians' table next to the piano. I had gone out with one of his waitresses before I met Melanie and because I played there all the time, I was almost like one of the staff. I had never sat down in the elegant early-dinner-crowd part of the restaurant.

"Are you sure you want us sitting here, Casey?" I asked.

"Positive," he said.

He brought Melanie and me over to a small table for two. On top of the table, between two lit candles, was a bottle of champagne in an ice bucket and a note attached: "Dear David, From Joan and me, from Evergreen, with thanks to you for remembering Jack. Barney."

Melanie and I ate and we drank champagne, and Freddie Redd came in at 9 P.M. to play.

"Damn, David," said Freddie smiling. "You're sitting here with all the white folks. Did you hit the number?"

"No, Freddie," I said. "I just wrote a memorial tribute for Jack for *Evergreen Review* and Barney Rossett gave us a surprise meal."

"That's beautiful," said Freddie. "We'll sure all miss that cat. I just talked to Sahib Shahib last week when he was visiting some folks in Brooklyn. He was talking about playing on the *Pull My Daisy* soundtrack, and what a righteous cat Jack was. They sure gave up on him when it looked like he wasn't going to make the big dollars anymore. Just like Bird. He was too beautiful to be here for a long time. He was such a warm cat."

Freddie played and I sat holding Melanie's hand, closed my eyes, and listened. As I heard Freddie's beautiful improvisations fill the room, I thought about all the times Jack and I spent together, and how he enjoyed life, and what an inspiration he was to others. I knew in my heart that his best days were yet to come.

The following is the memorial tribute I wrote for *Evergreen Review,* word for word, as I handed it to Barney Rossett, on October 24, 1969.

In Memory of Jack Kerouac

I used to see Jack often at the old Five Spot in the beginning of 1957, when I was working there. I knew he was a writer, and all musicians knew that he loved music. You could tell by the way he sat and listened. He never tried to seem hip. He was too interested in life around him to ever think of how he appeared. Musicians understood this and were always glad to see him, because we knew that meant at least *one* person would be listening. Jack was on the same wavelength as we were, so it was never necessary to talk.

A few months later, poets Howard Hart and Philip Lamantia came by my place with Jack. They had decided to read their poetry with music, and Jack said he would join in, reading, improvising, rapping with the audience, and singing along. Our first performance was in October of 1957 at the Brata Art Gallery on East 10th Street. It was the first jazz-poetry reading in New York. There was no advertising and it was raining, but the place was packed. Jack had become the most important figure of the time. His name was magic. In spite of the carping, whining put-downs by the furious critics, and the jealousy of some of his contemporaries for his overnight success (he had written ten books in addition to *On the Road* with almost no recognition), Jack hadn't changed. But people's reaction to him was sometimes frightening.

He was suddenly being billed as the "King of the Beatniks" and manufactured, against his will, as some kind of public guru for a movement that never existed. Jack was a private person, extremely shy, and dedicated to writing. When he drank, he became much more expansive, and this was the only part of his personality that became publicized. The people who came to the Brata Gallery weren't taste makers; they were friends.

A few months later, we began some readings at the Circle in the Square. Everyone improvised, including the light man, who had his first chance to wail on the lighting board. The audience joined in, heckling, requesting Jack that read parts of *On the Road,* and asking him to expound on anything that came into his head. He would also sing while I was playing the horn, sometimes making up verses. He had a phenomenal ear. It was like playing duets with a great musician.

Jack was proud of his knowledge of music and of the musicians of his time. He used to come by and play the piano by ear for hours. He had some wonderful ideas for combining the spoken word with music. A few weeks later, jazz-poetry became official entertainment, and a few months later was discarded as another bit of refuse, added to the huge mound of our junk culture. It was harder to dispose of Jack. The same journalists and radio and TV personalities who had heralded him were now ripping him to shreds. Fortunately, they couldn't rip up his manuscripts. His work was being published, more widely read, and translated.

In early 1958, all of us went to Brooklyn College, where Jack, Philip and Howard read. Jack spent most of the time answering the students' questions with questions of his own. He was the down-home Zen master, and the students finally realized he wasn't putting them on. He was showing them himself. If they wanted to meet the author Jack Kerouac, they would have to read his books.

His public appearances were never to promote his books. They were to share a state of mind and a way of being. The only journalist who picked up on this was Al Aronowitz. He saw Jack as an artist.

In January of 1959, the film *Pull My Daisy* was made. Allen Ginsberg, Gregory Corso, Peter Orlovsky, Larry Rivers, and myself—the 3rd Avenue All-Stars as one wit described us—appeared in it. Alfred Leslie directed it and Robert Frank filmed it. Jack had written the scenario, and after the film had been edited, Jack saw it.

Because it was a silent movie, Jack was to narrate it, and I was to write the music afterwards. He, Allen, and Neal Cassady also wrote the lyrics for the title song, "Pull My Daisy," for which I wrote the music and was sung in the film by Anita Ellis. Jack put on earphones and asked me to play, so that he could improvise the narration to music, the way we had done at our readings. He watched the film, and made up the narration on the spot. He did it two times through spontaneously, and that was it. He refused to do it again. He believed in spontaneity, and the narration turned out to be the very best thing about the film. We recorded it at Jerry Newman's studio. Jerry was an old friend of Jack's from the early '40s and afterwards we had a party jam session that lasted all night. Jack played the piano, sang, and improvised for hours.

In the early '60s I used to see Jack when he would come in from Northport to visit town. Once, he called up at one in the morning and told me I had to come over so that he could tell me a story. I brought over some music to copy and Jack spoke nonstop until 8:30 A.M., describing a trip he had made through North Africa and Europe. It was like hearing a whole book of his being read aloud, and Jack was the best reader of his own work, with the exception of Dylan Thomas, that I ever heard.

"That's a fantastic story," I told him. "It sounds just like your books."

"I try to make my writing sound just the way I talk," he said. His ideal was not to display his literary skill, but to have a conversation with the reader.

I told Jack about an idea I had for a cantata about the four seasons in America, using the works of American authors. He launched into a travelogue of his voyages around the country, and referred to writers I might look into. I took notes, and ended up reading nearly fifty books, to find the texts. I included a passage from his book *Lonesome Traveler*. The concert was at Town Hall in New York City, and Jack wrote that he couldn't come. It was the spring of 1965, and he didn't like being in New York.

Sometimes he would call from different parts of the country just to talk, and we continued to write to each other. In one letter he said "Ug-g-h. Fame is such a drag." He wanted time to work, but found that success robbed him of his freedom. At the same time, he felt that he was forgotten. I told him that all the young people I met when I toured colleges loved his books. To many, he was their favorite writer. But writer meant something different now. It was what was being said, not how it was said. It was content that counted, not style. Jack's message was a whole way of being, and he was becoming more of an influence than ever.

Truman Capote dismissed Jack's work as "typing." I never heard Jack put down another writer. He went out of his way to encourage young writers. His work reflects this spirit of generosity, kindness, and love. This is why his "typing" is so meaningful to young people today. Jack was ahead of his time spiritually. Like that of Charlie Parker, Lenny Bruce, and Lord Buckley, his work is constantly being rediscovered.

Through knowing Jack, I wrote some of my best music. Without knowing him, I never would have written my book. More important, young people all over the world are reading and rereading his work. His death only means the beginning of a new life for everyone who shares in the joy of knowing him through his books.

Twenty-five years later, in October of 1994, I was invited as the featured performer at Lowell Celebrates Kerouac! for the first time. A young writer, Attila Gyenis, asked if he could reprint the old *Evergreen Review* memorial tribute and have me add an afterward, twenty-five years later almost to the day, to accompany the tribute to Jack.

He told me he had ambivalent feelings about trying to make Jack into a cult figure, or creating a mythology about an era.

"Most of us here at the Festival and most of our readers were born after Jack died. Could you write a few paragraphs about what this all means today to go along with what you wrote twenty-five years ago?"

Here is what I gave Attila in October 1994 for his Spring 1995 issue of his magazine, *Dharma Beat*:

AFTERWORD

Twenty-five years after I wrote this, I was at Jack's memorial site in Lowell, for the first time. David Orr, a lifelong friend of Jack's family, and someone who reminded me of Jack in spirit and being, took me on a voyage to the Stations of the Cross, Jack's grave, and the Kerouac Memorial, where I ran into Attila Gyenis, coeditor of *Dharma Beat*.

I liked the magazine because it felt to me to be connected to the feelings of what Jack was about, and contained the broad, yea-saying, multifaceted, unsnobbish, communicative styles that he would have enjoyed reading himself.

After a beautiful few days in Lowell, I learned a whole new lesson about Jack and his life. Sitting in the living room of John Sampas and his gifted nephew singer-songwriter Jim, both of whom are devoting endless hours to organizing and preserving Jack's work, I met many people who had also grown up with Jack in Lowell. All of these people are helping to paint the picture of where Jack came from, and where his heart always was—in his hometown of Lowell, Massachusetts.

It was the completion of a long journey. Being with others who truly loved Jack and created the festival Lowell Celebrates Kerouac! was for me like going to the Wailing Wall in Jerusalem. I felt I had finally come home to a place I had always dreamed about, and longed for.

I could finally understand that Jack's physical passing was another continuing chapter in the Duluoz Legend, not the final one The night our group played our concert in his honor, we felt that we were surrounded by his spirit.

The final Sunday afternoon of Lowell Celebrates Kerouac! was climaxed by a reading at a coffeehouse, where I backed up twenty-three terrific area poets, just as I had backed up Jack in the 1950s. I went home and dug up the tribute to Jack I had written for the *Evergreen Review* twenty-five years before. Everything in it turned out to be true.

It made me happy that a quarter of a century later, the joy and inspiration Jack gave to those of us lucky enough to be with him was now being shared all over the world by young people. Through his books, his unique and soulful journey has been immortalized.

All the pain and sorrow, the Beatnik myth, the jealous and embittered detractors are part of the past. Through his glorious writings, Jack is a shining light to all of us in 1995, and gives us all energy and inspiration.

Merci Jack!

Now in the new millennium, Jack's work has gained the recognition and appreciation that all of us prayed for and believed would be awarded to him someday. There is a new generation that is continuing the pursuit of artistic excellence and the creation of work to enoble the spirit and the global society. The Children of the American Bop Night now have children and grandchildren of their own. Looking back at our era makes ensuing generations stronger and better informed than any of us were. We share our joy with them in knowing that the seeds we planted are flowering all over the world.

Book Two

Keeping the Flame Alive

In the 1970s and '80s, many people felt that all the goals and ideals many of us had struggled for were no longer relevant to our society.

"Full greed ahead!" was the battle cry. Now a new group of young people had their own stereotype to deal with. The fictitious Me Generation replaced the equally specious Beat Generation.

The great recording company in the sky that Jack always spoke about finally materialized. Just as in the case of my score for *The Manchurian Candidate,* I was allowed to do my best the way I best knew how to do it. I was able to present the dual aspects of what so many in our generation strived to do, usually in complete obscurity. Spontaneity and formality now had a home with the oldest classical music recording company in the world.

My 1971 RCA Red Seal double album *No More Walls* consisted of two LP records. The first contained three orchestral compositions I conducted: *Autobiography for Strings, The Shakespearean Concerto* (both of which I had written while in the company of Jack), and *King Lear Variations* for wind symphony (which Jack also heard when the New York Philharmonic broadcast their performance of it in 1967).

The second LP of the double album contained compositions of mine where I played instruments from all over the world and improvised in different musical idioms ranging from a jazz waltz written for Arthur Miller's play *After the Fall* to my compositions inspired by my trips to Brazil, the West Indies, musical styles from the Middle East, a guitar duet with Ramblin' Jack Elliot, and the song "Pull My Daisy," finally recorded for the first time, with the original chamber music ensemble I had scored for the film.

The whole album was formality and spontaneity, what Jack and I talked about and practiced in our daily lives, and hoped would become accepted by others as a natural principal for any artist to base his or her work on. The song "Pull My Daisy" was finally available, using the same chamber music and jazz style and instrumentation I created for the film score. Now, in the new millennium, there are college courses called No More Walls. There were no such courses, or any recording ever made like this when *No More Walls* was issued in 1971. I was able to present ideas and ideals that Jack and I shared, and open up doors as he had done.

"What are you trying to do?" asked a perplexed RCA executive.

"Exactly what I'm doing," I responded.

"You're all over the place," he said. "You're a symphonic composer and conductor and a jazz musician who also plays a dozen weird instruments. What's your specialty?"

"Music," I responded. "My specialty is music. I'm a composer. All my formal compositions come from my life experiences. Just like Jack Kerouac's books came from his life's experiences."

"Jack Kerouac?" asked the RCA executive incredulously. "Jack Kerouac? He's from the '50s. He's passé. That stuff's dead. No one wants to hear classical music or jazz or poetry or look at some half-ass oil painting. This is the '70s. Get with it. You're committing professional suicide. All those people you talk about in your interviews . . . Charlie Parker, Bela Bartok, Jack Kerouac. Grow up. That stuff's all dead. We're a rock and roll culture. If you're still hung up being a Beatnik, how can you be such a square? This is 1971. Get hip."

"Thank you for your advice," I said. "We'll see what the future brings. I was never into being a Beatnik, so I'll never be capable of transporting myself to your concept and level of hipness. But I will do my best and keep improving, and get others to feel welcome to all I do and share my joy in doing it. That's as hip as I can be."

"Well, you're dead in the water," he said. "You're committing professional suicide."

"I'm keeping myself alive by doing what I was put here to do," I said. "I'm following my heart and walking down my chosen path."

I continued on my chosen path and gradually saw the ideas Jack and I shared becoming institutionalized. Finally categories were created that our ideas and approach to art could fit into.

World music, multiculturalism, and spoken word slowly entered into our vocabulary. Since what our generation had strived for was always the presentation of ideas rather than the creation of labels, I continued to do what I had been doing all my life and tried to do it better than ever.

Remarkably, with no promotion of any kind, the work of Jack Kerouac and much of the music, art, poetry, theater, and film of our era not only refused to die, but, like Rasputin, kept leaping from the grave and persevered. By the '90s, Jack Kerouac was suddenly hot again.

In 1994, the Whitney Museum planned an exhibition for 1995 and NYU had a historic conference dealing with the legacy of Jack Kerouac and our generation. Under the direction of Helen Kelly, an event took place that received coverage in the media from all around the world. Jack was back.

New York University was the first major university to acknowledge Jack as a giant of American letters. Twenty-five years after his death, the influence of his work could no longer be denied. His books literally sold themselves. Like Lawrence Ferlinghetti's *Coney Island of the Mind,* one of the the best-selling books of poetry by an American poet in history, Jack's *On the Road* and all his other books, like Lawrence's other books of poetry, were being read around the world.

The NYU show even featured artwork by Lawrence and Jack. *Vanity Fair* magazine had Annie Liebowitz take a group photo of all of us.

"This is outrageous," I said to one of Annie's assistants outside Town Hall, where we were posing for our picture. "We're the most unfashionable group of people ever assembled."

"That's true, David," she said, smiling. "But you all made a lasting contribution to our culture and continue to do so."

I had met Annie when she first came to New York, at the Art Food Delicatessen, where I used to make my giant sandwiches. She was full of life and talent. She took an amazing photograph of us, in spite of Gregory Corso not only heckling her but also haranguing amused passersby as we huddled together on the street in front of Town Hall.

There were seminars with writers like Hunter Thompson and poet Ron Whitehead, who came from Kentucky to give a twenty-four-hour Insomniacathon nonstop poetry reading with a group of astounding young poets from Kentucky and the South. A whole new community of young poets like Casey Cyr, in their '20s, mingled joyously with all of us who had been there in the '50s. They reminded us of what it meant to be young. We tried to give them reason to hope and make them know how proud we were to see them there, leading their generation to a higher level.

I gave a four-hour concert with my quartet, Keeping the Flame Alive, that featured not only music that Jack and I loved, but readings by Terry Southern, Michael McClure, Jan Kerouac, Dan Wakefield, Ann Charters, Allen Ginsberg, Ted Joans (singing scat duets with me), and many others.

Young academics, devoted and eager to create new courses in American literature and American Studies programs presented papers, and swarms of students joined us in readings, jam sessions, lectures, and seminars. Distinguished scholars like author, university professor, and journalist Ann Douglas attended the event. Ann Douglas's presence added a whole level of distinction to the conference. This was the first time any of us from our era could remember anyone of her importance having a genuine interest in our work. And she was gracious to everyone who wished to speak to her about the experiences she so eloquently documented in her books.

There were programs about the rigorous role that women were assigned in the '50s. Crowds came for this exciting panel discussion that featured Joyce Johnson and Carolyn Cassady. There was a special program devoted to the enduring influence of jazz, hosted by author, scholar, and recording executive Sam Charters with Art d'Lugoff, founder of the Village Gate. Cecil Taylor and I were joyously reunited for the first time since 1955, and spoke about our community of artists drawn from so many disciplines who found jazz a common meeting ground and a point of departure for all forms of creativity.

Throughout the week, Native American poet-musician-architect Geoff Carpentier and I talked and played music for and with hundreds of young people eager to share part of the shining spirit they felt emanated from Jack's writings and now was playing an important part in their lives.

Just a few blocks from the Brata Art Gallery, where Jack and I, with Howard Hart and Philip Lamantia, had given New York City's first-ever jazz-poetry reading in 1957, there were now thousands of people participating in an event that embodied the same exalted feeling. Carolyn Cassady had arrived so late from London that she asked me if she could postpone her reading at my concert and wait to participate with me the next day.

"Of course," I said. "We're just so happy that you could come. What a beautiful thing for Jack and Neal to have you here bearing witness."

Carolyn was terrific as always, surrounded by young people, and all of us had a great time.

Jack Goes to the Kennedy Center

When E. G. Marshall asked me to set the words of Thomas Jefferson to music in 1993, I was thrilled to have a chance to work with him again. In the late '60s, we gave a series of free readings together for young people. He and other actors like Kevin McCarthy, and authors like Kurt Vonnegut, would read from classic works of the theater, recite contemporary poetry, and read their own writings. I would play music and occasionally make up a rhymed blues, getting the audience to participate by dividing them up into different choirs and having them sing something I dictated to them. I also often sang "Pull My Daisy," and when I did, E.G. and most of the other participants told me how much they admired Jack's work.

"It's a shame," said E.G. one afternoon, after we had given a free performance in a park in Manhattan. "He writes so lovingly about America. The critics don't seem to get it. The theater critics have the same problem. They still want to be the subjects of a king and queen. They positively *grovel* whenever they see English theater, no matter how dreadful it may be. They find the Actor's Studio to be an embarrassment. Marlon Brando is a great classical actor and their perception of his work, in spite of his versatility, is that he's typecast for life as Stanley Kowalski in *A Street Car Named Desire*, running around scratching himself in his torn undershirt, yelling 'Stella!' I think the same is true of Kerouac. I find his writing to be unique and personal. And he has an ongoing love affair with America. That's not fashionable at the moment. I love it when you improvise music and words. I wish I could do that sort of thing. I need a *script*. Give me a good script and I'll give you a great performance. I saw *Pull My Daisy*. Obviously none of you could act, and to your credit, it seemed you didn't even try. But the narration was so brilliant, it didn't matter. I'd like to do something of Kerouac's someday, if the right situation made it possible. I don't ever want to read in coffeehouses, as you all did several years ago. I'd like to do something in a concert hall or in the theater."

Finally in 1993, after he arranged for the Library of Congress to commission me to compose music for narrator and orchestra, accompanying the words of Thomas Jefferson, we had our chance to honor Jack's writing as well.

"I like the idea, David. Having you conduct the orchestra accompanying Kerouac's words in some of the selections from *On the Road* and then having you jump off the podium and play some jazz or whatever you feel at the moment behind my narration. We'll give 'em hell at the Kennedy Center and still make them feel like they're in heaven. Jefferson and Kerouac. Makes perfect sense to me."

Over the next year and a half, I completed the settings of Jefferson's texts, all twelve movements, for woodwind quintet, percussion, and string orchestra. I was so exhilarated to have completed a forty-minute new piece that the extra energy made it even more fun to finally set Jack's words with an orchestral accompaniment.

Finally, on October 22, 1995, I conducted members of the National Symphony Orchestra in an evening I'll never forget. The concert went amazingly well. When E. G. Marshall narrated my piece, he rose to a whole other level. He *was* Thomas Jefferson. The orchestra, as well as the audience, was galvanized. The piece got a warm and enthusiastic reception, and when we went backstage during intermission, E.G. was beaming.

"Well, David, my boy, after years of toiling in the vineyards, we have a hit! The director of the Air Force Band attended a rehearsal and wants to program it at Constitution Hall later on this year, so we already have a repeat performance!"

"E.G., you were great," I said. "Thank you for giving me the chance to work with you again."

"And this time, we got *paid*!" said E.G., smiling. "But don't let your energy level flag. Don't rest on your laurels yet. We've still got Kerouac to dispense with. We'll shake 'em up! I'm so happy this is being nationally broadcast. People need to hear this kind of programming. How many thousands of times do we have to hear the same few pieces ground to death?"

On the second half of the program, the good feelings kept building and when E.G. Marshall reentered following the performance of Chavez's *Four Ecuadorian Indian Melodies*, the audience rose to its feet. He created a warm and intimate atmosphere, transforming the Kennedy Center into his living room. He began reading the Kerouac excerpts, and I conducted the orchestra and listened to Jack's words describing the Children of the American Bop Night. I had accompanied Jack when he read this brilliant descriptive passage from *On the Road* at painters' lofts, coffeehouses, Lucien Carr's all-night jam session parties, in Washington Square Park after midnight, in my 6th Avenue pad, and in the readings we gave together anyplace else. I could see Jack, hunched over, smoking a cigarette, listening with his hand cocked slightly, intense and brooding.

E.G. made the words honest and moving, and I knew at that moment that the dreams Jack and I had of doing this someday together were finally being realized. It was a giant first step to more collaborations to come. And I realized that when I finally join him in that Great Jam Session in the Sky, as we all used to say in the '50s, some young composer would do the same for Jack's words, and keep the flame alive.

The Jefferson piece is now being performed in many places, and the Kerouac narrations are soon to be published as a work for narrator and orchestra. I often think of Jack when I conduct this piece, and how he wanted to go out on the road and narrate it with symphony orchestras.

"We can have an act," he would tell me. "Spontaneity and formality. Two old codgers with canes, spreading unconditional love as we make the musicians in the orchestra see past the gloom and allow them to bathe in the holy light and *smile*!"

At the time this book is being published, in 2002, the final version of Kerouac's excerpts from *On the Road* for narrator and orchestra is being completed. It is a work in progress. Since I have no guarantee of living forever and I don't wish to leave the parts I improvise myself to others, I am continually composing new music to substitute the parts where I play myself, so that the music and the words will complement each other long after I meet up with Jack again in the Great Jam Session in the Sky. As with so much else of what I have done, I'm asked to sign bootleg copies of cassette tapes and CDs taken off the air from the radio broadcast of our Kennedy Center performance with E. G. Marshall in 1995.

"I'm happy you liked what we did," I always say. "I was honored to be able to get Jefferson's and Kerouac's words shared on the same program."

"When is this coming out on a commercial CD?" I am asked.

"Someday," I always answer.

"No offense, Mr. Amram, but aren't you getting kinda old to be waiting around?" I was asked recently by a teenage bassoonist after a rehearsal of *Little Rebellion* where I was the guest conductor.

"I am getting older," I said. "But my music and Jack's words will stay young forever."

"Oh, that's awesome," he said. "What a great way to look at things. Would you say that's Beat?"

"No," I said. "I'd say that's the truth."

Back with Jack: The 1998 *On the Road* Recordings

In the 1950s, we never had adequate or affordable electronic equipment to document ourselves. Tape recorders were bulky and heavy, most portable microphones were limited in their capacity, and those of us who made recordings in studios figured that these sessions were enough to show the world what we had to offer as improvisers.

In jazz, we were working our six–eight hour club appearances from 9 P.M. to 3 A.M., six nights a week, and often going to jam sessions after work. We were constantly being creative, innovative, and exploring new ways of playing.

In this heady environment of the '50s, combined with the concert music I was composing by day, I never worried about a great phrase or melody or harmony disappearing. I knew there were a million more for me to find. I never thought that the well would run dry. It never has. It was the same with improvised lyrics.

All of us loved to hang out together. (My milieu, like Jack's, was never restricted to four or five gloomy people snarling at the world, contrary to some people's version of Beat Generation history.) All of us, wherever we were and whoever we were with at the moment, expected the unexpected. Since anybody within hearing range was an automatic member of an unsolicited audience, we always got instant feedback. We never worried about recording what we did for fun. We honestly felt that not that many people were interested.

What is now known in the hip hop world as free-styling we

called scat singing or scatting. Scatting was also a term used to describe a vocal style that reinterpreted the way various instruments in the band played by singing sounds that emulated the great jazz instrumentalists as they played their solos.

The exponents of Latin music, especially those who played Afro-Cuban style congas, could sing all the drum sounds. In addition to this instrumental style of singing, improvised words and rhymes were also part of the daily bill of fare. It was a constant floating feast of words and sounds.

Almost none of this that Jack and I and so many others did was ever recorded. The one time it was, at Jerry Newman's studio in 1959, the night after Jack finished recording the improvised narration for *Pull My Daisy* with my improvised accompaniment, Jack and I took turns playing piano for one another, and also took turns making up rhymed stories and songs on the spot. We wailed away for almost four hours, as Jerry recorded us, occasionally emerging from the control room to give us a variety of legal and illegal refreshments.

All of this has been lost, except in the memories of those who were there. We did this all the time at Lucien Carr's house, at my apartment on the lower East Side in 1956, Christopher Street in 1957–58, and 6th Avenue from 1959 until the last time I played a duet with Jack over the phone a few weeks before he died, in 1969.

I encouraged Jack to play piano, congas, and sing. He encouraged me to rap, scat, and write. Except for my 465-page book *Vibrations,* completed in 1968, all my writing was minimal. An occasional article, journal, diaries, letters, notes, or lyrics for a song made up for an occasion. I never gave much thought about preserving anything except my formal compositions. I just enjoyed what was happening at the moment.

The exception of course was what I wrote down on my scores for orchestral, chamber, choral, ballet, theater, operatic, and film composition. Those were done with loving care, and no matter where I was, or what I was doing, they have happily survived to this day.

"The old yin and yang," said Jack. "Spontaneity and formality, hand in hand, Davey. But my archives are even more meticulous than your perfectly notated scores." Jack's notebooks, paintings, his homemade baseball dynasty and his tapes were all incredibly well organized.

In 1996 I drove about an hour and a half from our farm to go a tiny studio in Woodstock, New York, to make a preliminary demo tape of Jack reading archival recordings he had made himself on his own reel-to-reel tape of his "Orizaba 210 Blues." My van was packed with my instruments. I didn't know what to expect. Since there was no budget for musicians, I was the band as well as the composer. Jack's nephew, Jim Sampas, was producing this recording with Lee Ranaldo, an accomplished poet as well as member of the innovative and pioneering group Sonic Youth. Geffen Records was planning to release a CD of archival tapes of Jack reading his own work. I was selected to provide the music, as I had done for him so many times. Since this was to be a recording to give the executives of Geffen Records a sense of what my music and Jack's words would sound like together, Jim asked me to come alone and improvise everything. Later on, I could write a score, when the company signed all the legal documents.

I brought along my *dumbek*, an hourglass-shaped Middle Eastern drum, my *shanai* (the Arabic forerunner of the oboe), my French horn, a Lakota frame drum and courting flute, my penny-whistles, double ocharinas, congas, and percussion instruments. There was a gorgeous acoustic baby grand piano, looking like a relic from a bygone era. It was like going to the Mystic Seaport Museum in Connecticut and seeing the old sailing ships. A true blast from the past. A real instrument with a voice of its own where you could make an infinite amount of subtle phrasings and tonal textures. I sat down and played it. Jack and I never had a piano that fine to work with in the '50s.

"Shall we try one, David?" said Jim Sampas. "I know you and Jack liked to do it spontaneously."

"Right," I said. "Let's hit it."

" 'Orizaba 210 Blues' piano track. Take one," said Jim. I winked at him through the glass of the recording booth. I had on earphones and suddenly I heard Jack's voice.

I wanted to swivel around from the piano bench and see where he was standing behind me. I could feel him over my shoulder, just the way the Mexican Indians themselves could feel the presence of certain spirits perched on their shoulders. Without a second thought, I began to play, making music that complemented his voice, rising and falling with his phrases, able to somehow feel what he was going to do before he did it, as we had always done together.

I felt such a warm feeling playing with Jack's recorded reading; it was as if the thirty-five years that had elapsed were telescoped into thirty-five seconds. As I played I got the eerie feeling that I already knew this poem. I couldn't really concentrate on listening to the poem as a poem, though. I couldn't just lie back and allow myself to soar like Charlie Parker's bird in flight, on the wings of any poet or reader whose work I was trying to complement, whether it was Jack or anyone else. I had to concentrate, like an astronaut landing on a newly discovered planet. I had to make music at the same time and always think a little ahead.

"That was amazing David," said Jim Sampas when I finished. "It sounded like you composed that."

"I did, Jim," I said. "But I did it on the spot."

"Are you familiar with this poem?"

"I think so. I don't know. Can I see a copy?" Jim showed it to me.

"Oh my God. I remember this," I said. "Jack read me this in 1959 one night when we were talking about his search for his Indian heritage that he said he could feel but was afraid he could never find. He talked about the Mexican Indians and how some of the dialect spoken in parts of Mexico and Central America contained sounds and fragments of ancient Toltec, and how he felt that reverberate in him, even though the Iroquois, if they were his ancestors, were a different nation, with a whole different tradition. He understood that all of this was a mystery world he could only be in touch with in his dreams. He had it in a notebook. He had other poems with him the same night. He read them from a small scroll that looked like it was made from shelving paper or teletype paper. He and Allen and Gregory were all hanging out with Rocco and Buddy the wino."

I reread "Orizaba 210 Blues" about four times. "I know what to do," I said to Jim. "Since there is no budget, I'll use the piano track I did spontaneously and build a whole score around it, with all the instruments I brought with me."

"How long will it take to compose it and write it down?" asked Jim.

"I'll do it right now. It's in my head," I said. "We'll harness the beast of technology and make it the servant of Jack's poetry honoring the heartbeat of all the Indian people who survived the Conquistadors and are still the heart and soul of Mexico. I'll use a different track for each instrument, but we'll make it sound like an acoustic orchestra playing on a plaza on a Sunday afternoon in Amatlan, which is an Indian village about an hour outside of Mexico City."

The great thing about working with Jim Sampas was that he allowed you to do your best. His own background as a bandleader and songwriter made him sensitive to other musicians and he was always able to make constructive suggestions. He also had a deep respect and understanding for Jack and his life's work.

I began adding different instruments, and we finished it in about two hours. We left the studio exhilarated. Jim and I had already worked on a Kerouac CD and a three-hour cassette of *Visions of Cody* for Viking Penguin Audiobooks, with Graham Parker reading Kerouac's words.

"This is going to an incredible CD," said Jim. "Geffen Records has worldwide distribution. It will get Jack's words and your music everywhere."

"It was worth the wait," I said.

A short while later Jim called me from Lowell. "David, I've got some bad news. Our man at Geffen Records who is supporting the Kerouac CD just called and told me that a whole bunch of people at the company have just been fired. The new regime has no interest in Kerouac in any way. We have to take the project to another company so it doesn't die in the warehouse six months after release."

"Well, Jim, we'll have to wait a little longer," I said. "Beaver

Harris, the great drummer from Pittsburgh, once told me 'some critics say jazz will never be popular because the modern drummers play too many offbeat rhythms and that we're late in showing up, but when our music starts . . . it's always on time.' "

"I hope you're not disappointed," Jim said.

"When this does get released, no one will know what any of us went through in order to make it happen," I said. "There will just be Jack's words and my music. And it will be right on time. I thank you for going through all of this to get Jack's own voice and my music out there. I got to play with Jack again. I'm ready for more."

Two years later, in 1998, Jim called me with some good news. Rykodisc Records wanted to make an entire CD of Jack's readings, taken from old tapes preserved in the archives of the Kerouac estate. Some of the tapes Jack had recorded himself on his own reel-to-reel tape recorder. Some were done by our mutual friend and Jack's old buddy from Columbia days, Jerry Newman.

"We'll finish up 'Orizaba 210 Blues.' I've listened back to it and its amazing!" said Jim.

"I'd love to hear it," I said. "I can't remember a lot of what I played."

"It sounds like a composition," said Jim.

"That's good," I said. "Composed music should sound spontaneous and spontaneous music should sound composed."

"We have a poem," Jim said, " 'Washington D.C. Blues,' almost eighteen minutes long. It needs music throughout. We have a budget for musicians if you'd like to hire some of the good players you know."

"I've love that," I said. "Let me read the poem."

Jim sent me a photocopy of "Washington D.C. Blues" and a cassette of Jack reading it. Jack sounded at his best. I felt like I was hanging out with him again. Since the poem hadn't been published, I kept the photocopy under my farm equipment catalog. I didn't want it added to the list of bootlegged copies of the film and soundtrack of *Pull My Daisy* that have been floating around since 1959.

I played the cassette for my kids. "He sounds *great*, Daddy," said my second daughter, Adira, then seventeen. "Now when I read his writing in public at your concerts, I'll do a lot better."

"Jack was the best reader of his work," I said, "and the best writer about his life. I'm so happy that you can hear him."

"He sounds so real," said Adira. "And funny. I can see why you guys had such a good time together."

"He sounds really cool," said Alana, then nineteen. "I like his voice."

"I like him more than rappers," said Adam, my fourteen-year-old. "He's got some crazy ideas."

I was happy that my own kids could relate to Jack's work through the communicative power of his voice. I was sure their friends and contemporaries would, too.

I called Jim Sampas and said, "I know what to do. We'll have two three-hour sessions. The first will be a group with alto sax, guitar, bass, drums, congas, and me playing piano, French horn, dumbek, shanai, pennywhistles, and everything else. That will be for our jazz–Latin–World music sound. I'll get Jerry Dodgion on alto, my quartet with Vic Juris on guitar, Victor Venegas on bass. We'll get Johnny Almendra on drums, and Candido on congas. Jack used to see Candido when he played with Dizzy's band after Chano Pozo died in 1949."

"Great," said Jim. "What will the second session be?"

"We'll have our neo-classical ensemble. We can have Jerry Dodgion come again to play alto sax, almost like Marcel Mule, the great classical French saxophonist who used to solo with the Boston Symphony when Jack still lived in Lowell. Jack used to tell me how he loved that French way of playing the alto that was from another planet, compared to the way Charlie Parker approached the instrument. "Then we'll have a viola, a bassoon, and an oboe doubling on English horn."

"That's interesting," said Jim. "An alto saxophone, viola, English horn, and bassoon."

"It's the same instrumentation I used thirty-nine years ago for the classical musical segments of *Pull My Daisy*. And the biggest kick of all: I called the three classical players who recorded the original *Pull My Daisy* soundtrack to play this recording—Midhat Serbagi, viola, Jane Taylor on bassoon, and Ronnie Roseman on oboe and English horn. They're all going to make it."

"How can you coordinate the two different groups recording at different times?" said Jim.

"I'll write everything out," I said. "It will be like a ballet or opera score. We can record it out of sequence, like a film score, and then fit it together. 'Washington D.C. Blues' will be fully composed and notated on paper. 'Orizaba 210 Blues' was made up out of my head at the moment. Spontaneity and formality, side by side. Jack would have loved it. That's what we did alone, together, and with others. That's what we had to offer when so few thought that way."

"I can hardly wait to hear it," said Jim. "I loved hearing the radio broadcast of E. G. Marshall reading Jack with your orchestral music from the Kennedy Center. My uncle John really liked it, too."

"This will be different," I said. "We've got Jack himself doing the readings, and his poems reflect a different part of his whole approach toward writing. It will be an extension of what we used to talk about doing."

I sat at home for hours, listening to the tape of Jack's recording of "Washington D.C. Blues." The long seventeen-and-a-half-minute series of short poetic vignettes and his dynamic reading were mesmerizing. He sounded just as he did when we first began to play together. *On the Road* was still unpublished, and he was full of energy and laughter.

I flashed back to when we would terrorize guests at various loft parties and disturb unwitting coffeehouse customers who thought we were two Village moving men trying to be artsy. No one else back then would have dared to walk into a room full of strangers and take turns playing music on any available instrument, read poetry of their own and others', in English and French, and make up scat-story-raps, while sipping on brown-paper-bagged bottles of Thunderbird wine and flirting with women. Still, Jack always, and I not quite always, tried to maintain *gentillesse* even if we sometimes appeared to be bulls in someone else's China shop.

"Il faut être gentil tout le temps" was our motto. Jack would say that in the same Lowell-tinted New England accent that I was now listening to on this 1956 recording, the year I started to work with him.

As I listened to him read "Washington D.C. Blues," I remembered the gentle way Jack had of expressing himself. He was usually out-shouted by most of his friends, so he never blew out his vocal chords trying to out-shout them. His speaking voice was beautiful and he was a surprisingly good singer. When he wasn't reading aloud, scat singing, bashing out at the piano, or hammering on the bongos, he would sit quietly in the middle of pandemonium. His voice was like a magnet to women. If he was sitting between two women, he would speak softly and try to relate to both of them, in an old-fashioned gentlemanly way that Carolyn Cassady described as "courtly."

Hearing him all these years later reading "Washington D.C. Blues" reminded me of the light that he brought with him and shared with everyone around him.

I wanted the music I wrote for this reading of "Washington D.C. Blues" to reflect the tapestry of the people and places that were packed together like a crazy quilt in this series of short poems and vignettes. The piece was made up of a series of over thirty short readings of recollections and impressions that were like taking a trip to the countryside. I tried to frame the poems and vignettes with music and at the same time make the whole reading flow and have the feeling of seamlessness.

When I came to the studio for the first session, Jim Sampas and co-producer Lee Ranaldo both looked surprised to see me loaded down with folders of music as well as all my instruments and a stopwatch.

"I don't know how you're possibly going to pull this one off, David, but I know you will," said Jim Sampas.

Our first ensemble came in to play. Candido, now approaching eighty, still played the congas like no one else. Jack had seen him when he performed with Dizzy Gillespie, Charlie Parker, and hundreds of other musicians. I first worked opposite Candido in the fall of 1955 when I was with Charles Mingus Quartet and Candido was a solo performer between our sets. He took me under his wing back then, because he could see I was interested in what he was doing, and respectful of him. He had played on almost every recording of my own, and concerts with my quartet and symphony concerts I conducted.

"*Que tal,* Candy?" I asked.

"*Mas viejo que ayer y mas joven que manana*" (older than yesterday and younger than tomorrow), he said, smiling.

"*Este dia, Kerouac,*" I said.

"Jack Kerouac," he said. "You always talk of him and sing that funny song you wrote with him. Today, we play with him. That's good."

Jim put on a tape of Jack reading for all the musicians to hear as they entered the Manhattan Beach Studios to unpack. Jack's voice filled the room.

"Man, he sounds great," said Vic Juris, the young guitarist who had played with me since 1978. "I've really been looking forward to this. His reading is so *musical.*"

"He sounds like he is right next door," said Victor Venegas, our bassist. "When did he record this?"

"Nineteen fifty-six," I said. "At Bob Giroux's house, in Washington, D.C."

"OK, David, we're ready," said Jim Sampas. "Let's begin recording."

I had the ensemble play the main theme. It was bittersweet, similar to a melody of the second movement of my violin concerto—melancholy but still full of hope. I knew Jerry Dodgion's artistry could make this simple song-like theme complement all the feelings that Jack's series of poems evoked in the one long seventeen-and-a-half-minute piece. After we finished playing it, I saw Jim Sampas, Lee Ranaldo, and the engineer smiling.

"That's perfect, David," said Jim. "Let's record it." We continued to record, section by section, and finished the session ahead of time.

"Since we have an extra ten minutes, I want to do something for old time's sake," I said. "Let me redo one section we've already recorded and play a new part behind Jack's narration on the French horn, the way I often did. There's one part on the soundtrack of *Pull My Daisy* where you can hear him half-singing a mournful ditty, keening and wailing, while I make up a second part that mirrors that old-country-lost-the-mountains sound that he is creating. I think the sound of my horn and his voice will pull people into the imagery of this poem without them knowing it's happening."

"I'm not quite sure I get it," said Jim. "But if you feel it's something Jack would want, go for it." We cued up the tape and got ready to record over the take that already existed.

"This better be a good one," whispered Victor Venegas. "The one we're erasing was *mean*! I hope your chops are up."

"This one's for Jack," I said. "He'll give me a psychic temporary chops transplant."

The tape rolled and I knew I couldn't miss. As I played, listening to Jack's recorded voice through my earphones, I could literally feel his presence just above my left shoulder, like the spirit that perches itself above the shoulder of the Indians of Mexico and the American Southwest.

"Nice, Dave," said Vic Juris when I finished. "You sound like you've been practicing. Next thing you know, you're going to actually have a rehearsal with the quartet."

"You're all so great I'd just rather let it happen," I said. "Whenever the four of us play as a group or when we add someone special who is tuned in to really listening, we can't go wrong.

"Naturally when we rehearse for my symphony programs, we're part of a large group that has to rehearse. They wouldn't be comfortable if they didn't have any idea what we're going to do at the concert. When you played in the small orchestra I conducted for the ballet score I composed for Jacques d'Amboise, we had a bunch of rehearsals so the dancers could get used to my music, how we played it, and how we could adjust to them. That gave the dancers confidence to know that they could soar and we would be right there with them, whatever they did.

"But when it's just us playing a concert, you're all so great, and creative, I know it will always happen. All of us know how to follow each other, and when the music itself takes over, we follow that. That's the same thing Jack and I always did every time we got together.

"Mingus told me my first week with him in 1955, 'Practice at home. Having rehearsals don't mean anything. Go home and woodshed. When you come to the gig tonight, you're here to *create*!' "

"I wish more bandleaders thought that way," said Vic Juris.

"I think they would if they could follow the Plains Indians' saying: 'The leader is the follower.' Kerouac came up at a time when the jazz philosophy made a contribution to the whole society with this way of looking at things," I said. "Young people need to know about this. I thank you guys for being here. You were all wonderful. We'll have another adventure into the unknown at our Central Park Concert 'From Cairo to Kerouac.' We'll all have a reunion and the actor Keir Dullea will read Kerouac and we'll play about two hours of wailing music till the Parks Department tells us to stop. Tomorrow I'm recording with three of the original players of the *Pull My Daisy* original film score."

"Another first," said Jerry Dodgion. "See ya tomorrow."

"We'll be smokin' in Central Park," said Vic Venegas.

"I'll be there early," said Vic Juris.

"*Coje lo suave, Dave y gracias*," said Candido.

"This was a ball. Come hear my band at Gonzales Gonzales Restaurant," said Johnny Almendra.

"It's all just starting," I said "It's a whole new day. Tomorrow we'll record with the chamber group and put it all together."

I went home and spent most of the night going over the rest of the music. I thought about how my sister Mariana and I used to sit on the floor of our farmhouse in Feasterville, Pennsylvania, in the late 1930s putting together jigsaw puzzles. I remember our squeals of delight when we would finally put the last piece in place, and could see a perfect picture that gave no indication of our struggles in assembling it.

This was what it was like fitting together the rest of the music I had composed for "Washington D.C. Blues."

If I could have had the chance to do it live, Jack and I would have been able to adjust to one another at any given moment and make whatever we were doing sound rehearsed. But Jack's recording was fixed in time. It sounded natural and was read as well as I had ever heard him in a recorded performance because he was recording himself for himself. It was a one-way street that I had to make into a thoroughfare musically, implying a give-and-take by responding to every nuance in his reading. We couldn't change one second of what he had already recorded without ruining the perfect pace he had established.

All my experience in composing for the theater, film, and ballet, where you had to adjust to someone else's creativity, made it possible for me to plan out this jigsaw puzzle in sound. I knew I had to figured out in advance how to put it all together. Then when we started recording, there would be a calm atmosphere in which the musicians could discover personal moments of hidden beauty as they played the written notes. They could bring the music to life in the same way that Jack could make his words sing in a thousand different ways.

The next morning, I got up early and drove back to New York City. The musicians arrived one by one. Midhat Serbagi, who knew Jack in our forays together at Lucien Carr's jam sessions in 1958, a year before he played on the soundtrack of *Pull My Daisy*, came early. He loved Jack's work, and always appreciated Jack's down-home Lowell soul and his strong regional accent. Unlike Jack's friend and one-year classmate from Horace Mann Prep School, William F. Buckley, who traded in his Texas roots and learned to speak like an English butler, Jack retained the speech patterns of his youth.

When I arrived, Jim was playing the tape of Jack reading over the playback system in the studio. He wanted the musicians to hear him as they walked in.

"My God, that's *wild*!" said Midhat. "That guy sounds just like Kerouac. Who is that? He's great!"

"That's Jack," I said.

"Come on, man. Don't put me on. He's been dead for thirty years."

"It's Jack," I said. "This is an old recording he made on his home tape machine in 1956. His nephew Jim Sampas and Lee Ranaldo got it remastered and cleaned it up. Isn't it fantastic?"

"It's *fantissimo,*" said Midhat. "Man, that's spooky. It sounds like he's right here. Let me see my music. I hope you wrote something good for the viola."

Midhat sat down, crinkled up his nose, adjusted his glasses, pulled down his hat, and began practicing his music. The rich sound of his viola, played in his personal heartwarming style, filled the small recording studio.

Jane Taylor arrived, carrying her bassoon case, and greeted us all with smiles, jokes, and hugs. She was one of the most beloved musicians in New York City, the founder and still member of one of the oldest and best woodwind quintets in the world. When she recorded on the *Pull My Daisy* soundtrack in 1959, she was already a musician who brought a freshness and idealism to every place she traveled on her constant tours. She toured the globe, bringing chamber music to new audiences and inspiring two generations of students to always think positively and exceed all expectations.

Her dark eyes had the serene glow you find in the eyes of holy men and loving parents.

"Well, fellahs, you're still all looking robust. Is that Kerouac reading? It's hard to ever forget that voice, even after forty years."

"I'm glad you're here," I said. "Wait till Ronnie Roseman comes and see us all together again. The Pull My Daisy Vegetarian Chamber Music All-Stars, reunited."

A few minutes later Ronnie arrived. Since 1959, when all four of us had recorded the soundtrack for *Pull My Daisy,* Ronnie had been with the New York Philharmonic, appeared as a soloist around the world, played in chamber ensembles, and was a highly respected composer and popular teacher. Like all of us, it never occurred to him to slow down. He lived for music and all the places making music brought him to.

"This is amazing," said Ronnie. "It's like a high school reunion. We have to get a picture of this. My young students now know that I played on the *Pull My Daisy* soundtrack. They ask me all about

Jack Kerouac. I'm trying to show them how to phrase, how to project their sound in all the situations we become part of, how to make the proper reed for the style that is right for each composer whose work you're playing, and they're asking me about Jack Kerouac."

Ebet Roberts, the Memphis-born photographer whom I knew from Farm Aid, arrived, carrying her cameras. A renowned photographer, she had the gift of making the people she was photographing feel at ease.

"I wouldn't miss this for the world," she said. "I've got great shots of you and Willie Nelson and Neil Young at Farm Aid. I'll shoot the recording session for your book."

I introduced Ebet to everyone, and we posed for a group photo. While we stood together and Ebet shot her pictures, we could hear Jack's voice, over the studio's speaker, reading to himself, now us, and eventually the whole world.

His unpublished poem "Washington D.C. Blues" was now alive again, and I got the eerie feeling that this must have been somehow fated, even though we both worked so hard to not end up like Diogenes, hiding our light beneath a barrel.

"Like you say, there's no rush," I would say to Jack, when he agonized over *Visions of Cody* not being published, and Marlon Brando never responding after expressing an interest in starring in a feature film version of *On The Road.*

"Be patient. *Soit tranquille.* It's never too late," Jack would admonish me, when I would rail against the conductors and record companies who would return my orchestral scores and recordings a year later, still unopened.

"Our day will come," said Jack over and over. "Stick to your guns." His voice that surrounded us as we stood in the studio was full of affirmation and life. It was the voice of a young man talking to himself and to the whole world if the world cared to listen. Like just about everything that we ever did together, his reading welcomed everyone to the party.

After Ebet finished photographing us she went into the control room to take pictures through the glass partition.

We were now ready to record. The same opening theme that I had written for the ensemble the day before was used again, scored this time for English horn doubling on oboe, viola, bassoon, alto saxophone, and myself playing occasional piano and other instruments.

Some of the music sounded almost Elizabethan, to match the elegance of Jack's words, much like portions of the music for *Pull My Daisy* when I wrote a sprightly minuet and trio to accompany the Bishop and his wife's visit to the apartment of Carolyn and Neal Cassady. We did almost all the music in one or two takes. All the players were so in tune to one another that each small piece sounded as if we had been on tour and knew it cold.

"Good stuff," said Midhat. "You've got promise."

"Will you guarantee to call me back in forty years?" said Ronnie Roseman. "I'll tell my students to stop calling you and asking about what Jack Kerouac was really like."

Ebet took one more farewell photo of us, and then Jim and I went over all the tapes, and assembled everything in order.

"We'll meet tomorrow," he said. "We can hear it with a fresh ear and mix it."

Jim left and I sat in the studio, collecting all the music and my instruments.

"Where do you go from here?" asked the young engineer.

"Home," I said.

I remembered the victory celebration Jack and Jerry Newman and I had after completing the recording of the narration with my original improvised music for *Pull My Daisy*. It took an hour to record. Then Jerry recorded hours of Jack and me singing, playing, telling stories and jokes, making up everything off the top of our heads with each of us accompanying the other. Like so much of what I did in the early days, I let it go, went on to the next adventure and let it all float downstream. I lived from day to day and only saved my music and my instruments. I never worried about the well running dry, or growing old. I thought that only happened to other people. After I got a family, I started trying to organize the rest of my life, as well as my music.

"Somewhere a copy must exist," I have said to myself and others thousands of times over the past four decades. There must be a copy somewhere of that midnight-to-morning landslide of words and music that we created for our own entertainment. Just as *Pull My Daisy* was a glorified home movie that now was considered a document of our era, I realized that the recording we did that night for fun would now be a document of what Jack and I did for years, whenever the spirit moved us.

Perhaps it was all for the best. If those 1959 tapes had been preserved and bootlegged, there is a good chance that some of the best moments might have been edited out. With modern technology, anyone with his own homemade studio could add tracks of music that would have no relationship to what we had done. A commercial recording could also be issued, altering what Jack and I had done. There is precedent for this. A recent film biography of Charlie Parker featured some of Bird's priceless recordings. His solos remained intact, but the rest of the recording had been electronically altered. Someone, undoubtedly with good intentions, had removed the entire rhythm section that was part of the original sessions and rerecorded the same performance with different musicians. Charlie Parker's solos were preserved, but he was now playing with a different band.

No one seemed to realize that even though the new rhythm section was comprised of great musicians, and well recorded, Parker would have played totally different solos if he had played with them. He always based his spontaneous creations on who he was playing with and how he felt at that moment. Hollywood's addiction to plastic surgery was now permeating the music industry. My music could easily be altered electronically or completely replaced by the latest Eurotrash techno-pop-funk band that not only wouldn't listen to Jack, but whose members wouldn't even listen to each other. A battery of lawyers and self-appointed youth culture experts of the moment would probably bring in a battery of drum machines and electronic effects to doom Jack's natural lyrical readings to a hell worse than any he suffered in his darkest days.

I felt some sense of closure for the first time since 1959 just because those tapes we made with Jerry Newman *had* disappeared. Jack and I wouldn't have altered them, but we would have selected the ones that we felt were the best. I realized how lucky we both were in 1998 to finally have a recording issued that represented both of us at our best, still collaborating. Even though Jack couldn't adjust his readings to my music, I could adjust my music to his readings in a way that could achieve the same effect because of our years together.

The recordings I had just completed sounded remarkably natural. Each section flowed effortlessly into the next. We had all spent a great deal of time and given a lot of painstaking effort to ensure that this new recording would sound effortless and spontaneous. Jim, Lee, and I also were determined not to have these readings with music sound like a New Year's Eve bash in a mental institution, poorly played and out of tune. All three of us agreed that the idea of the recording was not to reinforce the old image of the tone-deaf Beatnik.

This new recording presented Jack in his prime, accompanied by the best musicians I knew, produced with enough of a budget to record under optimum conditions. There was nobody involved in the creation of this beautiful new CD who was in the position of being able to come in after it was finished and ruin the results. The impeccable taste and talents of Jim Sampas and Lee Ranaldo as producers, my own best work as a composer and performer, and Jack's glorious reading were now documented for all time and available to a worldwide audience.

"Maybe the great Career Planner in the Sky has a reason for all this," I thought. Certainly other work on Jack's behalf that I had done a few years earlier with Jim Sampas had also come out remarkably well. I had done music for a Kerouac CD and an audiobook of Jack's beloved *Visions of Cody*. Graham Parker had been the narrator and both the events were done in a short time and had turned out extremely well. They were the very best I was capable of doing.

Jack's readings of "Washington D.C. Blues" and "Orizaba 210 Blues" were magnificent renditions. All of us involved felt that this new CD would set a high standard for how to combine poetry and music in a natural way. We all felt that this recording would paint a better picture in sound of what Jack and I had pioneered as a new way to combine music and the spoken word. We never called it jazz-poetry. We called it poetry-music music-poetry. Now it didn't matter what anyone called it. No brand name or packaging could alter the outcome.

As I drove back to our farm, feeling a rare moment of contentment, I realized how lucky I was to finally have a recording of us collaborating, even if it was done in this way, with the music added to Jack's reading forty-two years later. It occurred to me, as I battled my way through New York rush hour traffic, that if I had not lived long enough to make this recording, there would be no documentation of the collaborative approach that Jack and I pioneered, except for *Pull My Daisy*. Much as I wished that Jack had been with us and could sit next to me now, listening to the rough mix of the cassette I was playing in the car, at least I knew it would inspire a new generation to collaborate with their brother and sister artists.

I tried to imagine what it would be like for young musicians, poets, and writers who were now studying our work to finally be able to read about us. If Jerry Newman's legendary missing tapes resurfaced someday and I was no longer there, who would be able to mind the store? If Jim and Lee hadn't made it possible to make this CD, would all our efforts be represented by four hours of one recording of our crazed bombed-out victory party? Would this have become the only remaining document of our work together? There certainly would have been at the very least some portions of those lost tapes that might have been better sent to the wastebasket. Jack or I would have asked Jerry to record something else over them if they weren't up to our standards. That night in 1959, we were just having a party. Perhaps it was fate to have it happen this way.

As I listened to the rough mix of the afternoon session in my car, I knew this was just the beginning, not the end. Jim had discussed the debut on CD of the entire soundtrack of *Pull My Daisy* originally scheduled for release in 1959 by Columbia Records, which had somehow gotten sidetracked and never been released. All the people who had purchased bootleg copies of *Pull My Daisy* over the decades felt it was a document in sound that stood on its own.

Many journalists, scholars, and listeners have said that the complete twenty-nine-minute soundtrack of *Pull My Daisy* continues to paint a picture of a time and place, just by hearing Jack's words and my music, even without seeing the film.

My cantata *A Year in Our Land* with the excerpts from Jack's *The Lonesome Traveler* was now getting performed frequently and due to be recorded. The orchestral settings of three of his narrations from *On the Road* and the second movement of my flute concerto *Giants of the Night,* written for James Galway and dedicated to Jack, were also formal works that sum up the results of our collaborations. These compositions are written down and published, so that they can be presented whether I am around to conduct or play when they are performed. Like Jack's novels, books of poetry, paintings, and my symphonies, concertos, operas, and chamber works, they are self-contained. They don't require Jack or me to be there in person to spread our message. These works can be performed without us and still speak to people. They are no longer considered offbeat. They are now books on our shelves, available for all to read. They are now sound recordings on our shelves, ready to listen to.

As I drove the last remaining miles to our farm, listening to our new recording, I wondered what Jack and I would have done if he were still here physically to celebrate our latest collaboration at the end of the twentieth century. Would we party until 5 A.M.? I guess we probably would, but instead of crashing on the floor of my old 6th Avenue apartment wherever he or I could find a spot to lie down as the sun was rising, we could both come to our farm, the kind of place he always talked about wanting to settle down in someday. He could meet my family, and have a meal, hang out with my kids, and see all the copies of his books, now reissued in paperback, that line our shelves.

"Be patient, Stick to your guns. It's never too late," he used to say. I saw that he was right. Still, as I pulled into the driveway of our farm, I couldn't help wishing that all this was happening forty years earlier, so that we could enjoy this special moment together.

The Orlando Connection: The House That Jack Built

In March, 1997, I read a wonderful article by Bob Kealing of WESH-TV in the *Orlando Sentinel*. It described in detail the house in Orlando, Florida, where Jack and his mother lived. Joyce Johnson had sent thirty dollars to Jack to take the Greyhound bus to New York City, so that if *On the Road* was reviewed favorably he would be there. What happened the morning of September 5, 1957, when Gilbert Millstein's amazing review was published in *The New York Times* is lovingly documented by Joyce Johnson in *Minor Characters*.

What was never documented was the history of that house. In addition to Bob Kealing, two other people living in Orlando in 1997 shared his vision. Marty Cummins, a retired lawyer who had started Chapters Books, a coffeehouse, restaurant, and bookstore in Orlando, loved Jack's work and wanted to see the house saved. Summer Rodman, a twenty-three-year-old woman in the construction pipe business, also wanted to see the house and adjoining building purchased and turned into a writers' residence in Jack's name. We corresponded, Marty Cummins wrote me, and we talked on the phone.

"I feel it would be appropriate to make this writers' residence open to all styles of writing, and focus on Jack Kerouac, but not the Beat Generation. Do you think I'm making a mistake?"

"Marty," I said. "I've been waiting since 1969 when Jack left us to hear someone say this. I can also tell you the vast majority of all of us still alive would thank you. I think Jack would jump down from Heaven and buy all three of you a round of drinks if he could get a leave of absence."

We talked and I suggested to Marty that he get in touch with Sterling Lord, Jack's literary representative, John Sampas, his brother-in-law and executor of his estate, and editor David Stanford, who was responsible for the republishing of Jack's classic works and previously unpublished ones as well.

"We have just enough money to make a down payment on a down payment," said Marty. "We all love Jack's work and we are proud of his presence in Orlando. We want the whole world to know he was here, and a writers' residence honoring him would keep that flame he kindled here so long ago alive for today's young people. We also hope to establish a fund for improving literacy in the central Florida school systems and establishing a prize for high school students in his name to encourage artistic activity. And eventually, if we can purchase the other house, we can have a music residency as well. I know all this sounds overly ambitious, but I'm still a believer in the American Dream. I think Jack's work personifies that dream. I hope you don't think all this sounds crazy."

"I think it sounds great," I said. "I'll be there if I can help out."

Marty called a few weeks later.

"Do you think you could come down and play for a fund-raiser at Chapters Books and Cafe to help us raise a little money? We can cover the cost of your plane ticket and a room in a hotel."

"I'm on my way," I said.

Marty also invited Douglas Brinkley, a great young historian who had been chosen as Jack's first authorized biographer. Jim Sampas, Jack's nephew, whom I was working with creating music for unreleased archival tapes of Jack's readings, was also invited. We all came to Orlando and had an old-fashioned reading with music and a small concert, which I created celebrating world music, jazz, and some examples of the great variety of sounds that influenced us all in those long gone days of the mid-fifties. There was a small press conference, and we had a great time. Everyone involved loved Jack's work. There was not a Beatnik-style *poseur* or sour-faced person to be seen.

"What a breath of fresh air," said Jim Sampas. "Everyone is here to honor Jack. I can't believe this is finally happening."

"Jim," I said. "It's the beginning of a new era. As Charlie Parker always said, 'Now's the time.' "

A few weeks later, Marty Cummins called me again.

"David, I have great news. There was a tiny article in *USA Today* and Jeffrey Cole, who owns a large eyewear company, read the article in *USA Today* and contacted me. He's a huge fan of Kerouac's work and your work and has offered us enough money from stocks he holds to place a substantial downpayment for the first house. We want to honor Jeffrey Cole with an event. Could you come down again? We can't pay you but we'll cover expenses."

"I'll be there," I said.

Doug Brinkley came down and joined us, and we met Jeffrey Cole, who arrived with his whole family.

"I used to see all of you in the Village when I was still a kid visiting New York. I admired your daring and spirit. I'm happy and honored to contribute to this writers' residence in memory of Jack. I'd like to read some of his work at your concert and have you back me up."

"That sounds fine to me," I said. "Thank you for honoring Jack. Your generosity will be a big help towards making the impossible happen."

We had another marathon old style reading, jam session, storytelling, fun-filled night. Afterwards, Bob Kealing; his fiancée Karen; Doug Brinkley; and Susan Bennett, a young poet, painter, and Kerouac scholar who was visiting her grandmother in Florida, all went out to Alexander's Outdoor Restaurant to celebrate what seemed to be a giant step toward purchasing the small house and making it into a writers' residence.

We talked about the new wave of interest in Jack's work, and the reevaluation of the informal 1950s community of artists from many disciplines, of which Jack and all of us were members. I felt as if a true appreciation of our era had finally arrived.

"Each generation rediscovers Kerouac on their own terms," said Doug Brinkley. "When David and I first met in 1982 in Boulder at the twenty-fifth-anniversary celebration of *On the Road* being published, there was only a serious interest among a small group of devotees of Jack's work. Now, that interest has become worldwide. There is so much more to Jack than the Beat Generation. His presence in Orlando, and later in St. Petersburg, is fascinating. His early life in Lowell and all the accounts of his daily life that are part of his unpublished journals make an amazing story. I've got my work cut out for me. Don't you think he would be happy to have a writers' residence named for him?"

"I know he would be," I said. "He always supported his brother and sister struggling artists. After all his years of rejection he almost seemed to feel guilty whenever he met anyone who was striving to achieve something. He was empathetic when anyone would tell him about the pain they were suffering by being ignored.

"Jack never apologized for being an overnight success. He couldn't get his first ten books published, and *The Town and the City* received almost no attention when it came out. He would always mention to anyone who felt neglected that until *On the Road* was finally published after being rejected so many times, *The Town and the City* was his only proof to the world that he was a writer."

"*The Town and the City* is a beautiful book," said Susan Bennett. "All of his books have their own special qualities."

"I'm so interested in your work with Jack," said Bob Kealing. "I understand you and Jim Sampas are adding your music to unreleased tapes of Jack reading. I can hardly wait to hear them. All that we do together for the writers' residence might make people here aware of Orlando's contributions to the culture of the South. We have something as noteworthy to offer as Disney World. We have the legacy of Jack Kerouac's presence here."

"We also have a great art museum here in Orlando," said Summer Rodman. "We have a collection of contemporary art, including the work of a lot of the painters you and Jack spent time with. Tomorrow I'll take you all there. Disney World and the Space Center have put us on the map, but we have an artistic community here, and a lot of young people who need to know about our history."

The next time I came to Orlando, in October, 1998, Carolyn Cassady, the painter and author of *Off the Road,* joined me from London to help the cause of the Kerouac Writers' Residence. She was a central figure in Jack's life as well as Neal's, and a repository of stories of Jack's early struggles when she gave him love and support. Everyone in Orlando was excited at the prospect of meeting her in person, and hearing her speak and read excerpts of her book. Carolyn always reminded people that Jack and Neal had had a great friendship and the ability to stimulate each other intellectually and keep an open door and a seat at the table for anyone who wanted to join them on their ride. Marty Cummins, Bob Kealing, and Summer Rodman all wanted the Residence to reflect the egalitarian and inclusive approach that most of us championed in the '50s. They knew that Carolyn would be a perfect person to spread that message.

"We want to create a broad-based group of supporters from all over the country from different fields who admire Jack's work. We'd like to invite them to be on our Honorary Advisory Board," said Marty.

I wrote a form letter to many old friends, all of whom supported Jack's work. Some of the writers who responded enthusiastically were Norman Mailer, Lawrence Ferlinghetti, Douglas Brinkley, Dan Wakefield, and Ben Bova. Musicians included Pete Seeger, Floyd "Red Crow" Westerman, and Jerry Jeff Walker; from the film world British actor Michael York and Steve Allen. Photographers Patricia York and Chris Felver also lent their names.

The full-time Board of Directors was located in Orlando. The board kept growing with the addition of men and women who all had their own special contributions to make. They all worked tirelessly to raise money and awareness. The world premiere of the film made by the Sharples, *Go Moan for Man,* was shown during this event. I gave some concerts, and Carolyn Cassady read and talked to throngs of people, and we had a chance to stay up till nearly dawn every night talking and sharing stories about Jack and Neal and the lasting value of their influence on one another and on several later generations of writers and readers. We also talked about the collaborative nature of our era and the importance of getting young people motivated to tap into their own creativity.

"This is so much fun, to see our dear Jack being honored in this way," said Carolyn. "I had a friend who worked for the University of Missouri who could not believe that Jack and Neal and I all shared a passion for literature, art, and music of all kinds. He clung to the cliché image perpetuated by people that read articles *about* Jack that Jack was some kind of eccentric boor and that Neal was a semiliterate career criminal. He didn't understand that both of them were brilliant and enormously well read, and had a passion for the arts as much as they had for earthly pleasures. In addition to their talents and energies, they were true gentlemen.

"I mentioned all this to my friend. I asked him to please tell his colleagues that the mythology and so-called biographies written about Jack and Neal were mostly fiction and had nothing to do with how they were in real life.

"I said to him, 'I know. I was there. I am as primary a source as one could be.'

"My friend turned to me and said, 'Carolyn, my colleagues have a policy of never consulting primary sources. They feel they are unreliable and therefore they have no value in scholarly research.' "

Carolyn and I, along with everyone else at the table, roared with laughter.

"You have to remember, Carolyn, that truth is always stranger than fiction," said Bob Kealing. "Perhaps what you told them it was really like was too much for them to handle."

Carolyn smiled. "One poor little fellow, whom I took into my house, pronounced himself an expert on Jack. He began lecturing me one day on what I had done during a crucial week in my life. 'Excuse me,' I said. 'That never happened. You've got it all wrong.' 'No, I don't,' he said, and plowed ahead, oblivious to everything I said. They make it all up as they go along. There are some I know who have done remarkable work. Hopefully, with the doors opening up, there will finally be some accurate reporting done on all of this. We have to share what we experienced with the new generation of scholars. I'm not going to be here forever. Neither are you, dear David. We have to get a message out there. There should be more events and organizations like this one and Lowell Celebrates Kerouac! Douglas Brinkley is a professional historian. I know he'll take the time and make the effort to get it right."

Carolyn's presence in Orlando was a turning point in the struggle to establish the Writers' Residence. Everyone who met her was moved by her presence and wanted her back for future events. And everyone who met her gained a deeper appreciation of Marty Cummins's dream and was encouraged to lend their support.

I suddenly realized a major irony: in spite of the unappreciated and unheralded roles of women in the '50s, three of the writers whose work enriched the understanding of Kerouac's legacy were women: Carolyn Cassady, author of *Off the Road,* which recounted the accurate story of Jack's early years and struggles and his unique relationship with Neal; Joyce Johnson, prizewinning author whose *Minor Characters* was now considered a classic; and Regina Weinrich, a brilliant young academician whose critical analysis of Jack's work was acknowledged as a milestone in all circles. And every scholar was appreciative of the pioneering work of Ann Charters, Jack's first biographer. In addition to her biography, Charters compiled two volumes of Jack's selected letters that in themselves are an important portrait of Jack.

I returned to Orlando several times. In late October of 1999, I came back for another whirlwind tour, and over the next year, the Kerouac Writers' Residence became a reality. The old house was now to become the home for emerging writers from all nations, of all ages, and of all styles of writing. More money was being raised to restore the small adjoining house as a second residence.

I received another phone call from Marty Cummins.

"David, hold on to your seat. This is a dream come true. Steve Allen has agreed to come to do a concert with you as a fund-raiser for the Writers' Residence. It will be videoed as a document, and both of you as primary sources can also speak about your work with him. Everyone here is excited, and we already have a guaranteed sellout of tickets."

In September, 2000, I flew down to Orlando to do the concert with Steve Allen. Chris Felver, the great documentarian of the poetry and art world since the '70s, came from Sausalito, California, to video, shoot still pictures, and add his upbeat fun-filled manic personality to the whole event. His sunny personality reminded me of Danny Kaye singing and dancing in a Technicolor musical.

"What a great guy," said Marty Cummins. "So unpretentious and fun to be with. I love his work. His book of photographs, *Anarchists and Angels,* is a classic. I'm sure Steve Allen will love him."

"Everyone does," I said. "He was a golf pro, and a fine guitarist and folk singer. He's from Akron, Ohio, and has a good old-fashioned Midwest way of distinguishing what's for real and what is just a hustler's hype of the moment."

After Steve Allen arrived, Chris and I were sent by limo to pick him up.

"Well, David," he said, "after all your descriptions of the gurus with limos who've set back Eastern religions in the United States a hundred years, now *we're* the new leisure class, golfers with one limo. I think in five more minutes I'll be accustomed to this for life. I'm junking my old car and becoming a limousine liberal. I love this. Check out this air-conditioned interior. Forget about suffering for your art. Live it up, baby. Have a soda. Turn on the TV. Let's use the cell phone in the limo and order some sushi. Play your ocharina for the driver. We're riding in the style we should have always been accustomed to."

We arrived at the hotel where Steve Allen was staying and parked. I went inside alone. Chris stayed in the limo and waited. I had the desk clerk call Steve and he came down. He looked at me, touched the middle of his eyeglasses frame on the bridge of his nose, and then extended his hand palm up as we all did in the '40s and '50s when "giving skin" was at most a ritual and sign of respect and affection in the world of African American musicians, and used sparingly among non-African-Americans for special occasions. After a gentle slide and tap of hands, we gave each other an old-fashioned handshake.

"Steve, it's wonderful of you to come. And so great to see you. After so many years. The last time was 1956. The benefit for Adlai Stevenson."

"I know," said Steve. "I hope we can do this again without having to wait another forty-four years. I've followed your progress since that show we did together when you knocked the drum set over. You're doing some fine work."

We reminisced until about twenty people had gathered around, and began asking Steve for his autograph. He graciously obliged.

"Well, David, we'd better meet everyone at the Writers' Residence and then go to Dubsdread in College Park and do some playing. I was told the piano would be tuned. We'll just wing it. Just like we did with Jack. We'll just follow each other."

"Okay," I said. "I'll bring all my instruments and play some of your tunes like 'The Gravy Waltz' and then we can play some four-hand piano and then you read Kerouac and I'll accompany you and I'll read Kerouac and you accompany me. And then I'll do 'Pull My Daisy' and we'll end with a tune we can all play together with Orlando's Moore Than Jazz band. Then we'll answer questions from the audience with Doug Brinkley about what it was like working with Jack."

"Fine," said Steve. "We've just rehearsed the whole show for tonight right here in the hotel lobby."

We rode back to the Kerouac Writers' Residence in the limo and Chris Felver, quietly huddled at the front end of the huge air-conditioned car, filmed our conversation.

I was actually interviewing Steve. I told him I would give a copy to the Kerouac House, to John Sampas for Jack's estate, and to Doug Brinkley, so that in the future the story of how Steve came to hear Jack at the Vanguard and offered his help could finally be told by the person who was there.

"He was a natural," said Steve. "I loved playing for him."

By coincidence, the night Steve went to hear Jack at the Vanguard, Bob Theile was in the small audience, and this resulted in the recording Bob arranged for Steve and Jack to make together. All of what Steve was saying was videoed by Chris Felver, with the understanding that it would be given to Doug Brinkley to transcribe for his authorized biography of Jack.

We were following Carolyn Cassady's idea of sharing information with primary sources. We were trying to correct the years of misinformation, so clearly explained to me by Joyce Johnson with these simple words: "David, they weren't there."

I realized at that moment that all us still living had an obligation to try to pass on some of the beauty of all that had happened so long ago. The new generation, through no fault of their own, were still assaulted with the cliché of the Beatnik Myth. So much written about Jack missed the whole flavor of the era, the ambience, and the nature of Jack himself.

As Steve continued his remarkable reminiscing, I flashed back on conversations about Jack I'd had with Dizzy Gillespie, Sahib Shihab, Edie Parker, Joan Haverty, Jan Kerouac, Paddy Chayefsky, Leonard Bernstein, Jack's mother, Lew Welch, John Clellon Holmes, Langston Hughes, Zoot Sims, Al Cohn, Jerry Newman, Allen Ginsberg, Joan Mitchell, Franz Kline, de Kooning, Joan Mitchell, Edgar Varese, Bob Donlin, Bob Kaufman, W. H. Auden, Seymour Krim, E. G. Marshall . . . and so many other people whose lives had been touched by Jack. They were no longer with us to tell Doug Brinkley how they felt and what they remembered.

Now in the limo with Steve Allen, I realized that what he was saying was the basis of true history. His conversation flowed as if all this had happened yesterday. He remembered all the same people I, too, remembered in our 1956 encounters. He recalled the names of the people, where we were, and what had happened, including my overturning the drum set when I sat down to accompany him.

"I'm sorry, Mr. Allen," I had said. "I'm really a classical composer and jazz French hornist. I'm not really a drummer."

"I assumed you weren't," he had replied in a dry but gentle way.

All these years later, he still retained his warmth and humor. I wished that we were driving to Los Angeles instead of a short distance to College Park in Orlando. Then Steve could have rapped out a whole history course for Chris to record on video as we made our way across America. Steve was like an African griot, recounting an oral history of times and places that he recalled in a concise and vivid fashion. Chris Felver and I both knew how lucky we were to be alone with him. His love of Jack and his writing, his respect for jazz and artists who created it, and his desire to share this with the world transformed the limo into a classroom-church-temple-1950s coffee house.

The limo finally arrived at the Kerouac Writers' Residence, a small modest house in a quiet section of College Park that looked like most of the Orlando I recalled seeing as a child on the way to Passe-a-Grille, Florida, in 1937–38. This part of Orlando was untouched by the enormous changes that had occurred since Disney World and the Space Center had brought in armies of tourists and subsequent housing developments.

There was a small crowd of people waiting in front of the writers' residence. There were journalists from TV, newspapers, and magazines. Fans of Steve who also had home video cameras and tape recorders were waiting patiently. There were people from the same block and one elderly woman who remembered Jack as an affectionate neighbor.

Steve exited the limo and was swamped by everybody. Even the journalists asked him for his autograph. Standing tall, like a statesman visiting another country, he graciously obliged, answering questions, telling stories, speaking to each person in a warm and genuine way that relaxed everyone.

"Phew," said Chris Felver, half whispering in my ear, while all this was going on. "This is fan*tastic,* man. I've never seen anyone like him except when I was with you at Irving Plaza when you played that show with Willie Nelson. He's like Willie. He digs *everybody*. What a great cat. The footage we have is priceless. All that stuff he said, I've never heard before. He's like you. He remembers *every*thing."

"He remembers the parts that were meaningful and stay with him," I said. "We both have great *selective* memories."

"Well, he sure selected some great stories," said Chris. "I can hardly wait to film your concert together. That should be out of sight."

After about an hour at the Writers' Residence, we went to a 6 P.M. dinner. Somehow, Steve managed to finish his meal, in spite of people coming up to ask him to sign old LPs, books he had written, T-shirts, autograph books, and old photos from the '50s. One young woman asked him to sign her forearm with a Magic Marker. He was gracious to each person, and continued his conversation when they left as if there had been no interruption.

When it was time for us to play, we rose from the table and, after being introduced, walked to the bandstand.

"This one is for Jack," said Steve, just before we turned to acknowledge the applause.

We played some jazz standards together. I played pennywhistles and French horn and Steve played piano. We played some four-hand piano duets together. Steve read some of Jack's excerpts from *On the Road* and I played piano for him. I imagined Jack back in 1957 a few miles away, taking the thirty dollars Joyce Johnson had sent him, buying his bus ticket from Orlando to New York, just in case *On the Road* got some favorable reviews up there.

Here were two of his collaborators, forty-three years later, honoring him and his work. It had been our good fortune to share part of our lives with his, in his all-too-quick transit through the world. Steve read simply and beautifully, as if he were telling one of his own stories. You could feel Jack's presence.

Then it was my turn to read, while Steve played the piano. I began to read and Steve played his lyrical 1950s-style piano improvisations as he had done with Jack. Rather than tailoring his music to the words, as I always did, he provided an atmosphere that captured the whole era in an uncanny way. I felt literally transported back in time like the cast in the film *Back to the Future*. I felt like the twenty-five-year-old David Amram in 1956 hanging out with Jack, and when I started to read, my own voice made me feel that Jack was talking to me, or through me.

I had never experienced anything before that night, nor have I since, that equaled this experience. The night was documented on film and audio, and was donated to the Writers' Residence, the Kerouac Estate, and Douglas Brinkley. I realized as it was happening that it would be preserved beyond the memories of those who were there.

Steve and I then played another duet, and I sat with him at the piano and played "Pull My Daisy." He occasionally tapped his hands, like the members of the congregation in the amen corner in a sanctified church, as I improvised lyrics and scatted and was joined by the Moore Than Jazz ensemble for our grand finale. Then we answered questions from the audience. Douglas Brinkley joined us. He spoke movingly of his years of research for his monumental task of completing Jack's first authorized biography, and what Jack meant historically to several generations. Steve answered every question with priceless stories and anecdotes.

We then raced over to Chapters Book Store for signings of all our books and recordings and more questions, interviews, and conversations.

Finally, we drove Steve to his hotel.

"David, I know we'll see each other soon," Steve said. "We'll do some family programs together. We can even do some of your symphony family programs, and include readings of Jack and Thomas Jefferson, as you did with E. G. Marshall, and we can play jazz and answer questions from the audience."

"We plan to do that with the symphony down here in Orlando," I said. "You can narrate and I'll conduct, and we'll play some jazz duets together. Have a great trip back and send love to your family. It was a great night for Jack."

"It was a great night for all of us," said Steve. "I'll look forward to many more."

"Me too," I said.

Chris and I drove back to where we were staying for a nightcap.

"What a fantastic cat. What a fantastic night," said Chris. "You guys are great together. It's obvious why Jack liked to have you both play for him. I can hardly wait to see the footage."

"For God's sake, don't lose it," I said. "This might never happen again."

"The next time you guys play together it will be even better," said Chris.

There never was a next time. Five weeks later, on October 30, 2000, Steve Allen passed away. I watched the news reports and felt a sadness as if I had lost a family member. He was so much a part of our time and he gave so much joy to so many. I realized how lucky I was to have shared those precious moments with him. Jack had brought us together for this final session, and Jack would have loved sharing that night with us, reading aloud, playing the bongos, scat singing, and talking to everybody.

Our night in Orlando was about the joyous energy of Jack's writings as it affected all our lives. And how joining forces in artistic expression is mutually inspiring and makes you stronger and more creative when you are alone, giving your work extra resonance and luster.

As a result of this concert, the Writers' Residence gained a whole new group of sponsors from the private sector, foundations, local and state arts funding, and governmental organizations. The Kerouac Writers' Residence in a few short years evolved from a dream to a reality.

Now, many people who have seen the success of what happened in Orlando are trying to encourage other communities around the country to honor their own artists. The Kerouac Writers' Residence was created to honor lasting values and creation of new works. Like Walt Whitman and the Indian legend Kokopelli, Jack and his legacy were about spreading energy and opportunity to others.

The seeds that had been sewn nearly half a century earlier were bearing fruit.

A Down-Home Louisville Insomniacathon

Flying from New York to Louisville in February 2001 for a forty-eight-hour "Insomniacathon," produced by poet extraordinaire, teacher, and keeper of the Jack Kerouac spirit flame Ron Whitehead, I sat across the aisle from a young rapper.

"You a writer?" he asked.

"Kind of," I said. "I'm a composer, musician, conductor, and I'm writing a second book and a short stanza to start off a 12-bar blues at a three-day festival I'm going to. After I more or less stick to the first few lines, I'll just take off and see what happens, like a guy walking on a tightrope or a high wire act, or falling off an ocean liner all alone at midnight in the Caribbean and having to sink or swim."

"You mean you freestyle?" he said, leaning over.

"No. I wouldn't disrespect the hip hop tradition by calling it that. I hear and feel a different style I've been doing the last fifty years, since I was eighteen and started scatting spontaneous poems for fun. We called that scat."

"I'd like to check you out," he said, reaching in the small duffel bag he had stored at the foot of the seat in front of him. "Take some of my merchandise. Here's a CD of my music and a T-shirt."

"Let me look in my bag," I said. I searched through my Mexican shopping bag and came across the photocopy of the old flyer of Jack Kerouac and me with poet Howard Hart and Philip Lamantia from our 1957 jazz-poetry collaboration at the Circle in the Square Theater. On the back of the flyer was an old photo of Jack, Allen, and myself and an article in the *London Times* from 1994. I handed it to him. He read the article, turned over the pages, and stared at the flyer.

"You got some illustrious past," he said, smiling. "Kerouac . . . he was saying something they didn't want to hear back then. I loved that book *Tristessa,* and *The Subterraneans*. He must have been one of the first white dudes that wasn't afraid of black people."

"He wasn't afraid of anybody," I said. "His mind didn't work that way. He was checking out the world and all its people, and always searching for the beauty."

"I liked *On the Road,* too," he said. "All that was in my father's time. My Pops used to talk about Dizzy and Charlie Parker and Monk. One of my brothers won all-state as a trombone player, and my other brother plays saxophone and he talked about these guys, but I never got interested enough to check them out until I read about them in *On the Road*. He made me feel I was part of that. I went out and bought their music and checked them out. Those cats were bad! Hearing them made me feel closer to my father. He's a little younger than you. I like the way Kerouac lets it all out and speaks his mind. He's telling *his* truth. That's what I do when I rap."

We talked for a while about all the different ways poetry and music could complement one another. We exchanged numbers.

"I'll see you in Chicago next month when you're playing the Waltz III benefit concert for the homeless," he said. "I got some friends who are playing the show too. I'd like to come and check you all out."

"I'll get you a ticket," I said.

"I'll be there. Don't forget to send me a tape of your daughter singing and doing readings," he said.

"I won't forget. Give your three-year-old a hug," I said.

I walked to the Louisville Airport baggage claim and met Ron Whitehead. The last time we had been in Louisville together was when Hunter Thompson and Johnny Depp, both Kentucky natives, came to have Hunter honored in his hometown. Ron had organized an amazing event where I did a version of "My Old Kentucky Home" with Warren Zevon playing piano, with a Kentucky bluegrass band

and with Johnny Depp playing slide guitar. Since I had never met any of them before, and they all were arriving at different times, I had to rehearse for a few minutes with each of them and explain how I would cue them when to play.

It all worked like magic, and I used my conducting and composing skills to organize it so it sounded as though we had rehearsed for a month. After the concert, Hunter ambled backstage and gave me a hug.

"It's been too long a time, Amram," he said.

We used to live half a mile apart up in the hills in Huguenot, New York. Hunter had a cabin and I had a small farmhouse in the woods off a dirt road. We both went to the same tiny general store on Route 209 where the owner confided in us that he had seen flying saucers and saucer people make a landing in the field across the road from his store. He said we were the only ones he could trust to tell because he thought we were weirdos and would understand. This was in the middle of the 1960s when Hunter worked for the newspaper, the Middletown Record, before he lost his job for attacking a soda machine in one of his mischievous manic moments. I hadn't seen him since.

"I wish Jack were here," he said. "I know how you guys pioneered all this music-poetry stuff. It seems natural when you do it. You know what's appropriate."

"I just try to listen," I said. "That's all you have to do. If you listen, you can't go wrong. That's what Jack did all his life. He was a great listener."

"Well, this Ron Whitehead is a great listener too," said Hunter. "He's really crazy. I love him, he's totally out of his mind. He can understand what I'm saying."

"Ron does know how to listen," I said, "with his heart as well as his head. He doesn't let his education ruin his natural creativity."

Now I was in Louisville with Ron again at a forty-eight-hour Insomniacathon, with a hundred writers and a hundred musicians. In addition to performing my own music and demonstrating instruments and rhythms from around the world, and reading excerpts from my book, I was to accompany an army of young poets and musicians, in the same way I had accompanied Jack, Lord Buckley, and so many others so long ago.

Ron was waiting for me at the baggage claim.

"Welcome back to Louisville," he said.

"Glad I made it here again. In the spirit of Jack, I'm ready to wail," I said. "Do I have time to get a falafel before I accompany an army of underground Kentucky genius poets and musicians?"

"I don't know about falafels," said Ron. "But you've got everybody's heart."

"Then we'll eat some grits and collard greens when the sun comes up," I said. "Let's go over to the festival."

The Insomniacathon 2001 in Louisville was more than a déjà vu celebration. Refreshingly absent were people dressed in berets, dark glasses, paste-on goatees, speaking in monosyllabic bad imitations of a big-city street hustler or suburban white drug salesman, "like . . . duh . . . dig it, man . . . er-ah . . . like duh."

Louisville, the home of Muhammad Ali and Pee Wee Reese, as well as Hunter S. Thompson, was a community with a sense of self. In my first session (about thirty minutes after the plane landed) I told a bunch of young people of high school to college age that Jack had loved Southern culture, and that he had identified the influences of the King James Bible's flowing rhythms of speech and Shakespeare's stately poetic dramatic monologues on the writers of New England and the South.

Both New England and the South share a reverence for tradition. Both have a history of pride in that heritage. I told the kids that when I was invited to address the English Speakers Union when I was a visiting composer at Washington and Lee University, I talked about Jack and explained how classic French poetry and prose complemented the primal rhythms of Shakespeare and the Bible and had influenced his work. At the end of my rap for these people my own age, almost all of them came up and spoke to me. To my delight, they felt that Jack was sadly underrated as a stylistic innovator of twentieth-century letters.

"You mean those old dudes were Kerouac groupies?" said one young woman of about twenty.

"Not groupies," I said. "They were people who prided themselves on their knowledge of the English language, and wanted to see Jack credited for changing what a novelist can or cannot do."

"You mean they could understand what he was writing about, even though it must have been so shocking for a bunch of stuffed shirts like that, in their tuxedos and evening gowns?"

"No," I said. "Each shirt is also stuffed with a heart and soul. Jack saw that he was dealing with the human condition. He saw *beyond* what Henry Miller, one of his supporters, referred to as the Air-Conditioned Nightmare."

I talked to them about how Jack saw past the negativity to see the beauty of every experience. All the people there that night were old enough to have lived through the times Jack wrote about. They all seemed to feel that he was one of the great reporters of our era. I was told by one of the professors at Washington and Lee that most of the members of the English Speakers Union were from distinguished Virginia families who had been here before the American Revolution. As I looked out at the people I was speaking to, I was sure that a lot of what Jack wrote about was unfamiliar territory for many of them. And yet, like all gifted authors, his writing made you part of the scenes he described, and I felt the people warm up as I spoke of some of our adventures playing together. I knew Jack would have basked in the glow of all that Southern warmth that made the room feel like an incarnation of a more gentle time, when people showed off the brilliance of their intellect, rather than the sparkle of their jewelry.

"People came up, smiling and talking as if they had spent a night in the Village hanging out with us," I said. "Many of them said they had read Jack, and were fascinated and touched by all the places he had been and all the wild scenes he always seemed to become involved in."

"Wow," she said, smiling. "I can see that you guys were on the fringes, way ahead of your times."

"No, we were right on time. We were *of* the time. We were dealing with what was there at the moment, just like I'm dealing with what's here right now. Trying to pay attention. Trying to be respectful of you, and where you're coming from. Trying to bear witness to an era that is still misunderstood by many."

"Wow," she said. "You mean you Beatniks were *historians*?"

"First of all, none of us were Beatniks. That word didn't enter the picture until later, when Herb Caen, the columnist from the *San Francisco Chronicle*, wrote that the Russians had their Sputniks but we had our Beatniks. The phrase caught on and became a stereotype to dismiss all of us as a bunch of ignorant, America-hating, sociopathic, untalented mediocrities."

"Just like most of you people up North call us all rednecks, even if we get a Ph.D. or become President of the United States?" she said.

"Exactly," I said. "The Beatnik myth has no more to do with the writing of Jack Kerouac, the music of Charlie Parker, Monk, and Dizzy, or the paintings of Joan Mitchell and Franz Kline than the *Beverly Hillbillies* and *Hee Haw* has to do with the great Southern writers like Carson McCullers, Thomas Wolfe, William Styron, William Faulkner, Willie Morris, Tennessee Williams, Truman Capote, and Terry Southern."

"So Jack never was a New York snob?" she asked, looking somewhat relieved.

"He was brutalized by the snobbery of New York in the 1950s," I said.

"Well," she said, "they never tell us any of this stuff in English class at college."

"They will," I said. "The remaining primary sources are being interviewed extensively, and with the Internet, more information is readily available than ever before. That includes information about us. Your whole generation, born in the 1980s, has it available for the first time.

"Jack Kerouac's books were never promoted during his lifetime, after *On the Road*. Most people my age still don't regard him that highly. That's because they still believe what they read about him a long time ago about the Beat scene. They believe what was written *about him* by others. Those early savage criticisms were written by people who felt a successful man of letters should write and act in a certain prescribed way. They were horrified by Jack's natural down-home, inclusive, friendly, and good-natured boisterous style. Because most of them had led sheltered and often uneventful lives, they had no idea what Jack was writing about or why he would possibly write about what they were trained to think were the dregs of society.

"All that has changed. Jack's books now sell themselves. Charlie Parker's music sells itself. Doug Brinkley, the head of the Eisenhower Center for American Studies down in New Orleans, told me recently that each generation rediscovers Kerouac on its own terms. I'm here to support you in also rediscovering your own natural-born creativity and encourage you to get your friends to read books, look at paintings, go to concerts, enjoy dance programs, attend film festivals, and be creative yourselves. That's what Jack did all the time with kids he ran into. They would expect him to be Mr. Beatnik, and he would end up getting them interested in developing their minds and spirits. He was a lot different than the clichéd image we've been force-fed. I know, because I was there. I was a part of it. I still am."

"Well, I sure like Kerouac's books," said the young woman. "That's what brought me to this Insomniacathon. Ron Whitehead says the same thing you do. He makes you feel you're a part of it, not some nerd or geek or total loser sitting on the outside looking in. Could I go home and get my boyfriend and go out with you for a sandwich? I see on the program you have an hour before your next session. My boyfriend plays guitar and writes poems and goes to college with me, but his parents want him to be an insurance broker or businessman. His dad was a coal miner, but now most of the mines are closed. His dad grew up real poor. He wants my boyfriend to be secure in life. Maybe you could talk to him. My name is Katy."

"I'd be glad to, Katy," I said.

Katy left and came back about ten minutes later with a young kid who couldn't have been more than fifteen.

"My boyfriend couldn't make it till later," she said. "This is my neighbor Ted. He wanted to meet you."

We went around the corner to a down-home barbecue fast food eatery, where the heavenly smell of grease, barbecue sauce, fried fish, simmering okra, and smoldering beef and pork were like an intoxicating perfume of the soul to a Yankee with Southern roots like myself.

"You like this kind of food?" she asked. "I thought you were some kind of non-meat-eating Buddhist or something."

"No," I said. "I'm what they call a Jewish fallen vegetarian. I'm like Jack. I respect Buddhism as a perfect way to be in your heart and actions towards others, but I love the religion I was born into, just as Jack loved the church and went to Mass."

We sat down and started demolishing mounds of rich Southern food, as I told them both how happy Jack would be to know two young Kentuckians were reading his books. Ted, the fifteen-year-old, finally spoke.

"Katy invited me to come eat so I could talk to you. I just have two questions. Are you a Beatnik?"

Katy looked horrified, since she had just been to an hour session where I had talked about all the work I had done and was still doing involving Jack's writings.

"No," I said patiently, and went into a fifteen-minute monologue about the subject.

"Oh-h-h-h," he said. "I have one more question. All the people you talk about are amazing. But do you know any famous *models*?"

"No, I'm afraid not," I said. "You can see by the way I dress I'm not too aware of the fashion world, even though it's an interesting and powerful influence on our culture."

"Oh, no," said Katy. "Don't say that. You're very *retro*. That outfit you have on is neat. That garage-type shirt with the two patches on your pockets that says 'Dave' and 'Peekskill Hollow Farm.' We all look for ones like that at the thrift shops."

"Well, Katy," I said, "this shirt was given to me by Dave Orr from Lowell, Massachusetts, in 1994, after he took me all around Lowell and showed me the Stations of the Cross where Jack used to go as a boy at the French Catholic school he attended. Dave's family was French-Canadian too, and he had this shirt made for me and I wear it for special occasions like this. I wore it when I recorded with Jim Sampas, Jack's nephew, providing music for *Visions of Cody* and 'Jack Kerouac Reads On the Road.' I still wear this shirt for special occasions like this Insomniacathon. It's my Lowell spirit connection. And when I'm on the road, I can wear it each day, because I can wash it in the shower each night and it's dry the next morning."

"That's neat," said Ted. "I want to quit the tenth grade and hitchhike all over America with you. I'll be your roadie. I can meet beautiful models."

"Please," said Katy, looking mortified. "Mr. Amram is a distinguished guest at the festival."

"Uh-uh," said the kid. "He's a Beatnik like Jack Kerouac. I see it in his eyes. He's got girlfriends all over the world. I wanna go with you. We can travel together. I want to be a Beatnik like you and Jack were."

"We were never that," I said. "We were collaborators. We shared similar interests. We encouraged and confided in one another. We all hitchhiked in those days. It's different now. The spirit of adventure never changes. The bittersweet poetry of vanishing small-town America is still here. But you have to find your own way of finding it. You could do what my oldest daughter Alana did when she graduated high school. She and her boyfriend took a Greyhound bus across America and hung out at every place the bus stopped, talking to people and savoring the flavors of speech, dress, body language, food, smell, sight, and hidden feelings that every small place off the beaten path still possesses."

"That sounds stupid," he said. "I don't want to sit on a bus looking out the window. I don't want to go sit in some bus station with a bunch of losers. I want to hitchhike to New York and then to San Francisco and be a Beatnik and meet some famous models. I want to get out of Louisville and go with you and see the world. You should fire all your roadies. I'll be your roadie for nothing."

"I don't have any roadies," I said. "I carry my own stuff, and rent whatever I need. In our era, that's what everyone did. Duke Ellington crisscrossed America mostly in a car with his baritone saxophonist Harry Carney. Lionel Hampton often rode on the same bus as his band. Ramblin' Jack Elliot drove his own motor home to most of his gigs. Sometimes one or all of my three kids come with me and help out, driving and performing with me at jazz, folk, or world music and spoken word festivals. If I'm conducting a symphony they come along, but I don't have much to carry for those concerts."

"I could come with you and set up a booth and sell T-shirts of you and Jack Kerouac and photos and programs and recordings you guys did together," he said, looking unfazed.

Katy looked at Ted imploringly. "For heaven's sake, stop it right now. Don't you see Mr. Amram doesn't need you to do any of this? If he did he would ask you."

"Ted, I appreciate your offer," I said. "But I don't sell stuff like that. You can't merchandise a relationship. We were friends. We were collaborators. Jack just wanted people to read his books. I just want people to hear my music."

"Well," said Ted, "maybe you'll find a spot for me."

"You've got your own spot already. You have the most important thing. You're interested. You're aware. You want to search out new places and find out what they mean to you and other people. That's a lifetime journey you can take by yourself and with anybody and everybody you meet. Always try to pay attention to everything. I'm still doing that myself. That's what Jack did. Even with the grief of his final years, he kept on searching. All this has nothing to do with being a Beatnik. There really was no such thing. That was just a stereotype that became so popular, some people who felt they had no identity tried to play that role so that they could feel they were somebody, which of course they were. *Everybody* is somebody. That's what Hondo Crouch, mayor of Luckenbach, Texas, population seven, said was the motto of his town. Hondo had the saying 'Everybody is somebody in Luckenbach.' I wish you could have met him. He had more to do with the spirit of Jack Kerouac than all the Beat Mystique that ever existed."

"But I've seen Beatniks on TV. I saw Maynard G. Krebs on reruns of the old Doby Gillis show."

"They were actors, Ted. They were just doing their job, but the characters they were playing were built from stereotypes. None of us acted like that."

"Then how am I ever going to meet beautiful girls and famous models?" he said, looking crestfallen. "I'm the shortest kid in my tenth grade class. I'm overweight and wear glasses and other kids make fun of me. Katy's my only friend, and she's a foot taller than me. All the kids at school think I'm different from them. Can I read you a poem?"

"Sure," I said. "I'd like to hear it."

Ted took a neatly folded pack of papers from his pocket and read his poem. It was honest and touching, describing how he felt lonely and misunderstood, and how the clouds he saw moving over a Kentucky night were floating towards a place he had never been, and wanted to see.

"How was that?" he said.

"Great," I said. "That was you. That was all about how *you* felt."

"I can't finish it," he said. "I got stuck."

"Just continue the story," I said. "Talk about where the clouds might be going. Talk about following the clouds out of the picture frame of your mind, and follow them wherever they lead you. Put yourself and the reader up there in those clouds and tell us how we appear below. Just let your mind be free to travel to distant places and we'll be traveling right along with you. We'll be each other's roadies on those trips. That's what Jack did as a writer and what he did when we hung out together and shared each other's stories."

"How could you guys make up stuff on the spot? Did you plan all those things you did at those readings?"

"No," I said. "Whenever we got together, whether there was an audience or just us, we did whatever we felt we wanted to share. We always listened to each other. Just like I'm listening to you. We always tried to encourage each other to continue whatever it was we were working on, or wanted to work on at that moment. Just like I'm doing with you now."

"So what you're saying is I can be a poet and writer someday?"

"You already are," I said. "You just read me a poem you wrote.

You don't have to become a Beatnik. You don't have to leave Louisville. Come on later tonight to the Insomniacathon and read what you read me now and I'll back you up on piano and double D pennywhistle. Ron Whitehead can help you. He's a master poet and he has that same inclusive spirit that Kerouac had. You'll meet other young writers and musicians. You'll be starting your journey. Some young musician will hear you, and you'll inspire him to back you up, and to start reading himself. We're all put here to inspire each other. That's what Jack did. Through his work, he's still doing it today."

We finished eating and walked back to the Insomniacathon. At about 11:30, the poet Ed Sanders gave a reading of some of his exciting new work, and sang an exquisite song he had composed, accompanying himself on a miniature dulcimer strapped from his shoulder.

New Yorker Steve Dalichinsky read some of his short incisive moving poetry. His Brooklyn-flavored intonation was musical and gave all the young people in Louisville a glimpse of the beauty of New York's streets. In his way, Steve was showing everybody in Louisville, through the eloquence of his poetry, the luster of New York's own hidden diamonds in the sidewalk.

I was then introduced again and played music from around the world, and made up a spontaneous blues song with rhymes about meeting Katy and her young friend Ted a few hours earlier, and how we had gone out to eat, and all the things we had talked about.

Then I introduced Ted to read his poem. I adjusted the mike so that he would be able to speak directly into it.

"Take your time," I whispered. "There's no rush. Let everybody hear every beautiful word you wrote."

I turned to the audience. "Ladies and gentlemen," I said. "The little rap song I just made up never would have happened if what happened to make it possible to happen hadn't happened. Here is the young man responsible for the happenings. Jack used to always tell young writers that their questions to him would provide the answers to a lot of things in their life because searching for answers was in itself a path and a road toward understanding and sharing the spirit. People used to freak out because they wanted to be *told* what to do by him. He would always say, over and over again, that they had to find out for themselves in their own way by asking *anybody* and *everybody*.

"So after we hear Ted read his poem for the first time, please come up and ask him about it. So now, ladies and gentlemen, after hearing music from Cairo, Egypt, the Khyber Pass, which connects Pakistan to Afghanistan, a Lakota round dance melody from South Dakota, and a blues I just made up from the remaining brain cells of my once-promising mind, we're going to hear a new work from your own hometown of Louisville.

"Let's give a warm Abraham Lincoln rail-splitter Kentucky Derby mint julep Insomniac late-night early morning Southern welcome to that sentimental gentleman of swing and a poet, donchya know it, Louisville's own native son, the fabulous Mr. *Ted*!"

The bemused chuckles from the audience were accompanied by applause and enthusiastic rebel yells. I saw Ted's face change, and instead of being petrified, his eyes became clear. He stood up straight and for the first time that evening, he was smiling.

"Thank you, thank you, everybody. David used to play for Jack Kerouac. Now he's playing for me. I'm going to read you my new poem. Okay, David, take it away."

He sounded like an old Borscht belt summer program director, trapped in a fifteen-year-old's body. I started playing an ethereal high-register Chopinesque melody on the piano and Ted began reading. I flashed back forty-five years to a BYOB party at a loft in lower Manhattan, when Jack, after blowing everybody away with a reading of a still-unpublished portion of *On the Road*, invited a shy young painter to read her tribute to her grandmother who, in the poem, told her to dare to go for it and be an artist, and still love all the rest of her family who were constantly putting her down for daring to dream. After she completed reading her poem, he put his right arm over her shoulder like a big brother, and lifted her left arm up in the air as if she were a newly crowned world champion athlete acknowledging the thunderous applause of thousands of people in some distant stadium.

I remembered Jack smiling at her and telling her she was touched by angels. Ted was reading up a storm. He was transformed from a confused kid into a poet-performer young man. He finished his poem, which was much longer than the version he read in the restaurant, as he had included a lot of ad libs. There was a burst of applause and more rebel yells. He finally raised his hands.

"Thank you, thank you. That's the first and only poem so far from me. But I've got more to come."

Turning to me, his face flushed with happiness, he said, "Let's have a hand for my accompanist, David Ambranze . . . . Take a bow, David."

He walked off the little bandstand into the audience and Katy gave him a bear hug and kissed the top of his head. Other young men and women came up to him and congratulated him. Ted was beaming.

Ron Whitehead came up to me. "That was incredible, David," he said. "I've seen that kid at our events and he never said a word to anyone, except Katy. It's like he's discovered himself and his own worth."

"That's the job of the older cats," I said. "To take that holy moly out of the penitentiary and release it from its cell where it's been being pickled in bottles of formaldehyde. We have to grant creativity a presidential pardon and release the spirit from the maximum security prison of exclusivity."

"Don't go away," said Ron. "You're on again in an hour. See if you can round up some new talent to join you. We can't get enough of that holy moly."

An hour later I was ready for my next concert. I invited two musicians, both my own age, a tuba player and tenor sax player I met in the lobby, to join me in a mini-jam session. They were there to see younger members of their families participate in the Insomniacathon. I rapped with them for a few minutes, and found out they had a Dixieland band in Louisville and had just finished playing a concert.

"We'll play a blues in F and I'll make up a whole bunch of words about meeting you in the lobby and what it's like being in Louisville again, and meeting baseball immortal Pee Wee Reese and his wife and son Mark in Louisville when I was here to honor Hunter S. Thompson, and having my saxophone concerto recorded here by the Louisville symphony in the '80s."

"Have you got all that written down?" asked the tenor sax player.

"No," I said. "I just thought of it, and maybe I'll do something else, but the three of us together, all seventy years or older, can't go wrong. We'll show the kids three seventy-year-olds can give them more fun than paying sixty dollars to watch a group of musicians forced to play what they themselves can't stand. We'll sock it to 'em. What an ensemble! Tuba, tenor sax, and the remains of a French hornist, doubling on everything else I brought with me. Just the three of us. Big bands are back!"

"Well this sounds like too much fun to pass on," said the tenor sax player. "I'm ready to hit."

"I'm getting my horn," said the tuba player. "Wait until my grandkids hear this. What a gas. Big bands are back."

They left the lobby, went to their car, and returned with their instruments. I gave them a thumbnail sketch of what other tunes we'd play in addition to my made-up song, and we walked out on stage and played for about an hour. The younger members of the audience were transfixed, seeing three older men obviously having fun making music together for the first time. The musicians played their hearts out and were surrounded by everyone in the audience afterward.

"I didn't know you did that kind of stuff, Grandpa," said one of the younger kids as he hugged the pant leg of the tuba player.

"I didn't know I did, either, Bubba. But we did it," said the tuba player, picking his grandson off the ground and giving him a bear hug.

I went back with Ron to his place at about 2 A.M. and after we talked about the next day's program where I would introduce *Pull My Daisy* and *Lowell Blues*, two films I had worked on about Jack, Ron said, "What you and Jack started in those first jazz-poetry readings in New York City in 1957 has become a major influence."

"It just happened naturally," I said. "It would have happened anyway. We all need each other."

"Acknowledging the need and fulfilling that need in the right spirit makes all the months of work worth the effort," said Ron. "When you see these young kids discover that special part of themselves they never knew was there, and are able to share it with kids their own age and younger and bring their parents along to check it all out, well, that's what it's all about."

"That's what you and the Insomniacathon are all about," I said. "Meeting that need. Creating a loving space and a happy home for that spirit. Keeping it down-home and for real. In the spirit of Jack."

Jack in Northport: Off the Beaten Path

July 22, 2001, was a banner day for Jack and his novel *Big Sur*. A poet, journalist, historian, and visionary, George Wallace had the idea of multi-city marathon readings of *Big Sur*, all to occur on the same day. George was a native of Long Island and the curator of the Northport Historical Society. A year earlier on July 9, 2000, he had organized a tribute to Jack and the happy years he had spent in Northport.

Jack's old drinking buddy, the prolific and highly respected artist Stanley Twardowicz, spoke to an enthusiastic audience of young people about what it was like knowing Jack as a friend as well as a great writer. An old friend and neighbor described endless hours spent with Jack in Northport and how Jack was constantly trying to deal with the chaos of unwanted stardom and the sense of betrayal he felt from some of his old friends. Smith and other residents of Northport who had been Jack's friends reminisced about the Northport years. They spoke of Jack as a person, not a celebrity.

My daughter Adira, then nineteen years old, read selections of Jack's work with a trio of musicians: drummer Kevin Twigg, bassist John deWitt, and myself. We accompanied Adira's readings from five of the timeless passages from *On the Road* that Jack and I used to do all the time at loft parties, park benches, coffeehouses, Lucien Carr's apartment, and 4 A.M. impromptu, unsolicited, and often unappreciated spontaneous commotion-making sessions at the end of a party that would often either quiet the remaining guests or force them to leave. We did it whenever the spirit moved us, before *On the Road* was published in 1956 and for years after we did our last public performances in 1958. We had never performed together publicly in Northport. Now it felt like we were finally doing it, as I played with our trio and heard his words fill the room. You could feel the audience sensing Jack's presence, hearing the music of his prose read aloud, accompanied by music that complemented the images and characters he described in his unique poetic style.

Adira read with grace and dignity and humor. I felt it would have made Jack as proud of her as she made me proud to be her father. Adira and many of her friends I met through her and my other two kids, Alana and Adam, were part of a new generation that related to Jack's work in a fresh and personal way. They did not associate him in any way with the TV show Dobie Gillis character Maynard G. Krebs. They did not wear berets, dark glasses with no rims, paste-on goatees, and they did not restrict their conversations to ". . . like . . . well . . . crazy, man . . . like . . . you dig?" They also sensed that none of us had done so, either. For one thing, they *read Jack's books* and based their impressions of what our era was like from the works of Kerouac the author, just as the young musicians among them now saw Charlie Parker, Monk, Dizzy, Miles, and Bud Powell as extraordinary musicians who chose each note as exquisitely as Kerouac chose each word.

I shared reminiscences with the audience, as Stanley had done, about what the whole artistic atmosphere of the 1950s was like to be a part of, and what Jack and many of us had done together during those years. Our trio also played music that Jack and I were mutually interested in . . . classics of jazz, my own compositions, Native American, Latin American, French-Canadian, African and Irish folk music, all of which is now collectively labeled as world music.

Thirty-six years after Jack had moved to Northport, many residences of the town and surrounding communities were finding out for the first time that Jack had lived there for six years. They also learned that some of his most important work was done in this small hamlet that reminded him so much of Lowell.

The exhibition featured photographs, letters, and articles that were assembled with care and taste. Walking through the museum enabled you to get an authentic pictorial retrospective of Jack's life in Northport. Reading the letters and seeing the photographs was like a collage that summed up the period of transition from the end of the '50s to the early 1960s. We were informed a few months later that there had never been so many people visiting the museum as during the run of this show.

Our opening day presentation was videoed by MetroChannel, a subsidiary of PBS national television network. It was scheduled to run for a few performances for one week. It ran for several months throughout New York, New Jersey, and Connecticut. Another undocumented chapter in Jack's life was being reported. This chapter was being written by primary sources, people from all walks of life who had known Jack, and the story was enhanced by others whose lives had been touched in some way by his work as an artist.

Our 2000 opening day presentation was such a joyous event no one wanted to leave or have it end. After our last musical selection, I thanked the audience on behalf of so many of our generation who were no longer here. I also publicly thanked George Wallace and his devoted staff. I told George Wallace and the audience what Jack had told me when he decided to buy a house with the money he had received from *On the Road,* and move to Northport.

"Davey, the town reminds me of Lowell. We'll have a home. My mother will never have to work in a factory again in her life."

The success and interest generated by the 2000 exhibition gave George Wallace the idea of having a marathon reading of *Big Sur* in 2001. I put him in touch with Marty Cummins, who was one of the founders of the Kerouac Writers' Residence in Orlando, Florida. The members of the board in Orlando were enthusiastic and assembled a group of readers. I also put him in touch with John Sampas, Jack's brother-in-law and the executor of Jack's estate. I told George about Lowell Celebrates Kerouac!, the annual weekend festival each October where people come from all over the world for workshops, readings, tours of Lowell and Nashua,

New Hampshire—nonstop events, done in a soulful, down-home way, that reflect Jack's egalitarian, unpretentious, inclusive nature.

The organizers of Lowell Celebrates Kerouac! also joined forces to present a simultaneous reading of *Big Sur* in the towns of Northport and Orlando. George contacted poets he knew in San Francisco and they joined us as well. I wrote Carolyn Cassady in England, and she and her son John, now living in California, both agreed to come to Northport. Carolyn and I were the honorary co-chairs of the event, and I was invited by the Huntington Arts Council to give a "From Cairo to Kerouac" concert with my quartet in the evening of July 22, 2001, following our seven-hour reading of *Big Sur*.

For the Northport reading, George asked poets, authors, actors, painters, and people of all professions to each read a chapter. The readers included Carolyn Cassady and her son John Cassady, the keeper of the flame of Neal's legacy. Adira and I both read. Actors John Ventimiglia of *The Sopranos*, who had played Kerouac in Joyce Johnson's play, *Doors Wide Open*, and Tony Torn, who directed and acted in Joyce's play, both read brilliantly. Artist-poets China Blue, Casey Cyr, and Susan Bennett gave lyrical readings. Poet-actor George Dickerson, known for his role in *Blue Velvet*, gave a spellbinding reading. Building contractor–master carpenter Jason Eisenberg, the foremost interpreter of Lord Buckley, gave a joyous performance. George Wallace and a host of Long Island poets read with skill and grace. Poets Paul McDonald and Charles Newman came all the way from Louisville, Kentucky, to bring the lyrical sounds of the South, reading with skill and passion. Northport poet Kate Kelly brought sparkle and youthful energy to the event. Actors Michelle Esrick and Peter Garrity used their masterful theatrical skills to bring Jack's work to life. Drummer Kevin Twigg and bassist John deWitt and I played for the entire seven hours except during an hour when I had to drive like a maniac to Huntington, a few miles away, set up all my instruments at the Harry Chapin Rainbow Stage, and race back to Northport to play for a belly dancer who was also a classical concert pianist. Zoe Artemis, poet/world traveler, also did some belly dancing earlier during the readings. I then raced back to Huntington and arrived at the stage at 8:27 P.M., three minutes before our Heksher Park free concert was to begin. There were three thousand people in the audience, waiting to hear our quartet.

"Well, Maestro, I'm glad you showed up for the gig," said saxophonist Jerry Dodgion. "Now that we're finally drawing audiences that outnumber the band, we can enjoy being overnight successes for the three hundredth time."

I was tired after our seven-hour reading, but my mind was stimulated by creating new music on the spot for each of Kerouac's chapters of *Big Sur*. Now that it was time to play our three-hour concert, I got that rush of spirit-energy I used to get when I collaborated with Jack. After we played for forty minutes, we presented five short readings from *On the Road*. Our readers were Carolyn Cassady, her son John, my daughter Adira, John Ventimiglia, and George Wallace. Carolyn read in a way that got all three thousand people to feel they were in a room with her. Still gorgeous in her mid-seventies, her elegance and grace filled the stage, and the young people in the front rows sat in awe as she spoke about Jack and Neal and herself before reading her selected passage from *On the Road*. Carolyn needed no bombast, bluster, press agents, bodyguards, or interpreters to let everybody and anybody know who she was and what she was about. Her natural radiance and youthful spirit poured out and the whole audience was lifted by her presence as well as her performance.

John read with his father's joyous energy and warmth. John's keen intelligence was like medicine to all of us who spent most of our lives wading through the Beatnik sleaze-pit foisted upon our society by people who didn't have a clue about what we were doing back then and are still doing today.

John Ventimiglia read the thrilling description of Jack and Neal going to hear George Shearing play. John Ventimiglia sounded so much like Jack that the audience stood up and cheered after his reading.

Adira read one of the passages that Jack and I used to perform together before and after *On the Road* came out. I used to call it

"Children of the American Bop Night" and Jack liked that as an introductory title, even though it was the last line of the passage. It described the history of jazz and the generations of musicians and listeners. Adira's performance was mesmerizing. Her youthful exuberance combined with her uncanny understanding of Jack's musical way of writing was another milestone for her as a young performer.

George Wallace then read the epic last two pages of *On the Road* with great feeling, savoring each word and creating enough space to allow the audience to feel that they were part of a congregation.

Later that evening as we sat around talking in George's house, Carolyn said, "I have so much correspondence from young people all over the world. They've read *Off the Road*. They want to know about Jack and Neal as they really were. I try to answer them all and talk to them. I try to explain that Jack and Neal were almost Victorian in their manners and the way they behaved around me. They were really courtly. They were such gentlemen. What they did away from me was something else. Many of the people who have written about them have come to me and asked me to make corrections in case some of their information was inaccurate. I always give all of them huge amounts of corrections. When I read the books after they're published, all of the misinformation is still there, even when I am acknowledged by the authors for helping them. They are simply making most of it up. I can't understand it."

"I can," I said. "If they don't get to primary sources from all walks of life, and they don't read Jack's books carefully, how can they possibly understand what it was and still is all about?"

"I know," said Carolyn. "Jack wrote about Slim Gailliard. He and Neal and I loved to go to hear him. He was so brilliant. He spoke seventeen languages. I saw him again in England. He knew so much and was such a part of it all. Why didn't people interview him extensively or write a book about him? Why wasn't he or Dizzy Gillespie ever interviewed in depth about Jack? That's why I'm so happy that John was invited here. No one understands Neal either. They portray him as a semi-literate car thief and leave it at that. They don't seem interested in the intellectual stimulation he and Jack gave one another. It seems that literary people can't acknowledge or even comprehend how brilliant and well read they both were. How we used to sit and recite Shakespeare plays at our house with the three of us playing all of the roles."

"That's so true," said John. "And we had so much fun. For all his wild ways, Neal was such a great dad. He really loved his family."

"That's the part of the equation I've found missing," I said. "There's been a lot of grim judgmental scowls and negativity when people write about us. But whatever our shortcomings, we were all, in our own way, purveyors of joy, energy, hope, and sharing. We didn't whine and put down others, but searched for moments of beauty. We dug every precious moment of life."

"I don't know how you and Jack did it way back then," said John. "But I can feel it now when I read with you. You really listen. It's like you're talking back to me as I read, like a conversation. And tomorrow when this is all over, you can go compose a symphony or concerto, with every note written out, or go the day after one of these readings and conduct a symphony orchestra."

"It's all part of the same thing," I said. "It's about opening your mind and heart and *listening*."

"And spontaneity and formality," said Adira, chuckling. "I've got your whole rap down, Daddy. Whenever you get off your soapbox, I have your twenty-seven-hour prepared statement to the world ready to be delivered."

"In that case, let's all have one of our multilingual toasts to Jack and each other, and get some new material," I said. "Let's go play some music."

George Wallace, John, Carolyn, Adira, and George's beautiful and gracious wife, Peg, went from the outside deck into the living room, and I sat down at the piano. I made up a song with rhymes on the spot about when I worked as a carpenter's helper in Palo Alto and Los Gatos in the summer of 1948, so close to where the Cassadys lived, although I didn't know it at the time. I sang about how, in that summer of 1948, I visited North Beach before it became a mecca, and how all of us were here now bringing the Then to Now to a new beginning in the town where Jack and the fabled

Adolph the clammer would carouse till dawn, and what it was like to hitchhike back east in the summer of 1948.

Then John joined me playing four-hand piano and George sat down at the piano and played as well. Carolyn and Adira were giving us occasional encouraging comments or simply laughing, and at 1 A.M. all time was suspended and we could have been any place in the world in any year. As so many people have done since the beginning of time, we were sharing precious moments together, liberated from the tyranny of TV, canasta, small talk, blasting radios and CD players, simply having fun and celebrating our friendship and memories of Jack.

"Good God, Amram, you've been playing ten hours already today, which at 1:30 A.M. is now yesterday," said Jason Eisenberg. "Even Lord Buckley took a break once in a while. Don't you ever get tired?"

"All the time," I said. "But getting tired shouldn't stop you from pursuing that great New Orleans philosophical principle of survival. *Laissez le bon temps rouler*."

"Let the good times roll," said Jason. "Lord Buckley couldn't have said it better himself. I remember after your house burned down and I came to help you work one day. We put in twelve hours nonstop. You are a severe taskmaster, but we sure had fun."

"That's so important," said Carolyn. "The understanding that hard work in and out of the arts can be joyful. We've got to show these kids that there's something meaningful out there. This was so much a part of Jack and Neal's message."

"It's changing, David," said Jason. "During the time I've been involved in all this, I see the change. Since I live so near Lowell, I see the change there. All of New England is now in the process of adopting Jack as their native son, the way they did with Robert Frost. The way they're starting to with poet Robert Creeley. It's changing. The misconception that three people sat in a room and invented the Beat Generation is preposterous and now is no longer accepted, because these kids are reading Jack's books, or Joyce Johnson or Carolyn's books . . . written by people who actually knew him. *Atop the Underwood*, by Paul Marion, collections of the early writings of Jack in Lowell, shows he would have been just as great a writer even if he never came to New York. That's obvious."

"I've been saying that for years," I said. "All of us who got to know him in New York were *lucky*. Everybody influences everybody, but Jack was the giant of his time. His main influence was Neal Cassady. *On the Road* wasn't written about wandering around New York City. And his other many influences as he told me time and time again were Baudelaire, Céline, Rimbaud, Thomas Wolfe, Walt Whitman, Langston Hughes, Herman Melville, Charlie Parker, Dizzy Gillespie, John Dos Passos, Buddha, Carson McCullers, Bach, Slim Gailliard, and an army of musicians, painters, poets, working people . . ."

We continued talking. None of us could bear the thought that this day had to end. I had a concert to play in sixteen hours. Carolyn had to fly back to London. Jason had to drive back to New England for a construction job. Adira, Alana, and Adam all had to go home and go to work. George and his wife hadn't slept in a week. We all agreed that the special spirit of this event gave back to us more than we could ever give to it. We felt fulfilled. The common spirit we shared with Jack was enriching and nurturing.

New Millennium Blues: New Vistas, Final Thoughts, and Fond Farewells

As the twentieth century tottered to a close amid reports of impending catastrophes due to global computer crashes, which fortunately never occurred, lists were made up of some of the twentieth-century B.C. (before computers) achievements.

Some of the milestones in the arts read like scorecards, compiled by lists of anonymous experts. These mysterious experts included work that Jack and I had done together. Although no statuettes were presented, *Pull My Daisy* was included as one of the best documentary short subjects of the century. I called up Alfred Leslie to congratulate him and left a message on Robert Frank's answering machine. Lenny Gross called me up.

"Amram, you've arrived. I told you in 1959 that you should give up everything and launch a film career. You could be another Arnold Schwarzenegger, with more hair and less muscles. You could star in the new film being made about Genghis Khan. Go to the gym and get in shape. Go get some headshots. You've arrived. You're an overnight cinematic success."

"Well, Lenny," I said. "At least I don't have to ever feel guilty that I was overpaid for my nonperformance in *Pull My Daisy*. I'm still waiting for my $58.28."

"Well, you used to work in the post office," said Lenny. "You know how much volume there is in the mailrooms in New York. It's only forty-two years. Don't be in a rush. I have a feeling the check is in the mail."

"After this award, the next time Alfred and Robert have me in one of their films, I'm going to ask for a raise," I said. "Now that we're among the century's best, it's time to move on up."

"Judging from your acting performance, Amram, I'd say you should demand at least five dollars an hour and be able to keep your costume, or at least have it dry cleaned after the filming. Congratulations, Bubbalah. Don't let cinematic success go to your head. Do you think the soundtrack with Jack's narration and your music will finally come out? All the bootleg copies sound terrible."

"I know," I said. "Jack always tried to get them to put it out when he was alive. Several companies are interested in doing it now. It should finally be out by the end of 2002."

We talked for a while about how the perception of Jack and his work was finally changing.

"What you guys did that night in 1958 at Brooklyn College changed my life," said Lenny. "I always wanted to be a writer. I was serious, even at seventeen, but felt I couldn't possibly ever dare to try to be something I was brought up to know I could never be. After I heard your reading, and hung out all night with you and Jack, I knew I could do it. You both made me feel I could do anything if I wanted it badly enough. I tried to tell that to Jack, the last time I visited him in Northport. I reminded him of how much that night meant to me. I could tell he felt uncomfortable being praised. He never wanted to be complimented. 'I know you love my books, Lenny,' he told me. 'So I know you love me.' Now I've got some news for you, Amram. A dear friend of mine found out through the grapevine that in a few days there will be an announcement of the hundred best novels of the twentieth century. *On the Road* will be one of them."

"*Fantissimo*!" I said. "I've got some news for you. There's going to be a listing of the best feature films of the twentieth century and *Manchurian Candidate* is listed as one of them."

"I'm not surprised," said Lenny. "Your score was fantastic. I knew when I met you in 1958 that you'd become a one-man corporate entity. You're still an up-and-coming young composer. I want to go back and see the movie again."

"It was finally rereleased a few years ago, and it's on video now," I said. "Jack and composer Gil Evans were the only two people in the world who ever heard the entire soundtrack in its entirety. I sent them both reel-to-reel copies in 1963. Now everybody can hear it, including parts that were cut out."

"That's great, Davey. But why did it take so long? Couldn't they speed things up a little? Why did they have to wait for Jack to die before they published *Visions of Cody*? Why did it take forty years before a video VHS of *Pull My Daisy* came out? Before you answer me with one of your mega-raps, I'm going to turn on my tape recorder and get your answer. You can transcribe it later for your book or one of your presentations. OK, it's turned on. Testing, testing . . . Now tell me, Mr. Amram, why did it take forty years for so much of what you've been involved with to surface?"

"The same reason that Charlie Parker, Bartok, Jack himself, and so many others had to wait until they died," I said.

"Reason number one. Most people are unaware of what's happening at the moment and they're unable to accept the unfamiliar. As a result, we're always presented with repackaged versions that are watered down from the original. Then eventually, the original gets discovered.

"Reason number two. We're a necrophiliac culture. Dying is considered a brilliant career move. It's nuts. I tell kids: 'Ride a bike. Eat vegetables. Think positive thoughts. Count your blessings. Enjoy each moment. Live to be *old*! Longevity is the artist's best revenge.'

"If you get bitter, you've had it. If you get jealous of others who seem to have more for the moment, you're already ordering your own coffin. You've got to appreciate each other's work. Jack never put down another writer. When I boxed, you would always hug your opponent after the fight was over. Often you became friends. Our competitive society is largely responsible for the outrageous level of alcoholism, drug abuse, failed marriages, dysfunctional families, and pervasive sense of loneliness I see in so many people's faces. Here in this gorgeous country where we have so much, and enjoy so little, we've forgotten how to love each other.

"Jack and I always *supported* each other in everything we did. We were our own floating twelve-step program, even though the term didn't exist back then. It was a spontaneous, day-to-day homemade one that changed each day. It was really more of a do-it-yourself survivalist-style energy booster. It kept us fired up and reminded us that we should never give up.

"We were so concerned about trying to be real artists that we never gave a thought to our health. We were all so strong and determined and full of endless energy and ideas that we took it for granted that we would live forever no matter what we did to ourselves.

"We were fighting for our moment in the sun, trying to break out of the prison we felt we were assigned to. We felt that even the most successful artists in America were in someone else's jail. No one ever suggested we should be battling alcoholism or drug addiction. That's one of the reasons so many of us succumbed to it. We didn't even know those were diseases back then. We were already rebelling against all the negativity and hoping for a way out of our incarceration through what we did. We were battling selfishness, narcissism, greed, racism, and the self-loathing most of us were told we deserved. Today if we were killing ourselves with drinking and drugging, friends would tell us to cool out immediately or get help. But we were stupid. We thought it was natural that so many of us faded away because of our own self-destruction.

"A lot of our generation was done in by the negativity that was like a dark cloud following the triumph of World War II. But some of us refused to give up, and found ways to sidestep or ignore all that negativity. Instead of feeling sorry for ourselves, getting high twenty-four hours a day and spending our lives whining and blaming others, we worked even harder. We hung out with people who were searching out what was beautiful and practiced sharing love and compassion. Jack not only talked and wrote about this way of living his life, he practiced it. You know that, Lenny, because you knew him. He was warm and open to everybody. He didn't play the game. And he paid a price.

"He was like Mickey Mantle, the great baseball player. His willpower and desire to achieve his goals was so strong that his body couldn't handle it. Just like Mantle, playing on bad knees, in pain. They both tried to kill their pain with drinking. Drinking back then was considered a virtue. The better you could hold your liquor, the more of a man you were. My kids and their generation know better. They know that getting juiced doesn't kill the pain, it kills *you*. Jack and Mickey Mantle were both proud and compassionate people whose spirit demanded more than their bodies could handle. And they were both shy and modest, not cut out or trained to become public figures.

"Their achievements will always be part of our century's history. What a drag they're not here to see how much people love and respect what they left for us. Jack would have loved to know that *On the Road* was chosen as one of the one hundred best books of the century. If he were still alive and was interviewed by those who chose his novel to be honored, he would probably give a shy wave with his hand as a gesture of thanks, and mutter, '*Merci, mais ça suffit*' (Thanks, but that's enough). He would then tell the judges the names of a hundred great writers whose books *weren't* chosen, and would encourage the judges to read them. And he would give the judges the names of the publishers of each book he felt they should read. If Jack had time to spend with any of the judges during the course of the evening, he would most likely suggest a thousand or more books they should either discover or reread.

"Jack never compared himself to another writer. And he always tried to turn you on to the work of others. He would say 'You can't compare one gifted and sincere writer to another, any more than you can compare Jesus to Buddha or Mohammed to Moses. You could compare my statistics when I was playing football to those of my teammates who were playing the same position. You could compare me to my counterpart on my opponent's team, but in my writing, it's only what I write and who reads it that matters. I'm not in competition with other writers. I'm not in competition with myself. Each book is a song of its own, all part of one great Mahleresque symphony.

" 'When I was out at sea reading in my hammock, and writing when all my shipmates were sleeping, no one was keeping score.

As long as my critics can't make me stop writing, it really doesn't matter. They're like hit men, paid to assassinate. As long as they don't kill my readers, I will continue on my path. They may hurt my feelings, but they will never kill my desire to write, or my ability to do so, because that comes from God.

" 'They may dismiss me, but I won't ever dismiss myself. I'm an *author*, Davey. I'm a *writer*. I wonder if they even read my books all the way through, before tearing them to shreds, or ignoring them. Why are they so jealous? Can't they read? Why do they dismiss my work when so many readers love what I've written?' "

"Well, David," said Lenny. "It's good to know you're still a man of few words. I'm going to get ready to go up to my place in Oneonta with the kids to bring in the new millennium, and turn on my computer and see if cyberspace is still there. I'll see and talk to you in the next century."

"You know it, Lenny," I said. "We'll have a hundred years to get everything cooled out that went wrong in the last one. As Dizzy used to say, we'll 'put some new ingredients into the pot.' "

On New Year's Eve our whole family got together at Michele Berdy's house down the road from our farm. We all played music together and John Cohen, who was the still photographer for *Pull My Daisy*, was there, playing his banjo and guitar. He lived a mile from us.

While we all sat in a circle playing music, I thought about what was now the last century, and what those of us who were overlapping centuries had to do in this brand-new millennium. As we played old folk songs, I thought about what this new century would bring to my own three children and eventually to their children and their children's children. Miraculously, it seemed that our time so long ago had now arrived, and those of us who remained primary sources had an increasing obligation, whether we liked it or not, to clarify to others what we had all shared, each from our own personal perspective.

Even those of us in music, who would never dare to pass judgment on works of literature, were certain that Jack's work was never going to be dismissed again. Books like *Some of the Dharma* were recently published for the first time. Archival recordings of readings were finally being released for the first time. Jack's journals were going to be published and made available for the first time. He was now clearly viewed by a new generation of scholars as the engine that pulled the train. He seemed to be everywhere. Jack was right *now.* His presence was felt by a worldwide audience. At the dawn of this new millennium, more than twenty of his books were in print and more due to be published, in many languages all over the world. Artists in all fields were inspired by him. This shared inspiration came from reading his books.

"By your works ye shall be known," we used to tell each other during the course of endless conversations, as a reaffirmation of why we should never stop creating, no matter what setbacks occurred in our lives.

Ninety-nine percent of the great performances, conversations, shared ideas, words of advice, and moments of tenderness and compassion that we all shared were no longer with us. They were of the moment. Only the precious one percent of what had been written down, recorded, filmed, or accurately reported remained. That precious one percent was emblematic of our motto "By your works ye shall be known." What still remained to enrich our lives all these years later reminded me of the messenger in the Book of Job when he said "I alone am escaped to tell thee."

Jack was that messenger. Jack was our reporter. He escaped to tell us. By his works he now *was* known. His brakeman's shining lantern from his railroading days was still shedding light on a whole era, and shedding light on all of us as well. We were now in many ways the beneficiaries of his triumph over the neglect, misinterpretation, and pain that he endured. He was being set free at last, pardoned from a life sentence in the penitentiary of the Beat Generation. He was now viewed as Jack Kerouac, prolific author of over twenty published books you would like to share with all your friends. A long time ago, he had set up a mirror for America to see itself, and that reflection was now being seen for all of its true beauty. The light that he shed, and the reflection he cast, was helping the whole world to see those diamonds in the sidewalk that were the precious stones of our everyday life. Through his vision, we could see and take part in the beauty that surrounded us.

Like Walt Whitman's immortal lines in *Leaves of Grass*: "Take my leaves America . . . ," Jack had shared and spread his message. By a lifetime of documenting his own journey and spiritual quest, he had raised the spirits of people from every walk of life. Anyone reading his books felt that they were now able to pursue their own secret dreams in some way. He made his readers feel that they were all on their own road and that creating from your own experiences would always have a special meaning.

At the dawn of this new millenium, Jack's books were now like a sweet song in the early morning sunrise of a distant bird in flight, like Charlie 'Bird" Parker himself telling us through his music that we would make it through the night and the days to come. By his inclusive nature and appetite for experiences and knowledge, Jack personified through his writing the golden part of our era—those gifts that we all shared. We knew that the support we received from our elders was *our* Montezuma's buried treasure. It was our hidden gold, and a source for strength that nurtured all of us, and taught us to listen, to pay attention, to open up our minds and hearts and to appreciate one another.

"How beautiful to be playing music with a group of people who love it. What a great way to start the new millennium," I said to myself.

Jack understood, as all of us did, from the shared egalitarian environment of the late-night jam session, that each person blowing their solo was telling their own story in their own way. Even the cutting contest, where musicians would be inspired to new heights as they tried to blow each other off the bandstand, was really a good-natured dialogue and a sharing of ideas. It was about bringing out the greatness in you, not about who was the greatest.

As I watched the happy faces of everyone sitting in a circle and playing together, I hoped their serenading of this new millennium would be the harbinger of a new way of thinking about collaborating with one another, as Jack and I had done. I remembered those crazy nights in the '50s when everybody seemed in competition with everybody.

"Judge not that ye be not judged" would be thunderously pronounced by the lovable red-faced Greek artist Aristodemos Kaldis to Jack and me and all of us at the Cedar Tavern or a painter's loft party whenever any comparison of one artist to another took place:

"We are part of a continuum that goes back to ancient Greece. Your vitality in this young country of yours is intoxicating, but your immaturity is deplorable. You cannot compare oranges and apples. If you drank more of our modern-day Greek wine of the gods, *retsina,* instead of those terrible blended American whiskies, you would be closer to the ancient forces of the Hellenic civilization that made European culture and the New World possible. We were a nation of great playwrights, architects, sculptors, poets, and philosophers when you English-speaking people were living in caves. But . . . I am not judgmental or asking you to compare a person of English-speaking descent to a person like myself who is an heir to the Golden Age of Civilization. Comparing any one of you to me is impossible and unfair to you. That would be like trying to compare a child's tricycle to a chariot of the gods."

Aristodemos Kaldis's lack of modesty would usually precipitate a bigger argument than the one that occurred before Kaldis gave us his infomercial, but we loved his warmth, his lectures, and his personal style of painting. And after several *retsinas,* which he sometimes snuck into the Cedar Tavern in a bottle hidden inside his large coat, he would soar off into harangues worthy of the driver of one of those ancient Greek chariots. Kaldis told us that the athletic competitions in ancient Greece were also celebrations for the whole nation, and that our modern-day Olympics were a pale imitation of the original events that were viewed as a religious rite and huge weeklong party, almost like the Brazilian Carnival of a whole nation dancing together, rather than a "Who Is the Best Ego Fest."

Kaldis, along with so many other of our elders, made us understand that you shouldn't ever try to compare the relative merits of authors or poets, as if they were athletes competing against one another. We realized, by our proximity to seasoned artists like

Kaldis, that you could no more compare painters, poets, and architects to one another than you could compare whipped cream to Camembert cheese.

In the arts where interpretation of existing material is the cornerstone of creation, we understood that if thirty-five different actors played Hamlet, each actor would find his own truth in his own portrayal. All thirty-five of these actors shared one common goal. They were all, in their own way, trying to create a once-in-a-lifetime Hamlet, from their own bodies and psyches. Their fellow actors, the director, and the audience could choose which Hamlet touched them the most, but that had nothing to do with being best or worst. It had to do with how the people who judged each performance felt *themselves* about each experience. Shakespeare had already created Hamlet, so all thirty-five actors were starting their journey at the exact same point of departure. But what they did after that point of departure was unique for each performer. When comparing composers to one another, or authors to one another, we realized that we could only share our opinions and enthusiasm about special compositions or books that touched us. We could judge the creations, not the creators.

"Flaubert me no Flauberts," Thomas Wolfe wrote to F. Scott Fitzgerald. Wolfe knew he had his own voice. He wasn't trying to be an impersonator or a ventriloquist, and he felt that his work shouldn't be compared to the writing style of Flaubert, or anyone else.

Jack and I both knew that the relationship we had with our readers or listeners was crucial. Those readers or listeners had to become engaged in a dialogue with our work. If that dialogue didn't take place, they would close Jack's books or turn off their recordings of my music and turn on their TV set.

Jack used to always say that all he wanted was to tell a story and carry the reader along with him, the way Charlie Parker or Lester Young would improvise on a familiar song and take the listener to a new place. Jack also said to me and many others that the story of his life was a recounting of a great journey that was akin to a modern-day legend. All of his experiences were part of one huge lifelong novel, narrated by him. He wasn't interested in comparing himself to anybody. He never criticized other writers, and always encouraged budding authors, poets, musicians, and artists of all kinds because he felt that we were all doing God's work when we told our stories.

He often told me that writing was a form of confession, and that the deep spiritual gratification of the act of confession in church was akin to the expiation of all his feelings when he wrote. As a natural musician, he loved poetry as much as he loved prose and could let his mind soar along with the sounds of any poet whose work he was reading, and listen for the beauty.

I told Jack one night at the Cedar Tavern in 1959 how I was finally able to understand how he could hear and see the beauty in practically anything that occurred. I recounted to him the time I visited Thelonious Monk's apartment in the fall of 1955 when I was playing with Mingus. We both sat in silence for nearly an hour, while his radio was tuned into a country-and-western singer playing three chords, and moaning and groaning in a nasal near-monotone. It wasn't Jimmy Rogers, Patsy Cline, Tennessee Ernie Ford, or any of the hundreds of great country singers of the day who could captivate you immediately with their own individual soulfulness. It sounded like someone who was either related to the program director of the radio station we were listening to, or someone who had taken the station hostage. He was wheezing as if he had just finished loading up a barn full of hay.

I told Jack I never could figure out who that country singer was, but seeing Monk totally absorbed made me realize I had no right to be judgmental, and that perhaps, having just turned twenty-five, I should simply shut up and pay attention to what captivated him. After about an hour, I couldn't restrain myself.

"Thelonious," I said, "do you like that music?"

Monk sat motionless in silence. After about a minute, he said, "Listen to the drummer."

I told Jack that I almost fell off my chair when Monk said that. I began to listen as hard as I had ever consciously listened to anything in my life. I could hear, as faintly as the sound of a breeze blowing against a window, through the noise of distant traffic and occasional honking horns of a New York City afternoon, the sound of a drummer, muffled in tone.

I kept straining to hear the drum as the singer gasped and moaned,

"I don't know how,

They shot my cow . . . "

I focused all my energy on trying to hear that drummer who galvanized Monk's attention. Another song played. Toward the end of it, Monk slowly lifted his head and looked at me with his all-seeing gaze, and smiled.

"Check out his brush work."

I listened and sure enough, I was able to distinguish the sound of the drummer's subtle use of wire brushes on his high hat, ride cymbal, and snare drum, playing some original-sounding patterns, almost like a country version of Big Sid Cattlett, a master of the use of brushes in jazz drumming. I told Jack how Monk showed me how to listen and always look for the beauty, just as Jack himself had told me to look for the diamonds in the sidewalk.

"You have to listen," said Jack. "You always have to keep searching. The beauty is all around us. The Iroquois know about all of this. The Navajo prayer of the Twelfth Night addresses pursuing that trail of beauty by being on it.

"We are the messengers. We are telling our stories to inspire people to remember their own. I wish I could play a horn, Davey. Just be able to wail, in touch with the truth, no words, just pure truth. That's what the ancient Greek poets had in their work. And the Bible, in Latin, French, and English, is just like hearing God speak. Gregory knew this. He was brought up in the Church, too. When he went to jail, he read constantly. He understands the classic writers of Greece as well as Keats and Shelley and the poetry of the streets. He is a classicist, like Lamantia and Howard Hart, and he can swing. Phil Whalen and Creeley, Ferlinghetti and Dylan Thomas, Langston Hughes and William Carlos Williams . . . they're all like music. Gregory has that natural gift. Someday he'll be appreciated."

All of these memories played in my mind as I accompanied everyone in the room on my dumbek.

"Daddy, you look like you're totally spaced out," said Adira. "It's only 2 A.M. Don't tell me you're getting tired."

"No," I said. "I'm just going over the final playback of my own collection of The Greatest Hits of the Twentieth Century."

"We should be filming this," said John Cohen. "A rural upstate New York version of *Pull My Daisy*, fifty years later."

"We need Gregory here to be the leading man," I said.

I remembered again that winter in New York, January 1959, when we were making *Pull My Daisy*. Jack still had a real closeness to Gregory. Allen and Jack had differences as all friends do, and Allen, with his brilliant analytical mind, loved to argue loudly with everybody and deliver thunderous denunciations of society's inequities, almost like Leon Trotsky on speed, and often Jack would tune him out. I always enjoyed hearing Allen's tirades and would interrupt them by quoting Dylan Thomas' "rage, rage against the dying of the night," interrupting him until I could get him to burst out laughing or scream at me, which would then give Gregory a chance to shout at Allen.

When we all went to the Cedar Tavern, Allen and Gregory and many of us would have shouting arguments where we could scarcely hear each other. Since Allen was gifted with a huge voice that could fill a room when he really got enthusiastic or angry, Gregory developed a high-pitched braying sound, like a donkey, where he could occasionally provide an obligato to Allen's shouting by blasting out a Don Rickles–style series of comical insults about anybody present, including himself.

We always thought this was a good-humored way of letting off our mutual seemingly endless youthful energies, and were always surprised that some people found this behavior obnoxious. Jack was never comfortable when this kind of behavior occurred outside the confines of wherever he was staying. He never acted this way, nor did anyone else in the presence of his mother, who, contrary to so much of what was written about her, was a warm woman, with an endless love for Jack. She believed in good manners and demanded respect when you were in her home. I was brought up this way, and felt very comfortable with her. She did not care for Allen, which he found upsetting. But rather than thinking there might be some reason why she disliked him, he blamed her for disliking him. Even though Jack and Allen had slowly parted ways by the late '50s, Jack always had a soft spot in his heart for Gregory as we all did, and kept hoping that some sun would shine on his life, and that his star would ascend.

"He's a great lyric poet," Jack would say, sometimes muttering in my ear, so that Gregory wouldn't hear him.

"You're goddam right I am," Gregory would shout. "And I'm irresistible to women!"

Through the years, Gregory had good times and a lot of hard times. Those of us who knew him from the mid-fifties were his biggest cheering section. Once, at a big conference in 1994, where I had to play, speak, rap, accompany, and fill in for people who forgot to show up or were out in the hallway engaged in heated nonstop discussions, I took a breather during my two free hours before an afternoon concert of world music. My oldest daughter Alana, and my son, Adam, burst into our motel room, where I was lying down while copying some music I had written. They were at the auditorium, where Gregory was giving a reading and a talk. They both loved Gregory, as we all did.

"Daddy, you've got to hurry over to the auditorium right now. Gregory's been insulting you for ten minutes. He's so funny. He's hysterical! You'd love it!"

"That's a real compliment, Alana," I said. "It's like a roast that you see on TV when all the old comedians insult each other. It's a dying art form."

I rushed over, but by the time I got there, he was on another monologue, insulting all the great songwriters of the '60s that we all admired, beaming with a toothless devilish grin when a young person would look upset. When he was done, I went up on stage where he was talking to a group of high school-age kids who were showing him their poems. He talked to each one, read their poetry, made helpful comments and suggestions, and gave each of them encouragement.

"Well, Dave, you finally showed up. I saw your kids out there.

You missed it. You know all the poems of mine I read but you missed the zingers. I was really giving it to you, man. I got you good. You would have loved it!"

He turned to the kids who were still standing quietly, ready to show him more of their poetry or just hear him speak. "Do you know who this old guy is? He's Mezz McGillicuddy, a washed-up actor. He was in one movie called *Pull My Daisy*, in 1959. He hasn't been in a film since, or had another acting job. He's a one-shot total failure in show business. I was fabulous in the film. I still get fan mail from around the world, telling me how photogenic I am. Poor Mezz can't get a date. Even his dog feels sorry for him. These are two of Mezz's kids. He's lucky they look like his wife. He's got *three* kids. Planned Parenthood withdrew his membership. Look at him. He's ninety-three years old and still auditioning for a second movie role. We should take up a collection to get him a face-lift."

The high school kids looked stunned. My two kids burst into laughter. All the kids started laughing. Gregory threw his arm around me.

"We gotta show these kids how to stop taking themselves so seriously," he said. "Kids, don't take yourselves so seriously. Take what you *do* seriously. Stop watching TV and playing video games, and go to the library and read a book. Go to Mezz's concert this afternoon, if his respirator's hooked up, and learn to listen to something that's not coming out of a machine. Lemme see some more of those poems. Gregory has a high tolerance for pain. Maybe Mezz will back you up while you read one, the way he did for Kerouac, if you tip him a dollar."

"You can keep the dollar," I said. "I'd be happy to play for any of you, if you want to read with music, and I'm not scheduled to do anything else. That's why I'm here."

Gregory spent almost an hour, surrounded by teenage poets and authors, their parents, and anyone who happened to be there who wanted to talk to him.

"Dave, let's go out and eat, man. I'm burnt out."

My kids wanted to go back to the motel room and take a shower, and then meet us. We walked them to my room and then went to

Daddy Bruce's Barbecue to hang out with Daddy Bruce's son, who had an old upright piano and wanted me to show him different ways of voicing chords. Gregory and I both attacked some barbecue and talked.

"I get so tired of putting on an act," said Gregory. "I keep thinking of Jack and how he felt trapped by having to fulfill other people's expectations. He was supposed to be the King of the Beatniks. I guess I was supposed to be the Clown Prince. And you're supposed to be the Troubadour. Jesus Christ, man. Jack's one of the great literary innovators of the century. I know I'm a great lyric poet, a throwback to Keats and Shelley, and you write symphonies and operas and play all kinds of music . . . what do we have to do? At least you and Jack are now taken seriously. No one calls you a Beat composer or Beatnik musician or a Beat conductor. They still call me a Beat poet. Whadda bunch of crap." Gregory looked actually upset. "A bunch of *crap*!" He banged his fork on the table, and the succulent barbecue sauce speckled my old blue jacket, making it look like my blazer had caught measles.

"What's the trouble, Gregory? Is your barbecue too mild? I'll give you some more sauce," said Daddy Bruce's son.

"Nah," said Gregory. "The barbecue is great. It's just my life that's giving me problems."

Gregory continued talking about his role as the Clown Prince of Beat poetry.

"I get asked to do all these readings without getting paid very much. I don't want to read my poems once they're finished. I'm only interested in writing them. Once they're written and I know they're complete, they belong to the world. I'm done with them. I need the money. That's the only reason for me to leave the house. I don't want to do any more readings, unless I get paid well. I'm saying 'No' most of the time. Unless it's for Jack. If it's for Jack, I'll always do it. He deserves it. But this Beat Mythology trip is driving me crazy. Why don't they ask us, and get the facts straight? When they make an error about a scene I was part of, I tell them. Instead of thanking me for telling the truth, they get angry and they don't believe me, even when I get others who were there to back me up."

When we finished eating, Daddy Bruce's son came over and asked me to play some standards on the piano.

"You show me, and tomorrow bring your French horn and I'll play backup for you."

I played piano until my kids showed up and Gregory and I had second helpings as our kids wolfed down the secret recipe treasures of Daddy Bruce's grease-filled ecstasy barbecued chicken and ribs dinner. Even though I was a vegetarian most of the time, Daddy Bruce's barbecue canceled out all dietary restrictions.

In November of 1995 when the Whitney had the opening of its new show, "Beat Culture and the New America 1950–1965," Gregory attended the first night, standing inside the museum with Allen and me. Through the glass doors of the entrance we could see a mob of people crushed against the doors and windows, waiting to get into the building. They were all elegantly attired in opening-night tuxedos and evening gowns, Armani suits and trendy designer dresses. We could see their faces peering through the glass, like middle-aged groupies, ready to start a senior citizen riot if the doors weren't opened soon.

Allen surveyed the whole scene impassively. Gregory, dressed like a medieval prince, was agitated.

"Dave, let's get out of here. This isn't our scene anymore. Look at these people. They want to kill us because we're inside and they're outside. They've kept us outside their whole lives, and now instead of rejecting us they want to own us. Let's split."

"I think they want to honor us," I said.

"Are you crazy?" said Gregory. "They don't give a crap about Jack or his work. They just think this is another trendy event. It's like going to the circus."

"A patron of the Whitney told me last night at a dinner that Beat was the flavor of the month," said Allen. "I told him that his conception of being Beat had nothing to do with our work. I tried to remind him of our generation's struggle. He appeared to be the same age as us, but he didn't get what I was saying. 'Can you hear me?' I finally said. 'We were never what you assumed we were. We were finding ourselves and rediscovering America. We still are.' He couldn't hear me. He was incapable of listening."

"Then you better listen to me, Allen," shouted Gregory. "When those people come in, Gregory is leaving. Dave's going to play at the Broadway Bar for the big reception in an hour and a half. Let's go down with him. We'll get a seat there before the bar is filled. One of the Whitney staff has eyes for me. I've got to get her number. I'll get her to dance with me when Dave's band starts cooking. I'm a lousy dancer but a great hugger. Gregory is leaving. I want to score with some chicks."

Suddenly the entrance doors burst open, and hordes of well-dressed people came pouring in, as if there were a fire or a hurricane on the street and they were in a panic to get inside the Whitney. As the mob of intelligentsia charged the gates and filled the Whitney, blocking the view of almost all the exhibition, glad-handing one another, shouting greetings, craning their necks to see who of importance might be there, and often trying to maneuver their way into any group who were being photographed, Gregory, Allen, and I quietly disappeared.

"Thank God we're outta here," said Gregory. "We're not mummies. We don't belong here or in the Museum of Natural History. We're not dinosaurs or stuffed animals, fer Chrissakes. We're still creating, and these people still don't get it. Let's *party*!"

All of us arrived at the Bowery Bar, and I got my band set up to play. Larry Rivers, Alfred Leslie, Allen, and Gregory and others from the cast of *Pull My Daisy* and many other old friends were there. Those without invitations had snuck in, before the Whitney-selected list had arrived.

MTV was sponsoring the reception and had a whole Beat program assembled to play during our break, over television monitors placed all over the room. After our first tune, an MTV vice president came up to me.

"David, let's forget about MTV. Just play as long as you want, whatever you want. This is exciting. I was thrown out of three colleges. I've always been a rebel. You guys were heroes to me. You gave a damn. And you did some great work and never paid attention to the naysayers. Forget about the TV monitors. Just get up and jam. I want to meet Gregory Corso later on, if I may. I love his work."

"Me too," I said. "He's right over there, talking to that beautiful young woman."

We continued playing, and soon the bar was packed. People began dancing to the kinds of music Jack and I always had championed—jazz, Middle Eastern, Native American, and Latin American, with an occasional Irish and French-Canadian reel interspersed. Two young women broke the ice as they danced together, and one of the MTV employees joined in.

"This is so great, Mr. Amram," he said to me as he danced his way up to the bandstand. "All I hear is garbage all day at my job. Your band is playing real music."

Within five minutes almost everyone in the bar was dancing, some moving in place to the music while hugging each other. The whole scene had been transformed into the enduring spirit of our era. I played a Middle Eastern classic melody, "Aya Zehn," on my shanai, an Arabic forerunner of the modern-day oboe, and three of the women did spontaneous belly dancing. Then I played and sang my song "This Song's for You, Jack" and had the whole audience sing along. Toward the end of the night, I talked to Gregory.

"That was great, man," he said. "I wish Jack had been here. This is about one block from the old Five Spot and a five-minute walk to the Cedar Tavern, close to where Charlie Parker used to live. Close to your old pad on East 8th, between Avenues B and C. Remember those stairs? Man, how did we ever climb up and down all those stairs? This was a ball. We exorcised the demons. Have you seen that chick from the Whitney? She's crazy about me. Where is she? When I started dancing with someone else she split before I wrote down her number."

A few days later there was a showing of *Pull My Daisy* at the Whitney. Gregory gave a reading and I introduced him. On another night, my band played, as well as a string quartet that Midhat Serbagi assembled for one piece I had composed for the occasion. We had all had such a good time at the party and impromptu dance a few nights earlier that when we came to the Whitney to perform, everyone who worked there was as happy to see us as we were glad to be with them. Now that the show had opened and received a lot of praise in the press, most of the people coming to see the different events were really excited and enthusiastic about being there.

My band played some short pieces. It was wonderful to feel in touch with the audience as we all enjoyed one another, surrounded by drawings, paintings, photographs, and replicas of Jack's manuscripts. Then the film and stage actor Keir Dullea, whom I had known since 1960 before he starred in *2001*, read excerpts from Kerouac, accompanied by music I had composed for string quartet to complement Jack's words. I later orchestrated these for my concert at the Kennedy Center with E. G. Marshall reading Jack's words.

Michael McClure had come all the way from San Francisco with pianist Ray Manzarek to perform. He gave a wonderful reading and the audience awarded them both a thunderous ovation, and wanted him to do an encore. Michael, backed by Ray's peerless piano improvisations, read a long poem, captivating the audience with his dynamic reading style, powerful poetry, and movie star charisma. When he finished, he and Ray could have gone on another hour. Michael came back to the dressing room, followed by our band, to grab a sandwich from the array of delicacies the museum had provided us.

"It's like the old days," said Michael. "Everyone was listening. It was worth the trip, just for Ray and me to be here and for all of us to be together."

Allen came storming in, brandishing an alarm clock and pointing to the time like an infuriated Father Time, and began screaming at Michael. Because of the encore, which the audience had demanded, Michael had gone on longer than his allotted performance time. He kept eating his sandwich as Allen shouted until our band and the string quartet members, not realizing that his roars of anger were almost a sacramental rite of recapturing all those youthful years of yelling, left the room. I followed them into the hall to explain that his screaming was not an unusual or even a bad experience for anyone, and that Michael would just tune it out, and relish his memorable performance and continue enjoying his sandwich while the howling continued. Even through the closed door, we could hear Allen's mega-decibel harangue.

"What's the matter with that cat?" said Steve Berrios, our drummer. "This is such a laid-back scene. McClure and Manzarek could have performed all night. No one's in a rush. Is Ginsberg that much of a punctuality freak?"

"Not really," I said. "He hasn't seen McClure in a long time. Allen's a professor now, and finally become accepted, and I think he misses all the good times hanging out with old friends. All this shouting is a way of telling us he's happy we're all together."

"That's wild," said Steve. "That's a great way for you to look at it. Is that Beat?"

"No," said Victor Venegas, our bass player. "That's not Beat. It's offbeat. You know, like the *guaguanco*. Everybody asks, 'Where's the one? Where's the downbeat? Where is the one? *Donde esta uno, por favor*? Well, no one has to play the downbeat in our music. The *clave* tells you what to do. All the rhythms that *sound* on the beat are offbeat. They're correct, but hard for people in this culture to get down with. This culture makes people too concerned about being hip, and about being on the beat, instead of *on the case*!"

"Get down with the get down," said Steve.

"That's why I like to do these things with Dave," said Victor. "Whether it's with a symphony, or a folk festival, or a jazz or Latin festival, or a bunch of poets, we never know what's going to happen. But we're always on the case. And we never miss a beat."

About twenty minutes later, Gregory came down to join us and when Ed Sanders had finished his marvelous reading, we all went back in our little dressing room to attack the remaining food and joined Allen and Michael McClure, who were sitting and talking quietly, laughing and never giving an indication anything had happened. We all sat and talked, finishing up the food, until finally a museum guard told us we had to leave.

"Allen, I haven't heard you shout like that in years," I said.

"I know," said Allen. "I don't have anybody to argue with anymore. I'm getting respectable. It's awful."

"I can't scream like I used to," said Gregory. "It hurts my ears. You're not as frantic anymore, Dave. What's wrong with us? We must be getting old."

"No," said Michael. "We're just maturing gracefully."

In October of 1996, the exhibition opened at the de Young Museum in San Francisco. I was invited to perform and speak at the West Coast presentation of the Beat Culture and the New America show. Dennis Hopper, Diane diPrima, and many old friends I hadn't seen for years all participated, each contributing their own gifts. Diane and I performed together on a live radio show with an audience of millions with about thirty seconds' notice, and it sounded as though we had been rehearsing for years.

Jackie McClain came and created an unforgettable unaccompanied saxophone improvisation. He sounded better than ever, and we talked about our 1955 days as band mates with Charles Mingus at the Cafe Bohemia in New York when we would play until 3 A.M. and then stay up till dawn talking about music, or go to Small's Paradise or the 125 Club in Harlem for jam sessions.

"We never slept," said Jackie. "We just lived for the music. Now we sleep, but we still live for the music. My son plays with me. The last time I saw you was when my college had me present you with your honorary doctorate."

"I've still got the photo at home of us both dressed up in cap and gown, singing 'The Star Spangled Banner,' " I said. "Who would believe it? Professor Jackie McClain gives Dr. Amram a degree? Mingus must be laughing up in heaven. I wish I could take a year off and study with you."

"Come on down," said Jackie. "We need some older cats in the class."

Jackie had to leave. Allen Ginsberg asked me to play with him and Steve Taylor for his reading that night.

"I'd like you to play horn on the Blake songs the way you did on the recording with me. And also the pieces you recorded with Bob Dylan and me. And perhaps the ones at the ZBS studios in 1981 where you played all the instruments when I ran out of money. No . . . wait. Just come and play on everything."

Steven Taylor, who had played for years with Allen as well, is a consummate musician's musician who always senses the right thing to do, and as we both played for Allen, I told Steve that Allen sounded better than ever. He was really advancing musically.

After about forty minutes, he said to the audience, "You know, David hasn't even had one rehearsal with us."

There was a polite smattering of applause. "Ladies and gentlemen," I said, "Allen and I never had a rehearsal in the last forty years."

At the reception after the concert, Allen walked in slowly. "Thank you for playing with me, David. It helped my reading. I don't have the strength I did before."

"You sounded better than I ever heard you," I said.

"I love playing with Steven Taylor. You remember those first sessions we did with you and Dylan in 1971? Steve's been with me ever since."

"He knows just what to do," I said. "He really listens. He's great."

People came up to talk to Allen, and I saw he was not his old self. He was still energetic, but I sensed something was wrong. The de Young concert was the last time we ever played together. Ever since I brought Bob Dylan by Allen's apartment after Gregory and Allen gave an afternoon poetry reading at NYU, I always played whenever Allen needed help. He had championed Jack's work when Jack was unknown. I always appreciated that, and his early support of Jack remained our common bond.

In early 1997, Allen learned that he was terminally ill. I talked to him on the phone and he sounded wonderful. I was sure he would confound the doctors and live to be a hundred. On April 5, 1997, Bob Rosenthal called and told me Allen had passed away a few hours earlier. He said that we had to remember Allen for all he had done in his life, and that the private service would be at the Shambhala Center.

I couldn't believe he was gone. I always thought we would be able to see each other, eat health food, and argue about everything indefinitely. How could you possibly say goodbye to Allen?

"It's a private ceremony," said Bob. "Don't tell anyone. It is for his family and old friends. There will be a big memorial later on. There will be a few of us there. I wanted you to know."

I called Bob and Bill Morgan back the night before the funeral service to see if there was anything I could do.

"I haven't told anyone about the service except my sister and my wife and kids," I said.

"That's good of you, David, but you might as well tell everyone. It was printed in the *New York Post,* and radio station WBAI has been announcing it all day long so it will be a public mob scene. We'll do the best we can."

I arrived the next day, and there was a swarm of TV reporters, newspeople, and hundreds of people entering and leaving the Shambhala Center. Gregory came over and we hugged each other. We were surrounded by newspeople.

"Fellahs, I know at this time you have suffered a loss, and we all extend you our heartfelt condolences, but could you answer a question?" asked a TV newsman.

"Shoot," said Gregory.

"Mr. Corso and Mr. Amram, now that Allen Ginsberg has passed away, which of you will inherit the mantle of the Beat Generation?"

I felt myself start to feel sick, and then felt some of my old anger rise up inside. I gritted my teeth and gave Gregory a little poke.

"Not me," said Gregory. "I'm a poet. I don't have time for that crap. How about you, Dave?"

"Definitely not," I said. "A lot of us met and maintained lifetime friendships. Those of us still here will miss Allen as we have missed Jack and so many others, but we honor our collective spirit through our work. We are not a political organization."

"Which of you will inherit the mantle of the Beat Generation?" asked the reporter, as if we hadn't heard him the first time.

"Not Dave, not me," said Gregory. "I'll tell you who will." He gave me a conspiratorial wink. All the reporters either turned on their cameras or stood poised with pen and paper in hand, for a scoop.

"Call this number in Lawrence, Kansas. Are ya with me?" Gregory said, in a *sotto voce* rasping tone. There was a mumble of *yeses.* "Awright. Here's the area code and number." Gregory gave out the number slowly. "Ya got that?" Again with a mumble of *yeses.* "Ya sure?" asked Gregory. More affirmative head noddings.

"Ya want it one more time?"

"No," mumbled the chorus, almost beginning to resemble the chorus in a Greek tragedy with the call and response as part of the story line.

"Awright. When the phone gets picked up, ask for Bill. When Bill gets on the phone, tell him Gregory Corso and Dave Amram told you to call and gave you his unlisted number at home. Tell Bill we were asked who should inherit the mantle of the Beat Generation. Tell him we said we weren't interested but we know the perfect person. That perfect person is Bill himself. Ask him if he is now ready to inherit the mantle of the Beat Generation. Tell him he is Gregory and Dave's choice."

"Bill who?" asked one of the reporters.

"Just ask for Bill. They'll know who you mean," said Gregory.

"Thank you, Gregory, thank you, David. I know this is a sad time for you both. We'll let you go to pay your respects to your old friend."

Some of the reporters took out their cell phones to call Lawrence, Kansas, and speak to Bill. Others raced to find a pay phone to make the call. Gregory and I entered the Shambhala Center doorway, out of earshot of the reporters.

"I pity the first poor schmuck who gets through to Burroughs and asks him that question. Bill will tell him to shove it and hang up. Ha-ha-hah! What a stupid-ass thing to ask us. Why don't they ask about Allen's poetry? Why don't they ask us about Jack? At least Allen got recognized while he was alive. He worked hard. He earned it. It'll be awful quiet without him. But we gotta be happy. We can't stop working. Allen never did. He made it past seventy. We'll be old men together, Dave. We gotta stay healthy. I'm gonna miss him."

"Me too," I said. We both attended the service in silence. There wasn't much we could say.

I remembered meeting Allen at the same time I met Cecil Taylor. We were at the Cafe Bohemia, where I played with Mingus in the fall of 1955 and where I would go with Mingus and his band during our week off to hear Miles Davis when he was making his comeback. Where I first played with Sonny Rollins, where I met Monk and recorded with Mingus and Max Roach on a live album done at the Bohemia during that autumn. In the middle of all this I met Allen, young, dynamic, cantankerous, brilliant, full of dreams. Now he was gone.

So was Miles, whom I used to hang out with between sets and talk about Ravel and Debussy's harmonic innovations, and the French impressionist painters and how there was a correlation between music and painting back at the end of the nineteenth century. Miles often mentioned how the abstract expressionist painters of today were inspired by jazz, the way those French impressionist painters and composers interacted at the end of the nineteenth century. And we also talked about boxers and basketball players and how their improvised movement was so related to creative jazz improvisation.

All this interest in creative interaction, past and present, was something Allen and I took for granted. We never discussed the past that much, except when I talked about Jack.

"You're living in the past," Allen would tell me sternly.

"A thing of beauty is a joy forever," I would respond. "What is truly beautiful always stays young."

Then we would argue for hours about everything. Now we couldn't have any more arguments. Gregory and I were both quiet.

"I can't even invite him to sit in with our band and play the finger cymbals anymore," I said.

"Ahh, that's awright," said Gregory. "Just say a Kaddish for him. He's not going anywhere. He'll be around. He's still here."

More events occurred celebrating our era that Gregory and I were invited to. He was finally getting some of the recognition he had deserved for so long. Then Gregory started to gracefully bow out of appearing in public. I was traveling, playing concerts, conducting, writing music, spending every minute at home when I didn't have to perform, raising my kids. When I heard that Gregory was not able to show up at events where he was being acknowledged at last for his lifetime of work, I began to get worried. I began calling him so that we could talk. He had been the life of every party for over forty years. If it was a serious and often humorless occasion, Gregory made it a party as soon as he showed up. The thought of him not showing up to share his wild comic commentaries—charming, infuriating and always educating whoever was there—seemed impossible

"I'm getting help from Yamagata, so I can pay my rent, but I'm not feeling well, Mezz. Come by and see me when I feel better. We'll watch some ball games and talk about old times. I think about Jack a lot."

"Are you OK, Gregory? Is there anything wrong with your health?" I asked.

"Nah," he said softly. "I'm just getting older. I'm fine. We gotta go out when I feel better."

"OK, Pops," I said. "When I get back and am off the road for a while, I'll bring my kids and we'll all go down to the Nuyorican Poets Cafe for their open mike night and hear some of the young people reading. They've got some killer young poets, hip hoppers, and rappers, and a lot of them really appreciate your poetry."

"Yeah," said Gregory softly. "Like Jack always said, 'it takes time.' Tell your kids Uncle Gregory is watching them, so they better not mess around."

When I was in Colorado on tour I got a phone call from Roger Richards and his wife, Irvyne, Gregory's friends for years, saying that Gregory was terminally ill. As soon as I got back to the farm from the airport and unpacked, I drove into the city to see him. He was in bed. He had lost so much weight that at first I didn't believe it was him. I held his hand and we talked for about an hour. I played him some songs on my Irish double D pennywhistle and Lakota courting flute. I had written a new introduction to the paperback edition of his collection of poetry, *Mindfield,* which was added to the ones by Allen and Burroughs from an earlier limited edition. We talked about what we hoped we could leave behind to make our children proud. We talked about whether Keats or Shelley first said "A thing of beauty is a joy forever."

"They each stole from one another," said Gregory. "They were both great."

I went back to see him several times, brought my kids to visit, and saw his kids, now grown up, who were all terrific young people. I also got to know his oldest daughter, Sheri, whom I had never met before. She was an extraordinary person, a professional nurse with such a magical medicinal healing strength that she literally extended his life.

In his last few months, he was like the person I first met in 1956. All the innate sweetness and gentleness that most people never saw poured out of him. A few days before my seventieth birthday I was asked to be honorary chairman of the first New York Underground Poetry and Music Festival in New York City. Ron Whitehead and Casey Cyr agreed to be co-hosts with me in a tribute to Gregory where a group of gifted young poets would read his poetry. I called Sheri and Gregory and told them that since Gregory couldn't be there, we planned to videotape the performance and send him the tape so that he could watch it in bed, and share it with his family.

The night of the tribute was one of those rare experiences where something you wish had been recorded actually *was* recorded. My band played, I read the tattered copy of the Thanksgiving poem Gregory had dedicated and given to me in 1957, and poets Sharon Mesmer, Casey Cyr, Susan Bennett, Michelle Esrick, and Ron Whitehead all read. We mailed a VHS copy of the tribute to Minnesota, where Gregory was now living with his daughter, Sheri. She told me on the phone that at first he was hesitant to see it, but when he finally did he laughed and cried. He and the family watched it often. He was able to see young people honor his work.

Finally Gregory's time came to leave us. I talked on the phone to Sheri and tried to help as much as I could. At the funeral home the night before the church service, I saw Robert Frank for the first time in years. We talked about Gregory and all the good times. He was as sad as I was that Gregory was no longer with us. When he said goodbye, I ran out on the street, took my pennywhistle out of my coat pocket, and played him a little tune.

"That's very sweet of you," said Robert, smiling. "You didn't have to do that."

"Well, Gregory won't be able to make us laugh anymore, so this was for you and him. I remember when you were filming us and he would be so outrageous that your tripod would shake when you were laughing."

"Well, we can still laugh," said Robert. "We must never forget how to do that."

I gave Robert a hug goodbye.

Patti Smith came to the funeral home and Shari invited us to both say a few words at the service the next day at the church.

"Would you like to play with me on a hymn?" she asked.

"I'd love to," I said. "Let's meet at 9 A.M. and we can go over the piece."

We got together the next morning and rehearsed with the church organist. At the service, we each played a piece by ourselves, and then we played together. She sang with such sincerity and honesty I was really touched. I closed my eyes as I played with her, and could feel her love for Gregory so strongly that I almost started crying while playing. We sat down afterward in a pew with her fine young guitarist and I did cry. This church was where Gregory was baptized. I had met him on the streets of Greenwich Village. Now we were saying goodbye here, a few blocks from our meeting place back in 1956. I was asked the next day to write a tribute for *Long Shot* magazine for Gregory. This is what I wrote:

Remembering Gregory

When you've known someone forty-five years, it's hard if not impossible to ever feel that they have left you forever. If you believe in an afterlife, or the enduring strength of the spirit, there is no forever. There is only a separation in time till you are rejoined with all your old friends. In the case of Gregory Corso, his spirit was and is so strong that during his funeral service at Our Lady of Pompeii Church in Greenwich Village where he was born and baptized, his spirit filled the whole church and overflowed into the streets. These were the New York City streets he always loved and remembered no matter where his journeys led him in his life's travels.

We met in 1956, and with all the times we spent together in the '50s, walking those same streets of downtown New York City, engaged in heated discussions about music, poetry, baseball, mutual romances, and how we could survive and pursue our mutual seemingly impossible dreams, there was never a moment that we didn't have fun, laugh, shout, yell, and often share some reverent moments of silence, appreciating the magic spirit that seemed even then to be a part of that amazing era. We knew without even saying it that we were part of something special.

The energy filled the air. The new masters of jazz, painting, poetry, the theater, and all related arts were all sharing their gifts with all the rest of us and we had our own reporter to document it in a new novel that told the world about itself, as well as about all of us. In spite of the critical savaging of Jack Kerouac within a year after the publication of his monumental *On the Road*, we knew that we had a friend who was opening the door for all of us. And Gregory knew he had a lifelong friend in Jack as well as myself and many others who were walking the same path. We were all searching, each in his or her own way, to celebrate the beauty that was all around us and was screaming out for some soulfulness and joy.

Jack always knew that Gregory had a gift that was given to him at birth. Jack, like Gregory, never tried to merchandize his own deep spirituality. Like Gregory, he lived the life of his own spiritual quest. None of us ever asked people to sign up to become members of a cash cow organization designed to make you more holy. All that came later on in the '60s, and neither Jack, Gregory, nor I had anything to do with it. We all had religious roots that stayed with us for life. The only time Jack ever addressed any of his own feelings of his connection to a higher power was when he told me in a rare immodest moment after he had completed his extraordinary improvised rap-narration for the film *Pull My Daisy* that he, Jack Kerouac, was touched by the hand of God. Gregory never said this about himself, but a few of us knew then that he was born to be a poet. His knowledge of his own natural gifts freed him from any doubts about why he was here, and like so many of the major talents of this rich era, he let life take him to wherever he seemed destined to be at the moment, knowing that as long as he could keep writing, he was doing what he was here to do.

We talked many times about how we could pursue our dreams and still have some kind of family, since we also shared a mutual love of kids and wanted to have families of our own some day.

"Who would be crazy enough to marry either of us?" he often said to me during the wee hours of our late night-early morning field trips down the wilds of MacDougal Street.

With surprising frequency, "I would" was uttered at 6 A.M. by some young woman whom we had just met an hour ago. Gregory in those days was irresistible to many women, but he always had an intuitive bond that he maintained with whomever he was with at the moment. This innate sensitivity made him more empathetic than most of the rest of us. He took the time to care for others. He was not career oriented in any way, and as a result could talk to anybody about the beauty of the moment, rather than about himself. He knew how to listen, and how to share.

This is why in his final few months, his children, my children, and so many old friends came to see him so often. The love that he kept in his heart, often hidden to strangers, was as pure as his poetry. He was never comfortable with the whole Beat phenomenon. He often said to me that the myth-making about all of us, which none of us wanted or needed, clouded the whole picture. We all felt our work could speak for itself.

He would often poke me with his elbow, when we appeared together in the '80's and '90's, as Kerouac's genius was being rediscovered and we would attend conferences and all kinds of events where we were forced to listen to experts talk about the hidden meaning behind significant events in our lives that never actually occurred.

"See that Mezz?" Gregory would whisper in my ear, with enough volume to fill up the whole room. "It's the Beat mythology shot. They'd rather deal with myths than speak with us and find out what was happening and is still happening. I'm still a poet, man. So was Jack. It's all in our books. They can find out all they need to know up there on the shelf where our books lie. We'll be judged by our books on the shelf. Just like you with your symphonies. How can people that weren't even there tell us who we are and what we're thinking? Why don't they ask us first and get it right?"

When *Mindfields* was reissued by Thunder's Mouth Press, I was asked to write a new introduction to accompany the other forewords by Burroughs and Allen. I mentioned the fact that Gregory was such a colorful personality as a performer that people often overlooked his real value as a major poet and one of our true originals.

In the last few years as I crisscross the globe, in concerts and seminars, young people in many countries (and finally throughout the U.S. as well) inquire about Gregory's work, and about his life outside the imagery created by his public persona. They say, as they always say about Jack, that they feel they know him as a result of reading his books. Young people would give me messages, poems, songs, and stories to give to Gregory. I always tried in some way to relay these messages of love when I would see him or talk to him on the phone. I was also asked for years why Gregory wasn't acknowledged as much as he deserved to be. I always explained that he was only interested in being the best that he could be, and that the excellence of his work was all that concerned him. In the past few years he has gained recognition for his contributions by a larger audience than he ever dreamed of. He often told me how uncomfortable he was having to perform at events where he was supposed to portray the

Peck's Bad Boy image, or worse yet, be the Clown Prince of Beat poetry.

"I'm a classicist, Mezz," he used to say, "I'm a lyric poet from the tradition. When are they going to drop this Beat crap and judge me on my merits?"

That time has finally arrived. At last, Gregory is emerging in the peer culture as a unique artist whose work can be judged by its own intrinsic merit. Like Kerouac, he is being perceived as an original who, by virtue of his lifetime of achievement, can stand alone. No label is necessary to understand either of them.

In early fall when his devoted daughter Sheri took him to Minneapolis and I saw him for the last time in New York, I told Sheri and Roger that I would ask a group of young poets, musicians, and appreciators of Gregory's work to get together and make a video to send him in Minneapolis. This way, he and his family could watch his poetry being read with music, the way we did forty-five years ago, by a whole new generation of young artists. In November, I had the good fortune to be chosen as the honorary chairperson at the first New York Underground Music and Poetry Festival in New York. I asked the organizers, poets Casey Cyr and Ron Whitehead, if we could do this for Gregory while he was still with us. They were nice enough to get the Nuyorican Poets Cafe to give us a night during the festival where the featured performance would be a reading of Gregory's poetry with music. It went over beautifully, with a lot of joy and no maudlin or self-serving rants. The whole hour was filled with the sunshine of Gregory's spirit, guided by the beauty of his words. The musicians who played with me listened to every second of what was being spoken, and with our old tradition of no rehearsal, it all came out flawlessly. Everybody listened to everybody else. We all respected every line of Gregory's poetry.

I mailed him a copy of the video, and he watched it many times in Minneapolis. When I spoke to him on the phone for the last time, he said, "Mezz, I understand how you always confused Keats and Shelley, but I forgive you because the video was great. Tell all those people who read and played . . . Thanks."

We talked a little more that night. We reminisced about old times, about our unexpected grand reunion when we ran into each other in San Francisco with Neal and Allen in 1965 in a tiny bar in Haight Ashbury. We recalled the jam session in 1956 at a famous painter's loft when he played drum beats on a series of pots and pans while Jack and I were scat singing till we were all thrown out at 3 A.M. I reminded him about the great picture taken of him during the program we participated in at the National Portrait Gallery in Washington, D.C., in the late '90's, where he was photographed reading his poetry under an oil painting of George Washington. And finally we talked about his kids and my kids and how they were all so grown up.

"Old times, Dave. Good times. We'll be together soon again. Goodnight, Mezz."

Those were the last words I heard from Gregory. At the church, after I accompanied Patti Smith in a beautiful version of an old hymn that we played together for the first time, I spoke briefly. I began by reading touching statements by Lawrence Ferlinghetti and Robert Creeley, both of whom I called a few nights before the funeral. They weren't able to come, so they gave me their messages to read. Then I asked the people in the church to remember Gregory's shining spirit, and to celebrate the joy and laughter he brought to our lives. I mentioned that so many of us came from other places to New York and to Greenwich Village searching for something we knew was there. When we said hello to Gregory for the first time, he told us this was where he was born. Now we were in the same place to say goodbye.

I also thanked the priest for letting us share the place where Gregory began his life's journey, and where he told his daughter Sheri he wanted to have his farewell. I reminded everyone that Gregory, Jack, and I often would quote to other aspiring artists and dreamers the classic maxims—"an artist must burn with a hard and gemlike flame," "by your works ye shall be known" (the Bible), and "a thing of beauty is a joy forever" (we always argued whether Keats took it from Shelley or Shelley took it from Keats). And I told everyone that we had to remember Gregory's family and treasure the gift to the world of his beautiful children, his grandchildren, and his relatives who are still with us.

The church was full of people who wanted to read a poem, sing a song or tell a story. This will happen many times in many places for years to come because Gregory's star will shine brightly when all of us are gone. His work will always be here to remind us and future gener-

> ations that you can follow your heart, and if you remain honest and dedicated to what you dream to set out to do, you can lift people's spirits and make the world a better place through your work, just as Gregory did.
> David Amram, January 30th, 2001

The year 2001 became a banner year for Jack's legacy. With the sale of his scroll for *On the Road,* the completion of his archives finally being placed with the New York Public Library, I realized that those of us left who knew Jack and worked with him had an obligation to honor his memory. We also had to bear witness by sharing what we knew with anyone, fans and scholars alike, in a responsible and accurate way. Otherwise, the decades of misinformation and mythology would continue to obscure the remarkable spirit of the man who was our reporter.

As I sit writing this memoir, I can still hear Jack's voice. You can hear it too, because he spoke exactly the way he wrote. I remember the letter he wrote me about the cantata *A Year in Our Land* from Florida in 1965 after I had sent him a tape of the first performance at Town Hall. I told him we would do more together. He saw the 1968 telecast of the piece, and we talked on the phone for nearly two hours. Towards the end of the conversation, I played the horn and piano into the telephone so that we could do some long distance improvising together.

"We're still wailing, Jack," I said.

"Ah, Davey, we have to do more," he said. "I'm tired, man. Fame is such a drag."

I could hear the sadness in his voice, and even though I could still get him to chuckle, I sensed the overwhelming pain that seemed to engulf him.

He talked about his new book, *Vanity of Duluoz.* He said it was dedicated to his wife, Stella Sampas. He told me how she was saving his life and his mother's life.

"Someday, we'll all get together, if you ever settle down and get married, and we can all go off in the mountains, grow our own food, write an opera, and play music with the Indians, while our wives look after our adoring children. Ah-h-h, man. *C'est triste.* No one comes to see me, or calls. Neal's dead. But I'm writing. You'll have to read my new book, Davey. I can still write."

"I know that, Jack. *Bien sûr,*" I said.

"Read it soon, Davey," he said.

He knew I was always years late in reading his books. That was because being with him was exactly like reading his books. Often Jack would read me favorite passages of whatever he had written or was writing over the phone, as he used to do over the years when we were together in New York City.

"Someday, Davey, when we're old men, we'll sit in hammocks and rock back and forth, picking our teeth and discussing our life's works. You can read all my published books, and I'll study all your published symphony scores, and we'll show our grandchildren *Pull My Daisy* so that they can see how crazy we were and then we'll play the recordings of our symphonic collaborations and leap from our hammocks to give an impromptu *soirée* seminar on the secret joys of music and poetry, filling the air with Mozartean delights. Ah-h-h *mon dieu, cher* Davey . . . I feel tired, man. Don't lose your energy. 'An artist burns with a hard and gemlike flame.' Don't let the fire go out! Keep the flame alive."

The ranks of the keepers of the flame were slowly being diminished. When Dody Muller left us in the spring of 2001, I realized how lucky we were to have known her, how lucky Jack was to have had her bless his life, and what a joy it was to have had all of us reunited at her seventieth birthday on June 7, 1998, just a few years earlier.

Her daughter Maia had arranged a surprise party for her at 2 P.M. at the Frontier Restaurant in New York City. I knew it would be a chance to honor Dody and see a lot of wonderful people again. Richard Bellamy, who had played the Bishop in *Pull My Daisy,* was there, looking very much the same as he did in 1959, full of humor and warmth. Lucien Carr came, with his children all grown up now, looking like a patriarch sea captain with a beard. His son

Simon, an accomplished artist, gave me an announcement of his art show.

I remembered Simon as a child, staying up late as Jack and I played music, rapped, and carried on till dawn. Lucien's ex-wife Cessa, still close to him, greeted me warmly.

"Cessa," I said. "Here we are at an afternoon party. It's the first time I can remember saying hello to you in the daylight."

"We're maturing now," she said, laughing.

When I finally got to sit down with Lucien, he said, "I'm sailing a lot now. I live in Washington, D.C. Don't drink anymore. I have a good life."

"I'll never forget all the parties, and all the music at your house when Jack would come to town," I said. "We got so many ideas of things that we could do at those jam sessions. They went on for hours. Jack never read or scat-sang better than he did when we were carrying on at your house."

"Jack loved music," said Lucien. "He always felt it and understood it. All kinds of music."

"That's why his writing has such rhythm," I said. "His prose really swings, as we used to say. Now my kids would say it rocks."

"However they say it, it's still damn good," said Lucien. "Imagine if he were alive today, to see how much he is appreciated. Wouldn't it be great if he were here with us for Dody's birthday?"

"I'm so glad we can honor Dody," I said. "Jack really loved her, and I guess we all do. She's all spirit."

I talked to Lucien about the new era that seemed to be dawning. About the enormous number of young people I kept meeting who gravitated towards what we did because they sensed there was a generation and an era where a lot of people felt a connection to a higher purpose and mission in life than just staring in the mirror. There was music, art, theater, poetry, and dance that still makes your heart stand still and is now being appreciated, almost as though Alice from *Alice's Adventures in Wonderland* were checking us all out in a time machine.

"It's kind of like then is now," I said. "Like we used to remind each other every day, 'A thing of beauty is a joy forever.' " I told

Lucien of Doug Brinkley's new book and how important it would be to talk to Doug. "He's interested in Jack from the viewpoint of a historian, Jack's place in the history of America and the changes he helped to shape. You and Dody are both so important in Jack's life, and neither of you have been included in a meaningful way in most of the recent books about our era, except for the most important ones—the books that Jack wrote himself. If you'd agree to talk to Doug, I promise he won't come on like a tabloid scandal sheet reporter, looking for sleaze and dirt. He truly respects Jack's work and the importance of him as a major artist. I think his book will change everything. He'll remove Jack from the penitentiary of the Beat Generation. Doug will have full access to all Jack's journals. We'll finally have a true picture of what he was about. Jack *himself* will be the number one primary source. As Jack would say, 'It's never too late.' "

"You can give him my number," Lucien said. "I'll speak to him."

I managed to get a few minutes alone with Dody.

"I loved Jack," she said. "He was wonderful. He was so emotional. Sometimes it was almost like being with a dear woman friend. He always acted and reacted with feelings first. I don't know if we ever could have made it being married. I don't think his mother approved of me. He was so devoted to her. I still think about him. We all had so much fun making *Pull My Daisy* together. I want to come up with Maia and see your farm and the rest of your family. Jack always talked about living that way."

"I'm so glad we can all be together again," I said. "Alfred Leslie is out of town or he would be here. Your daughter is fantastic, the way she got all this together."

"I'm proud of her," said Dody. "She's not only beautiful, she's a really good person. I think we did pretty damn well with our children. Your daughter is a fine young lady."

"We certainly don't fit the official Beat image," I said.

"You'd better believe that," said Dody. "I don't even pay attention to any of that. I never did. We were artists and we remain artists. Jack's work had nothing to do with that."

"Why do you suppose they denigrated him all of these years,

bringing him down with that Beatnik myth?" I asked. "Were they jealous?"

"He was too damn good," said Dody. "They just couldn't handle it. And he was too damn real."

EPILOGUE: From Lowell to the Himalayas: The Trail of Beauty

As I finish this book, we are approaching the year 2002. The symmetry and perfect mirror image of this year is a feast for numerologists. To them, it is a number of great significance. For most of the world, Western culture determines our calendar. We are taught that our calendar is the only accurate keeper of time.

It is easy to forget that many places in the world have their *own* calendar that is thousands of years older than ours. Many places in the world are inhabited by people whose traditions and history are devoid of any type of calendar at all. Still, regardless of whose calendar you subscribe to, 2002 has a balance and appeal that makes you yearn for the good old days of 1001. The stark beauty of 2002 can whet your appetite for the fireworks and the excitement that will surely erupt all over the globe during the mammoth nationwide celebrations, including BYOB 1950s-style parties that will usher in the year 3003.

Waiting 1001 years from 2002 till 3003 is asking too much patience from any of us. Even Jack would have grown discouraged at the thought of such a long time between celebrations. The baseball dynasties he created and maintained were to an extent his antidote to the frustration of not being able to control the passage of time or alter the tempo of his hectic life. With his teams, games, batting averages, personal selection, and total control of the destiny of all the participants, he was able both to create a series of athletic events and master time, place, and destiny. If he couldn't control the Shakespearean outrageous fortunes of his own life, he could control the lives of all the members of his imaginary athletes, and create the outcome of each game they played. He didn't have to gamble and pull numbers out of the hat. He was in total control. Unlike the enormous risk that always comes when any of us dare to improvise, he could determine every second of every game.

The wire services went wild in August of 2001 when stories appeared that detailed Jack's homemade baseball dynasties following their acquisition, along with all his archives, by the New York Public Library. In interviews I had spoken about these games, which Jack had shown to me at Dody Muller's house in October of 1959, but most people thought I was either delusional or that Jack's time spent pursuing these activities was an ex-football player's silly juvenile hobby.

I knew, as did his friends, that this homemade sports dynasty was influenced by his early days in Lowell as an athlete and promising young sports reporter for *The Lowell Sun*. Paul Maher, Jr., a young scholar from Lowell, was one of the first people to see the newly acquired materials of Jack's archives. Paul spoke to one of the archivists at the New York Public Library and had him call me. The person in charge of Jack's enormous archives in New York was astonished when I described to him what I remembered seeing that afternoon in 1959, forty-two years ago, especially my description of the imaginary baseball team from Pawtucket.

"You have *some* memory," he exclaimed.

"So did Jack," I said. "He remembered *everything*. Now that the library has acquired so much of his writings, journals, diaries, poems, paintings, and random notes, the world will be able to judge him on his own merits. The preeminent Kerouac scholar was Jack himself."

"I find all this fascinating," the man said to me. "I want to know more about him as a person."

"Then come to Lowell Celebrates Kerouac!," I said. "I'm going there the first weekend of October. The town welcomes people from all over the world to come and see the places he lovingly described in many of his books, voices that sound the same way Jack's did. It's one of the few places in the Northeast, outside of rural Maine, Vermont, and New Hampshire, where there's still a unique regional style of speech. Even in the French language as spoken, *joual* is retained, an old dialect from Quebecois roots, with a special Lowell flavor. Like all living languages, always changing. Roger Brunelle not only teaches in Lowell, he gives tours during the Festival through Centralville, where you can see the remnants of the old French-Canadian community. He also can explain the subtle differences and nuances of the way French is spoken today. Now, groups from other parts of the world have moved to Lowell, but the old spirit is still there. All languages are part of Lowell's ever-changing tapestry."

"I'll try to come," he said.

"Bring your friends," I said. "They'll all feel welcome. Even Jack himself would feel welcome today. He is finally being acknowledged in the place that was the gyroscope of his life. I don't want to bankrupt the library with this phone call, but there are things you should know. 'Our place of birth is sacred to all of us, Davey,' Jack used to say. 'Poor Thomas Wolfe. After his success, he was afraid to set foot in his home town in Asheville, North Carolina. Now they have a statue of him there. Someday they'll recognize me. *Je m'en fou.*'

"But Jack did care, and now Lowell cares, as does the rest of the world. There is no street named after Neal Cassady in Denver yet, but he is immortalized in Jack's writings. Jack is now immortalized in Lowell. The Jack Kerouac Commemorative at Kerouac Park is the kind of caring that Jack always searched for, a park as beautiful as Stonehenge in England. Small obelisk-shaped monuments are engraved with excerpts from his writing. Etched in stone. Ready for 2002 and 3003. As symmetrical as the numbers themselves. I can hardly wait to get back. This year, the Festival honors Steve Allen and Gregory Corso, who both left us. I'll show excerpts of the film made with Steve and me playing together, speaking about Gregory and how these two totally different people had an important role in Jack's life, and how all of us collaborated with one another."

"You sound like you'll be busy," he said.

"The 2001 festival theme to usher in 2002 is 'Cross Cultural Kerouac: Jack in Any Language,' " I said. "What Jack and I talked about incessantly, what Dizzy Gillespie spent hours telling me in 1951, what my uncle David, a merchant seaman, instilled in me before I could even read and write, what I myself have tried to share with others is now being done in Jack's hometown, in his memory, for all in the community and all who visit Lowell. The whole town takes part for the weekend. I wish you all strength and energy in putting together all this new material. I understand in 2005 the whole world will have access to it. That's really right around the corner."

I hung up the phone. I began to look at the program that the festival organizer, poet Lawrence Carradini, had sent me. He and his wife Meg Smith, a journalist and dancer, are part of a large group who have made this annual event the premiere tribute to Kerouac since the '80s. I began to write a note to myself to plan what I was going to do in Lowell, as if I were writing a celestial press release to all the dearly departed. Here is what my imaginary celestial press release looked like in the mail room of my mind:

FOR EARTHLY AND CELESTIAL RELEASE
Lowell Celebrates Kerouac! 2001

The Athenian Corner Restaurant is honoring Jack (and his wife, Stella Sampas, and all his Greek-American lifelong friends) with 'A Night of Music and Poetry with a Greek Flavor.'

I'll have my dumbek and shanai, and play "Kalamatyano" as I have with my own Middle Eastern Trio with Avram Pengas and George Mgrdichian for thirty years. Jack loved this kind of music. I'll say a prayer for Dimitri Mitropoulos, great Greek-born conductor who set me on my journey in the 1940s by making me realize I could dare to try and be a composer, conductor, and improviser.

I'll also say a prayer for Sebastian Sampas,

who died in World War II, mortally wounded March 2, 1944. Sebstian inspired Jack to dare to become a writer. I'll say another prayer for my cousin, David Powell, an infantryman killed November 25, 1944, in the Battle of the Bulge. He played the trombone. Like Sebastian, he left his family with sweet memories and an empty space in our hearts. But the Greek music and message of the love of life will fill the restaurant and spill out into Market Street and we'll all have a glass of retsina and a rousing "Yassoo Kyrie" (great time Mr.) toast to Jack's memory, the way Aristodemos Kaldis used to shout above the din at the Cedar Tavern in 1958 when he told Jack and me that we should be like Homer and his anonymous accompanist on the lyre, and demonstrated by shouting excerpts from the *Iliad* and the *Odyssey* in Greek (or so he told us, as we only could relate to his passionate delivery, without knowing what he was saying).

If Kaldis were still here physically, he would go to the University Gallery in Lowell where Jack's paintings and drawings are to be shown, and undoubtedly become a spontaneous co-host with Ed Adler, who along with Bernie Mindich, created the visual portion of the historic 1994 Conference at NYU that featured art work by Kerouac and Ferlinghetti. Ed, a highly successful artist, is also one of NYU's most popular professors and a walking encyclopedia of history of the visual arts, theater, music, and poetry of the last fifty years. Like all of us, he comes to Lowell, where he attended the university years ago, to celebrate Jack as only a true-blue scholar could. With devotion, charm, grace, humor, and a trunk load full of knowledge, he shares with all who will look and listen.

A program celebrating Jack's involvement with Buddhism will feature performers from Lowell's burgeoning Asian community, with the Angkor Dance Troupe. The music and language of Vietnamese, Cambodian, and Laotian people, now part of Lowell, will be honored in Jack's name, as Jack himself will be honored by new arrivals to America.

There will be workshops and round table discussions with poets and writers from Cambodia, Montreal, and Bolivia, discussing Jack's French-Canadian roots, and the work of writers in other languages who are influenced by him. Hillary Holiday, who has organized the academic events for the festival, is a young professor from Virginia. She is an example of the new generation of scholars who are brilliant and tireless ambassadors for their own areas of expertise. Hillary is passionate that her knowledge be shared in a way that makes her students committed to excellence in their own work when they finish school, regardless of their chosen professions. She is also an accomplished poet and sets a standard for all who visit Lowell for her events, as well as for her devoted students. She is the kind of champion Jack dreamed of having during his lifetime.

Jack's love of Mexico, and his appreciation for Afro-Cuban and Puerto Rican music, which he heard in New York, is honored in a concert where I'll be sitting in with Los Pieneros del Coco. We'll play not only for Jack but for the memory of Tito Puente, a favorite of Jack's with whom I played many times.

I told Lawrence Carradini, the head of Lowell Celebrates Kerouac!, that if Jack and Tito could get an overnight pass from Heaven, we would be playing till dawn, without a break. They'd be sitting in with us and never stop.

There is also a showing of Henry Ferrini's classic film *Lowell Blues* with narrators Carolyn Cassady, Robert Creeley, Gregory Corso, Johnny Depp, Joyce Johnson, and myself, with music by Lee Konitz. The film has all Kerouac's words and the cinematography features the faces and places of an ever-changing Lowell, showing the excitement and freshness of people from around the world who now are residents of Jack's hometown.

Along with *Pull My Daisy*, *Lowell Blues* is already acknowledged as the classic film involving Jack's words and message. It sets a new standard. I'm also giving a concert, "From Cairo to Kerouac," at the high school Jack attended for children of all ages, and a festival grand finale which I do every year, "Improv with Amram."

Poets, musicians, and free-associators line up around the block and enter the Sugar Shack where I accompany each person as I did for Jack, to end the festival on the inclusive egalitarian note that our collaborations personified. After six hours, I drink some coffee, pack up my van, and bid adieu.

A new CD, *A Tribute to Kerouac*, recorded live at the Dove Cafe in the St. Joseph the Worker Shrine, will be formally released during the festival. All revenue will go towards supporting future festivals. On the CD, I performed with many of the local poets and musicians, and finally recorded my tune "This Song's for You, Jack" with young musicians I met in Lowell, some still in school, but full of desire to make a life in music and collaborate with others. I usually have improvised most of the lyrics, and I did quite a few on this CD, but for the first time also recorded the original ones that I have been adding to since 1982. Here is what I wrote down:

This Song's for You, Jack

As long as there's a tree
A flower
A river
Or a stream

As long as there's a swallow
A catfish
A storm cloud
And a dream

As long as there is summer rain
And early morning dew
This song's for you, Jack
This song is for you.

All the times you talked of Texas
As the sun set in the west
Across the New Jersey skyline
Those stories were the best

People from all over
We got to know through you
Cross the Rockies, down to Mexico
Far from New York 6th Avenue

Two floors up, one room, scat-singing
Laughing-dancing-poetry all night through
The good times and rivers roll along
So I wrote this song for you.

Moonlight bright October night
In Lowell, Massachusetts
Birds fly south
On their winter way

Casting moonlit shadows
On the road
You traveled
Yesterday

The wind blows east
From Denver
In San Francisco
Clouds are turning gray.

You stayed and left
A thousand places
Searching for Buddha
Brittany and Spain

Walked through Colorado holly
Heard the ancient South Dakota drum
Of Sitting Bull
Drank Oklahoma rain

You wrote us stories
By your brakeman's shining lantern
Through the night on rusty tracks in Texas
On the roadside by the train

The road
You shared with us
The road you showed us
We can ride on too

We share the ride
You're by our side
Jack, this song's
For you

Together on the road tonight
We share the holy highway light
This song's for you, Jack
This song's for you.

The audience sang the lyrics at the end in perfect harmony as if we had rehearsed for years. I am happy that I finally have a recording after twenty years of singing different versions—one that was made with poets and musicians from the greater Lowell area. Susan Bennett and I were the only people participating who did not live in the area. We both felt honored to be included as visitors who feel so at home in this special, mystical town that seems to withstand the destruction of its own multifaceted character. Lowell still represents what Jack saw disappearing in the mid-1950s. The indefinable, sometimes harsh, but always personal small town family-oriented poly-cultural communities that made traveling across America a path towards enlightenment. These plain and humble places were already being transformed in the late '40s into standardized models of what Henry Miller described as the Air-Conditioned Nightmare.

> Through his writing, Jack welcomed the world to Lowell. Now Lowell was welcoming Jack to the world through their annual Festival.
>
> I could hardly wait to get back to Lowell and visit Phil Chaput and his wife and family and eat French-Canadian moose pie and Greek food and speak French with Roger Brunelle and all Phil's friends in a homey atmosphere that was timeless. Phil had letters from Jack on the wall and pictures he has taken of Lowell that speak to the heart just as Jack's writing does. I'll look forward to hanging out with Dave Orr, who introduced me to the Stations of the Cross, where Jack attended French-speaking Catholic school as a boy, and who always shows me new places in Lowell where Jack spent his youth.
>
> I'll also spend time with Paul Marion, Billy Koumantzelis, Paul Maher, Jr., and Steven Eddington to learn new things about Jack that I never knew before. I'll visit John Sampas and his nephews Tony and Jim, their mother Betty, and hope to see all the other members of this remarkable family, and go with Adira to the Worthen Bar where Jack used to drink, and have a toast to the memory of Tony Sampatacacus, who used to tell Adira stories, jokes, and suggest books for her to read when she was too young to drink but just the right age to discover literature . . .

I finally stopped writing my celestial press release and realized it was better suited for this book than as a well-crafted terse and precise one-page announcement.

I realized I needed to call John Leite, a lifelong resident of Lowell. John was a trombonist in the Seventh Army Symphony in 1953–54. We were both members of the orchestra and have stayed friends through the years since then. I have been trying to track down primary sources, people who actually knew Jack, for Doug Brinkley to contact as he writes his biography of Kerouac.

John, it turned out, remembered Jack from encounters with him in 1948–49. It was only after my appearances in Lowell several times for Lowell Celebrates Kerouac! that he realized all I had done with Jack. In 1998, John told me of his first encounters, fifty years earlier. He is a lifelong resident of Lowell, and the president of the Musician's Union there. He told me he remembered seeing Jack at the Cosmopolitan, called the Cosmo for short. It was located between the Olympia Restaurant and the Highball Cafe, which became the Sac Club. This was after World War II, back in 1948–49.

It blew my mind to realize John had known Jack that far back. I told him I wanted to write down some of his remembrances. This is what he told me.

"Jack came into the club. I was playing trumpet then. I was only fifteen, and just beginning to play in public.

" 'You guys sound good,' he would always say. We believed him, because we could see he was really listening. Most customers came in for fast sex for fifty cents in a back booth. There was also a little patio in the back where people could make out. But Jack came for the music, not for broads. He would sit, and we knew he was checking out our music, even though we were all just kids—not even shaving. We were fourteen to fifteen years old, playing our first gigs.

" 'Good. Soundin' good,' he would say to us. I used to play off sheet music. Mostly songs from the '40s. People would dance. He just sat real quiet and listened. We knew who he was. He was a famous football player at Lowell High at one time. Some people thought he was strange, but he was nice to us. You could tell he was sincere. He would *listen*, not talk to others. Then he'd leave, and go hear the older guys, the famous players, that would work on Moody Street. He made you feel you were somebody. After he got so famous, people started to put him down. Jealousy is a terrible thing."

I am listening now to "Washington D.C. Blues." One of the themes I composed to accompany Jack's readings for this series of short poems stayed with me so many weeks that I rescored it as the principal theme of the second movement of my flute concerto *Giants of the Night* for James Galway. The second movement is dedicated to Jack.

In 2002, James Galway plans to premiere and then record the concerto. In 2002, Mark Reese, son of Pee Wee Reese, will complete a documentary film about my work that relates to what I have described in this book, where I will join the poet Ron Whitehead in a reading on Mount Everest for the Dalai Lama. I'll play a piece for Jack from the mountain, and in the film will include part of a one-hour documentation of Carolyn Cassady and myself in London at a festival organized by poet Richard Deakin where our panel "Primary Sources: Soul Survivors" will be just the two of us talking and reading from our own works about Jack and Neal. Mark has agreed to donate this hour of film to the Kerouac estate, and the Kerouac Writers' Residence in Orlando, so that the information will be available to students and future scholars, exactly as the two of us presented it.

In 2002, my saxophone concerto *Ode to Lord Buckley,* and *A Little Rebellion: Thomas Jefferson* are being recorded by the young American conductor Richard Aulden Clark.

Also in 2002, my recorded collaboration with Lawrence Ferlinghetti will be released. The CD *Poems from a Gone World* was made in four hours at Zoetrope Studios when I was in San Francisco in the spring of 2001. There was also a DVD made of Lawrence and me, performing together as if we had been working together all of our lives. Now students will always be able to see as well as hear how people can collaborate on the spot and come up with something of lasting value. Jim Sampas was the producer. The showing of Jack's original scroll for *On the Road* got me back to San Francisco and enabled Lawrence and me to collaborate.

And 2002 will be the year I continue to work guest conducting and soloing with symphony orchestras, presenting Jack's narrations with orchestra, my cantata *A Year in our Land,* and what we now call world music—reaching out to young people to build new audiences.

And with all these activities, I'll begin a new collaboration with author Frank McCourt, who I met in the beginning of the 1970s when I played at his brother Malachy's bar, The Bells of Hell, on 13th Street and 6th Avenue, two blocks from my old apartment. In 2000, Frank suggested we work on an ecumenical Mass, honoring three hundred years of immigration to New York and America, with each portion of the Mass celebrating a different immigrant culture. It will be composed for narrator, chorus and orchestra.

"Jack and I used to talk about collaborating like this," I told Frank.

"Well, we'll not only talk about it, we'll *do* it," said Frank. "You're the only composer who could write this, with all the various styles of music."

Malachy and Frank had both performed at my seventieth-birthday tribute at the Paramount Theater that Mark Morganelli had organized, along with Jane Alexander, Ed Sherin, Joanne Shenendoah, Odetta, Charles Castleman playing my violin concerto, and many others.

I knew Frank was as great a reader as he was a writer. Like Jack, he could make the words on paper sing when he spoke, and make the reader hear the music from the writing itself.

I could now see that what Jack and I dreamed of—spontaneity and formality—was not such an offbeat idea. I am now, more than ever, able to treasure those moments alone. I can compose in the delicious silence that in itself is a supreme element of all musical creation. And whenever I am in the world still on the road, in those places of silence composing, Dizzy's words stay in my memory:

"I'll do this forever. That's why God put me here. To play this music."

Sometimes when I'm composing, I spend a whole day writing and rewriting one measure of music, to get it just right. My orchestral scores are impeccable. I spend most of my commission money having the scores and parts copied and recopied, with every tiny nuance, tempo change, metronome marking, dynamic, and phrase clearly indicated. But the *music,* the breathing, living, human, mystical, mysterious part, comes *naturally.* That naturalness is what

Jack and I strived for when we performed together. When we wrote alone we created formal works (his books and my symphonies) inspired by the natural energy of these real-life experiences. When we performed together, we were celebrating the moment, dealing with the informal, and daring to improvise like tightrope walkers. We wanted to create formal works, built to last, that retained this same energy. That's what we were all about. That was the basis of our friendship and our work together.

When I go to high schools, colleges, or any place where there are young people today, they all know who Jack Kerouac is. None of them now tell me that he was the King of the Beatniks. They tell me that *they read his books*.

That is Jack's ultimate triumph. His work speaks for itself. Until the very end, through all the pain and rejection, he continued to write. When I talked to him on the phone in those last sad months, in late night–early morning phone calls, he still spoke of work he had to do, and dreams he wished to fulfill.

I feel blessed and lucky to still be here in my seventies. I try every day to share the joy of seeing my own dreams in music finally coming true. I also try every day, in some small way, to share that gift of Jack's spirit, energy, and human kindness with everyone I meet. Jack's work can enable future generations to look back on the second half of the twentieth century and see the beauty part.

When Jack and I used to talk about his desire to find his lost Canadian-Indian heritage, I reminded him of the Navajo Prayer of the Twelfth Night. How the men and women prayed as they walked on the trail of beauty. I sang him some of the old songs I had learned from Native American musicians. Jack and I both prayed in different languages, but the trail of beauty remained the same.

Many of us walked and still walk that trail today. It is accessible to anyone and it is endless. If you stand tall as Jack did throughout his life, and walk that trail of beauty, you will surely meet him there someday.

Acknowledgments

The first two women in my life, my mother, Emilie and my sister Mariana, gave me a love of both the French and English language, and they both encouraged me to read, speak, and listen to both.

I am also grateful to my father, Philip, and his brother, my uncle David. They taught me the value of hard work, the joy of sharing, and the importance of laughter.

My three children, Alana, Adira, and Adam, patiently listened to most of the stories about the events, people, and places that appear in this book, even after they knew them by heart. They remain a constant source of inspiration and energy, and fill my heart with pride and love every day of my life. And to Lora Lee, forever.

The skill and patience of my editor, Jim Ellison, were of enormous value. So were the tireless efforts of Jean and Tom Sweezey, Denise Carr, and Neville Hugelmeyer, who allowed me to burn the midnight oil, and gave me countless hours of help to finish the book on time.

I thank Stella Sampas for the love and comfort she gave Jack and his mother when they both needed her the most. Also, gratitude to the surviving members of the Sampas family who continue to stand by Jack and remain committed to seeing that he receives his rightful place in history.

To Roger Brunelle, Paul Marion, Phil Chaput, and Paul Maher Jr., of Lowell, Massachusetts, who work every day to help preserve the Franco-American heritage that Jack held so dear.

To the devoted members and supporters of Lowell Celebrates

Kerouac!, who provide an annual festival for people from around the world to study Jack's work by visiting the town of his birth. Among the hundreds of volunteers, I thank Lawrence Carradini, Steve Eddington, Brian Foye, Billy Koumentzalis, Meg Smith, Dave Orr, and so many others who open up their hearts and their homes to keep Jack's legacy alive.

The Kerouac Writers' Residence in Orlando, Florida, is now a dream come true thanks to the efforts of Marty Cummins, Summer Rodman, and Bob Kealing. The photographers and filmmakers Fred McDarrah, John Cohen, Robert Frank, Henry Ferrini, Mark Reese, Patti Brand, Betsey Blankenbaker, and Chris Felver have all exhibited extraordinary generosity in finding time over the decades to document precious moments, places and people that Jack and so many of us shared.

We all owe appreciation to the women who wrote so lovingly about Jack. Their work has also created a better understanding of the role of all women during our era. Joyce Johnson, Carolyn Cassady, Regina Weinreich, Hillary Holiday, Ann Charters, and Ann Douglas all deserve thanks for their outstanding scholarship.

Journalists who have painted a fresh picture of our era include Douglas Brinkley, Pat Fenton, George Wallace, Attila Gyenis, Bob Blumenthal, Dave Perry, Dennis Duggan, Steven Ronan, and Kevin Ring.

Special gratitude to those poets, authors, and loyal friends, young and old, still alive, whose individual work reflects their unique gifts and also honors the yea-saying spirit of Jack who wished in his lifetime to see a more joyous and compassionate America. This Honor Roll of the Road includes: Lawrence Ferlinghetti, Michael McClure, Lucien Carr, Ted Joans, Casey Cyr, Ron Whitehead, Lenny Gross, Neil Ortenberg, Sterling Lord, Herb Gold, David Stanford, Helen Kelly, Ed Adler, Malachy and Frank McCourt, Kurt Vonnegut, George Plimpton, Odetta, Pete Seeger, Willie Nelson, Floyd Red Crow Westerman, Joanne Shenendoah, Matoka Little Eagle, Lee Ranaldo, Johnny Depp, Keir Dullea, Jerry Stiller and Ann Meara, Arthur Miller, Mickey Raphael, Brooks Jones, Mark Morganelli, Art d'Lugoff, Vassar Clemmins, Mia

Muller, Alfred Leslie, John Cassady, Norman Mailer, Sharon Mesmer, Richard Deakin, Bob Holman, Frank Messina, Jason Eisenberg, Michelle Esrick, Jerry Jeff Walker, Dan Wakefield, Bill Morgan, Asher Levi, and Hunter S. Thompson.

For all the thousands of musicians, poets, painters, actors, dancers, and everyday down-home dreamers whose names I couldn't fit into the pages of *Offbeat*, I thank each of you for every precious moment spent together.

And finally, of course, this book is for Jack, whose brakeman's shining lantern still illuminates the diamonds in the sidewalk, reminding us that we were all put here to celebrate the joy of knowing one another, collaborating with one another, and living each day with an open mind and a loving heart.

—David Amram, Putnam Valley, New York
October 11, 2001

index